Structured Assembly Language

Contents

3   Simulated Extensions to Assembler Instruction Set   53

4 BIOS Video Procedures   77

—————————————————————PART II—————————————————————

Adding Structure to Assembly Programs

5 Introducing the CHUCK Programming Language   145

6 CHUCK: Subroutines, SWITCH/CASE, Looping   167

Acknowledgments

Norm, Jay, Dennis and the gang at TSR Systems Ltd. have always lent technical support and lively friendship for my programming and writing projects.

Stephen Moore, my editor at TAB/Windcrest, has championed my ideas and always encouraged me to follow my creative instincts.

Without the generous loving support of Barbara, my wife, and Rachel, our daughter, I would never have been able to undertake the writing of this book. And the master CHUCK, of course.

And finally, without the deep knowledge shared by the programming community in countless books and magazine articles, the content of this book would never have been conceived.

Thank you all.

About This Book

This book is not a run-of-the-mill assembly language subroutine book. Rather, it provides the theory and source code to add high-level language structure along with C- and Pascal-like procedures to your assembly programs. To use the book from the starting gate, you should have at least beginner-level knowledge of assembly language basics.

PART I discusses the creation and attributes of EXE and COM executable files generated from assembly language programs. Techniques for utilizing the power of macros are discussed and, in a deliberate and progressive fashion, macros soon replace the pure assembly directives and mnemonics. The notion of creating a new language defined by a macro script is introduced. Macro-simulated extensions to the 8086 instruction set follow. Part I ends with basic BIOS video procedures constructed so they have a C- or Pascal-like feel. When you finish Part I, you will have a solid knowledge of macros, the start of a structured assembly library, and understand concepts such as procedure-calling conventions, macro directives, conditional directives, and calling subroutines from within macro-defined procedures.

PART II begins by exploring considerations of program flow and thoughts on building a programming language utilizing the power of macros. The macro-defined language presented in this book is named CHUCK. Following a brief discussion, the comprehensive set of macros that form the foundation of CHUCK is described. Your assembly programs can now contain a structure similar to familiar high-level languages. Conditional branching, looping, and value filtering (such as SWITCH and CASE in C) are all defined using macros. Bountiful demonstration programs carefully describe the use of all the program-flow macros. Part II ends with a discussion on how to use CHUCK in a mixed-language programming environment.

PART III starts by exploring what categories of procedures should be added to the CHUCK library and follows by adding the procedures such as, direct video access, window management routines, making COM programs Terminate and Stay Resident (TSR), text prompts, integer-to-ASCII conversion, string handling, reading the keyboard, I/O disk operations, cursor control, and more. When Part III ends, you will have many library routines and will know how to write CHUCK programs. Your CHUCK programs will have the structure of high-level languages while retaining many attributes of pure assembly programming.

PART IV integrates the book's concepts and information through the presentation of demonstration programs. The executable size of the CHUCK-generated demonstration programs will often weigh in at 50 to 70 percent the size of comparable C programs.

The commercial version of a CHUCK language programming environment, ASMplus™ (containing CHUCK language macros, a CHUCK procedure library containing over 100 standard procedures, window and TSR procedures, and more), is currently under development by TSR Systems Ltd. and will be available by the time this book is published. The commercial version's introductory price after using the discount coupon provided at the back of the book is $59.95.

WHO IS THIS BOOK FOR?

This book will be useful to all programmers interested in improving their assembly language productivity. High-level language programmers who are interested in improving their programs' quality while reducing their code quantity will also find the material presented in the book useful.

Beginning assembly programmers will not be left hanging in the wind, even though many advanced concepts are discussed. Although beginners might find some new programming techniques or concepts challenging, fear not. I've taken great care in explaining all programming concepts and code in a step-by-step fashion.

The information in this book will prove useful to assembly and non-assembly programmers alike. Experienced assembly language programmers who wish to improve their productivity can make immediate use of the CHUCK language program flow control macros. The high-level language programmer who wishes to write programs with the power of assembly, but doesn't have time to learn all the esoterica associated with it, will appreciate both the CHUCK language and library.

MACRO ASSEMBLERS SUPPORTED

MicroSoft MASM (5.0 or later) or Borland's TASM is required to assemble the programs presented in this book. All programs in this book were assembled using Borland's TASM Macro Assembler in the MASM emulation mode.

PART I
Assembly Basics

Welcome to the magic world of assembly programming. Part I is an introduction to writing EXE files and COM files along with a very detailed look at how assembly code affects executable program size. The powerful macro facility of Borland's TASM and MicroSoft's MASM is introduced. Very basic macros are used to slowly modify the look of the EXE and COM demonstration programs. These basic macros provide a firm foundation for the more complex macros presented later. A set of macros that change the name of some assembly instructions and simulate new assembly instructions is presented. Part I ends by presenting BIOS-based video procedures and attendant subroutines. Your structured assembly library building has begun.

1

EXE and COM File Comparisons

In this book you'll be developing both COM and EXE programs. Because the methods and macro-defined procedures are slightly different for EXE and COM files, I suggest creating the following disk organizational scheme.

For floppy disk users, keep one disk labeled EXE and another labeled COM. For hard disk users, create a directory named CHUCK and two subdirectories named EXE and COM.

As you work your way through the text, the EXE versions of macros and subroutines called from within macros are presented before the COM version. Place the EXE macros on the EXE disk or in the \CHUCK\EXE subdirectory. Your TAB.LIB file will be placed on your EXE disk or \CHUCK\EXE subdirectory. Place the COM macros on the COM disk or in the \CHUCK\COM subdirectory.

This method of separation might seem a tad cumbersome at first, but because the EXE subroutine listings and macros can cause fatal disasters to your COM programs, total separation is required. I'm sure that there are other ways to manage the disk file organization, but the method I've described worked for me, and if you choose to purchase the TAB disk or the TSR disk, you'll find that their organization follows the one described here.

To summarize, when you type in an EXE macro or subroutine make sure that you are using your EXE disk or are in your \CHUCK\EXE directory. When you type in a COM macro or subroutine make sure that you are using your COM disk or are in your \CHUCK\COM directory.

SOME THOUGHTS

I often think of myself as quite lucky to have learned how to program in assembly language before any other. I found the 6502 microprocessors which populated the 8-bit Atari and Apple computers quite limited, but also quite fun to use. I always felt very in control while programming in assembly on those 8-

bit machines. Whenever I programmed in assembly it felt as though I were "laying hands" on the machine.

Following my affair with the 8-bit Atari computers, I switched to the 68000 Atari ST and took to the C programming language quickly, staying with C when I entered the IBM PC-dominated universe. After dabbling in the low-end page composition waters (TypeSetter PC) for a while, I began developing a C library which eventually grew into TSR's 'C'erious tools and Windcrest's *C Libraries: Menus and User Interfaces*. Much to my delight, 'C'erious received immediate reviews in some magazines and many kind words from the programming community.

Once 'C'erious Tools 1.0 (2.+ will be out when you are reading this) was safely put to bed, I began to dabble with the idea of writing a library for assembler programmers having the power of the standard C library combined with the specialized windowing, keyboard handling, data entry, and Terminate and Stay Resident-creating capabilities of 'C'erious. What a product!

Because programming is still wondrous fun for me, I quickly began prototyping this assembly library. Then dominoes began falling. Having an assembler library meant that I needed to decide on library procedure calling conventions. C compilers did very well in the function calling convention arena and I looked at two choices: passing parameters on the stack as Micro-Soft and Borland's Turbo C do, or with the registers (most of the time, that is), as Watcom's compiler does. Although Turbo C is my first choice for developing C code, I really am impressed with the code produced by the Watcom compiler. The last compile of any commercial C program I'd write would always be done using Watcom C.

Once I settled on the register parameter passing conventions for my library, it soon occurred to me that it made great sense to name these library procedures with namesakes from more familiar languages such as C or Pascal. Because I'm far more comfortable programing in C than any other high-level language, I began to select names for my assembly library from the standard C and 'C'erious function pool.

My first assembly demonstration program using macros for library procedure calls ran as expected. For fun I decided to code the demonstration program in C. I was shocked to see that the C generated EXE executable program was much larger than the assembly generated EXE file. When I re-wrote the demo program in assembly so a COM file was created it proved a whopping 97 percent smaller than the executable C file. My heart raced. Was there another product lurking about? Hmmm. . . .

Then one day my friend Jean Kahn, a highly gifted computer science teacher, and I were chatting. I shared a snippet of my macro-infused assembly source code. She glanced at the source and said, "What language is that, Len?"

What language is that? I felt frantic. Assembly of course. Or was it?

Jean and I spoke a bit more about computer language attributes and I decided if I could control program flow using macros I might really be able to write my own computer language.

"Len," I mused, *"who's going to want to buy a computer language written by a middle-aged ex-video game coder?"* My intellect tried to stop me

from writing this computer language but the creative process had no stopping and before long a new computer language bubbled in gestation.

Sure there were program flow considerations, library procedure selections to be made, but that wasn't enough. Borland's fine Turbo Assembler manual has a section on pitfalls in assembler programming. Could I reduce any of those pitfalls while keeping the executable program lean? The more I coded the better I began to feel about structured assembly.

What should I name this new language? The new language produced executable demonstration programs 50 to 80 percent smaller than C. A name is not something to be taken lightly. I sat at my kitchen table working out the SWITCH/CASE control flow sequence of C in this new language when my brown tabby cat Chuck jumped on my notebook. Chuck is flexible, compact, fast, elegant, his eyes glow in the dark . . . my goodness. And the rest is history.

USING ASSEMBLY TO
WRITE A SIMPLE EXE PROGRAM

MS DOS permits two types of executable files: EXE and COM. There are differences between EXE and COM files and these differences will often prove very telling when you wish to select an executable program file structure style. EXE programs allow the programmer to use the full capabilities of the 8086 family of microprocessors. You may write programs with multiple data and code segments. Writing large programs is very important and it is the EXE file header that provides the facility to handle all the necessary multi-segment addressing information. The EXE header is placed at the beginning of an EXE file and will never prove to be less than 512 bytes.

Under certain circumstances, though, the EXE file header can grow much larger, taking up more and more of your executable code. The COM file on the other hand, does not use a monstrous header. All the program CODE and DATA must reside in one 64K segment. COM programs can prove to be very compact. What happens if you wish to write a COM program but have more than the allotted 64K of CODE and DATA? Forget it. You must use an EXE file. What happens if you need to allocate memory dynamically during program execution using the DOS memory allocate function? Forget using a COM file format. DOS returns a segment address for the allocated memory. COM programs use only one segment.

I've read some assembly titles where the authors laud the properties of COM files while subtly taking pot shots at the EXE file structure. Of course, others feel differently. My view is use a COM whenever possible. Use a COM file for Terminate and Stay Resident applications. If your program must dynamically allocate memory, or contains more than 64K of CODE and DATA then use an EXE file format.

On to writing our first assembly program. Many of my programming buddies code at such a rate that they debug code while at the computer using the video monitor. I always try to print a source listing and work at a bit less frantic pace. The consequence of this habit is that I often print many listings. Sitting at my left is an Epson FX-286 printer. There is no convenient way for me to switch the printer into its condense printing mode. Let's write a utility to switch the Epson printer into condense so that it won't use up so much paper in printing my many listings.

If you send 0Fh (15 dec) to my Epson it will automatically kick into the condense mode. The PC BIOS interrupt 17h handles communication with the printer. Interrupt 17h, function 0, sends a byte to the printer. On entry:

- AH holds 0, = the interrupt function number
- AL holds 0Fh, = the byte to printer
- DX holds 0, = the printer number

Interrupt 17h returns the printer status in the AH register. Seems simple enough. Figure 1-1 is the assembly source listing for COND1.ASM.

Fig. 1-1. The source code listing to COND1.ASM.

```
;----------------------------------------
;
; Source Listing Start
;
; File Name: COND1.ASM
;
; Description:
;  Uses BIOS int 17h function 0h
;  to send a byte to printer number
;  0.
;

;
; Group segments according to the
; Microsoft ordering conventions
;

        DOSSEG

;
; Assemble in the small memory model
;

       .MODEL SMALL

;
; EXE files need a stack so set to 100h
;

       .STACK  100h

;
; Begin the CODE segment
;

        .CODE

;
; DX holds the printer number
; We select printer 0 by default
;
```

```
        mov     DX,0


;
; Invoke printer int 17h
; using function 0fh and send
; byte 0fh (condense) to the printer
;

        mov     AH,0
        mov     AL,0fh
        int     17h


;
; Terminate program via DOS
;

        mov     AH,4Ch
        int     21h


;
; Tell assembler no more instructions
; in this file
;

        END


;
; End of Source Listing
;-------------------------------------
;
```

Fig. 1-1 ends.

Note that the source code listing presented in Fig. 1-1 uses the new style directives available with Borland's TASM and MiscroSoft's MASM (5.0 +). If your macro assembler doesn't use these newer directives I'd suggest that you upgrade to get one that does. These directives greatly simplify assembly programming. COND1.ASM sets a stack size of 100h. All EXE files must allocate memory for a stack. Also note that this program is assembled in the SMALL memory model. The SMALL memory model restricts the code and data segments—each segment size must be less than 64K.

Because I'm using Borland's TASM Macro Assembler I've written two small batch files to help with program assembling and linking. The following file, AL.BAT, assembles the source code to an .OBJ file and automatically invokes Borland's linker to create the executable EXE file:

```
tasm %1
tlink %1;
```

Consult your MicroSoft assembler manual to write equivalent batch files.

Once COND1.ASM is assembled and linked, the executable program size is 525 bytes. Remembering that the EXE file header will always be greater than 512 bytes, you can see that the code segment size is fairly small.

USING ASSEMBLY TO
WRITE A SIMPLE COM PROGRAM

Remembering the previous discussion, COM files do not use a 512 bytes header, so the COM file should be considerably smaller. Let's see. Figure 1-2 presents the source code listing to COND2.ASM. This source file will assemble and link into a COM file. The COM file assembles in the same fashion as the EXE file, but Borland and MicroSoft provide two different linker arrangements to create the COM file. If you own the MASM from MicroSoft you'll have to assemble and link into an EXE file and then run the EXE2BIN utility to convert the EXE file to the COM file. TLINK, the Borland linker provides a switch (/t) which tells it to create a COM file. Needless to say, I like Borland's COM creation scheme far better than MicroSoft's. Consult your MicroSoft macro assembler and linker documentation for more information.

Fig. 1-2. The source code listing to COND2.ASM.

```
;------------------------------------
; Source Listing Start
;
; File Name: COND2.ASM
;
; Description:
;   Uses BIOS int 17h function 0h
;   to send a byte to printer number
;   0.
;


;
; Group segments according to the
; Microsoft ordering conventions
;

        DOSSEG

;
; Assemble in the small memory model
;

        .MODEL SMALL

;
; Begin the CODE segment
;

        .CODE

;
; ORG 100h sets code start at CS:100h
;

        ORG     100h


;
; COM Program start
;
```

```
ProgramStart:

;
; DX holds the printer number
; We select printer 0 by default
;

        mov     DX,0


;
; Invoke printer int 17h
; using function 0fh and send
; byte 0fh (condense) to the printer
;

        mov     AH,0
        mov     AL,0fh
        int     17h


;
; Terminate COM program via DOS
;

        int     20h


;
; Tell assembler no more instructions
; in this file
;

        END     ProgramStart


;
; End of Source Listing
;-------------------------------------
```

Fig. 1-2 ends.

Note that the COM file doesn't need a stack. The executable code does need to begin at 100h bytes after the start of the code segment. Also, the COM used a different BIOS terminate function. Substantively, though, the two files are the same. Except that the executable file size for COND2.COM is 11 bytes:

COND1.EXE   525 bytes
COND2.COM   11 bytes

In smaller programs the EXE file header can look comparatively large. When writing Terminate and Stay Resident application programs, it is very important to save every byte, and that is why I favor using COM programs for TSR programming.

USING C TO WRITE A SIMPLE EXE PROGRAM

This is not a C book, but nonetheless every once in a while I'll put in a small C program so you can see why I so passionately argue for the adoption of the CHUCK language.

Figure 1-3 is the source code listing for C-COND1.C. This program functions identically to the COND1.ASM program. To be fair I'll be comparing the assembly-generated EXE file and the C-generated EXE file.

Fig. 1-3. The source code listing to C-COND1.C.

```
/*-----------------------------------
 * Source Listing Start
 *
 * File Name: C-COND1.C
 *
 * Description:
 *  Uses BIOS int 17h function 0h
 *  to send a byte to printer number
 *  0.
 *
 */
#include <dos.h>

void main(void);

void
main()
{
union REGS ir,or;

/* Prepare registers for BIOS call */
ir.x.dx = 0;
ir.h.ah = 0;
ir.h.al = 15;

/* Invoke BIOS int 17h               */
int86(0x17,&ir,&or);

}

/*
 * End of Source Listing
 *-----------------------------------*/
```

Don't worry if the C program is "gobble-dee-gook" to you. C is a very solid language and produces fine code amongst the high-level language group. So, after compiling and linking C-COND1.C what is the EXE file size? How about 2706 bytes!

```
COND1.EXE    = >   525 bytes
COND2.COM    = >    11 bytes
C-COND1.EXE  = > 2706 bytes
```

What's going on here? The EXE header is only 512 bytes. Why does the Turbo C compiler produce 2706 bytes of code?

Oh, you say, C is so much easier to understand and maintain than assembly. Oh, you say, I can be so productive in C.

Just be patient. Chapter 2 introduces you to macros and a youngster with mighty potential named CHUCK.

2

Macros

Macro expansion is an elegant and powerful facility of macro assemblers. At their simplest level macros are simply text expansions. You assign a name to a block of text with the MACRO directive, and when the assembler detects the name associated with the macro, the text is then integrated into the program.

At deeper levels there are many conditional expressions that allow the programmer to create some complex macros. Macros can receive parameters just as they might be passed to a procedure or function in a higher-level language. Parameters passed into macros may be thoroughly analyzed using a simple yet powerful set of conditional directives. Once the parameters are analyzed the assembler can act in a clever fashion. But let's not get ahead of ourselves.

There are advantages and disadvantages to using macros in assembly programming. On the plus side of the scale, macros can be used to greatly simplify both the ease of coding and the readability of the code. In fact, later in this chapter a macro is described that will send a byte to the printer via the computer's BIOS. The macro will in fact create a procedure that will look identical and function in an identical fashion to the C function of the same name in my 'C'erious library.

There is a negative side to the scale, though, and it's a big negative. The negative occurs when the macro describes the text to many microprocessor instructions. If the macro needs to be invoked, say ten times, the instructions in the macro will be embedded in the assembly source code ten times. If the macro holds text which assembles into 250 bytes of code, invoking the macro will add a whopping 2500 bytes to your program size.

Writing subroutine procedures would be a far more efficient way of using the needed routine. You could call the 250-byte subroutine ten times for a price of 250 bytes, as opposed to invoking the 250-byte macro for a price of 2500 bytes.

The CHUCK language, though, manages to combine the advantage of code efficiency from subroutines and mingle it with the macro's readability and ease of coding. And there is a synergy which is hard to miss. Parameters are passed to procedures in CHUCK with the ease of Pascal or C. The technique that describe the process of nesting subroutines within macros is clearly described later in the book.

If the preceding discussion on advantages and disadvantages of macro usage isn't clear yet then don't despair, examples are always far better as descriptions than words.

SIMPLIFIED SEGMENT DIRECTIVES

Segment directives tell the assembler what segment to put the data and code into. Segment control is one of the more kludgy (in my humble opinion, that is) aspects of the 8086 microprocessor. I choose not to discuss the standard set of segment directives which have previously been used by assembly programmers. It would be too painful. The new simplified segment directives are nothing short of wonderful.

There are five simplified segment directives which I will discuss. They are DOSSEG, .DATA, .CODE, .STACK, .MODEL. Let's look at them one by one.

DOSSEG

The DOSSEG simplified directive tells the macro assembler to group the different segments according to the MicroSoft segment ordering convention. As a rule of thumb I suggest always using this directive at the top of every assembly file.

.DATA

The .DATA segment defines the start of your data segment. Simple enough on the surface, but there is a bit more that you need to know before you can use this directive properly. The DS (data segment register) must be loaded with the data segment value, such as:

```
mov   AX,@DATA
mov   DS,AX
```

In order to access the data in the data segment you need to execute this code before any data is obtained. Note that you cannot execute the previously mentioned code in a COM source file. CHUCK'S COM files are designed so that all the code and data reside in the code segment. This can be accomplished with code such as:

```
mov   AX,CS
mov   DS,AX
```

Once the CS equals DS, COM programs written in CHUCK will perform in fine fashion. The technique of using the .DATA directive in EXE files is fully demonstrated later in this book.

.CODE

The simplified .CODE directive marks the beginning of the code segment. The code segment holds your 8086 instructions.

.STACK

The simplified .STACK directive sets up a stack for EXE files. Stacks of 100h or 200h should prove sufficient for non-recursive programs.

.MODEL

The simplified .MODEL directive tells the assembler whether to use far or near RET instructions. There are six memory models supported by Borland's TASM. They are the tiny, small, medium, compact, large, and huge models.

For the purposes of this book all the demonstration programs are written in the small memory model mode. That means that all your code must fit into a 64K segment, and all your data must fit into a separate 64K segment, and that all the calls are near calls and all the data is near data.

The small memory model is invoked in the following way:

```
.MODEL SMALL
```

Putting all the simplified directives discussed together might look something like this:

```
    DOSSEG                ; Set MicroSoft standard segment order

    .MODEL SMALL          ; Small memory model
    .STACK 100h           ; Stack size 100h
    .DATA                 ; Begin data segment
; data here
    .CODE                 ; Begin code segment
; code here
    END
```

The new style simplified assembly directives should lure many new programmers to assembly language programming. I know that for me, when I migrated from the 6502, to the 68000, to the 8086 I felt in the twilight zone for a while when it came to the concepts of segments and offsets. Enough said, I think simplified directives are the best.

MACRO DIRECTIVES

As previously mentioned, macros permit you to assign a name to a block of text. The macro can also receive parameters in a similar fashion to that of high-level languages. There are four macro directives that will be discussed here. They are MACRO, ENDM, EXITM, LOCAL. You may also use Repeat Block directives from within macros.

MACRO

MACRO defines a macro name. The MACRO directive takes the form of:

macro_name MACRO [*parameter1*,[*parameter2*]...]

where macro_name must reflect a legal text name which may be used in the assembly source file. Once invoked the text following the macro invocation will be expanded into the assembly source file.

ENDM

ENDM defines the macro end. The ENDM directive tells the macro assembler when the block of text that has been assigned a macro name has ended. For example:

macro_name MACRO
        statement1
        statement2
        ENDM

demonstrates that a macro named macro_name was defined and that there are two statements associated with that definition. When macro_name is invoked statement1 and statement2 are included in the assembly source file. The ENDM directive tells the assembly that the macro expansion has now ended.

EXITM

EXITM exits from a macro expansion. There might be a time when you wish to have your macro expansion end prematurely. EXITM immediately stops the expansion of the macro as soon as the assembler comes across the directive. For example:

    IFB <*agrv1*>
        EXITM
    ENDIF

tells the assembler to abort the expansion if *argv1* is blank.

LOCAL

LOCAL defines symbols that may only be used within macros. LOCAL symbols are very useful for controlling program flow within a macro. The symbols declared as LOCAL are not visible outside the macro to the linker. This means that you may re-use the LOCAL names in other macros without harm.

There are more than a few CHUCK macros that use locals. The syntax for LOCAL is:

```
LOCAL      symbol1,[symbol2],...
```

An example of LOCAL usage within a macro, which exchanges the value in one word of memory with another might look like this:

```
xchangemem MACRO val1,val2
      LOCAL    loc_1,temp
      jmp      loc_1
temp DW        ?
loc_1:
      push     AX              ; save AX reg to stack
      mov      AX,val1         ; transfer val1 to temp
      mov      temp,AX
      mov      AX,val2         ; transfer val2 to val1
      mov      val1,AX
      mov      AX,temp         ; transfer temp (now holds val1)
      mov      val2,AX         ;    to val2
      pop      AX              ; restore AX and transfer complete
      ENDM
```

Although there are more efficient ways to code this macro, as is, it provides a clear look at how the LOCAL directive is used. The symbol temp allocates a WORD placed in the code segment. In order to allow the program to properly continue through the expanded macro there must be an unconditional jump over the word. If the jump over the WORD at temp were not there then the program would enter the "unknown zone."

By defining temp within the code segment you have created an area of memory that will function perfectly for storage of a WORD. The macro xchangemem receives WORD-sized memory locations and exchanges the values in them while preserving the values of all the registers.

REPEAT BLOCK MACROS

A *Repeat block macro* is a special form of macro that allows you to create blocks of repeated statements. The three repeat block directives are REPT, IRP, and IRPC. Take care not to confuse the string instruction REP with the repeat block directive REPT.

The syntax for the REPT directive is:

```
REPT expression
statement1
ENDM
```

The following example demonstrating the use of the REPT directive replaces

```
ascii_dig DB    '0'
          DB    '1'
          DB    '2'
          DB    '3'
          DB    '4'
          DB    '5'
          DB    '6'
          DB    '7'
          DB    '8'
          DB    '9'
```

with

```
ascii_dig LABEL     BYTE
x   =   0             ; initialize x to 0
    REPT 10           ; repeat 10 times
    DB    '0' + x     ; allocate ascii digit
x   =    x + 1        ; increment original '0'
    ENDM
```

In a way, the example for the REPT directive acts as a FOR/NEXT loop. The variable x is set to 0. The first byte in the buffer is '0' + 0. The next byte in the buffer is assembled to '0' + 1 or '1'. And so on.

The IRP directive is used to create repeat blocks where the number of repetitions, as well as the parameters for the repetitions are specified in a list of arguments. The syntax for the IRP directive is:

```
IRP parameter,<argument>
statement1
ENDM
```

The following example shows how to use the IRP directive to create the same ascii_dig which has been previously demonstrated.

```
ascii_dig LABEL   BYTE
    IRP   x,<'0','1','2','3','4','5','6','7','8','9'>
    DB   10 DUP(x)
    ENDM
```

The IRPC directive is similar to the IRP directive with the exception that the arguments are specified with a string. The syntax for the IRPC directive is:

```
IRPC parameter,string
statement1
ENDM
```

The following example shows how to create the now familiar ascii_dig buffer using IRPC:

```
ascii_dig LABEL     BYTE
          IRPC x, '01234567890'
          DB   x
          ENDM
```

MACRO OPERATORS

Macro operators are special to macro and conditional directives. The operators are:

Operator	Definition
&	Substitute operator
< >	Literal text operator
!	Literal character operator
%	Expression evaluate operator
;;	Suppress macro comment operator

& Substitute Operator

There are times when formal parameters mixed with other text is a potential problem. The Substitute Operator is useful in dealing with this potential problem. When you get to the section defining CHUCK's control flow macros you see extensive use of the Substitute Operator. An example follows:

```
macro_name    MACRO name
&name&:
.
.

@@&name&1:
.
.
.
```

The label declared as &name&: will appear in the source as name: and the label declared as @@&name&1: will appear in the source as @@name1:.

< > Literal Text Operator

The Literal Text Operator directs the assembler to treat what is contained within the brackets as a single string, as opposed to separate arguments. For example:

```
mvcur  10,10
```

passes two parameters (param 1 = 10, param 2 = 10) to mvcur and

```
mvcur   <10,10>
```

passes one two-element parameter (10,10) to mvcur.

!   Literal Character Operator

The Literal Character Operator tells the assembler to treat the following character literally, as opposed to being a symbol. For example, the statement:

```
<Value !> 128>
```

tells the assembler that there is a single literal element within the brackets. However, in this special case the greater than symbol (>) is to appear within the literal element and not function as a symbol. The ! operator tells the assembler that > is not a symbol in this special case.

%   Expression Operator

The Expression Operator tells the assembler to treat the argument following the operator as an expression. An example of the Expression Operator in use is:

```
set_width MACRO val
     IFB <val>
          %out     Parameter missing in set_width
     ENDIF
  .
  .
     ENDM
```

The example prints the message "Parameter missing in set_width" to the screen if the parameter val is blank.

;;   Macro Comment Operator

The Macro Comment Operator tells the assembler to ignore all the text after it. The regular comment operator ';' can also be used in macros, however it will still appear in the macro listing.

CONDITIONAL ASSEMBLY DIRECTIVES

Macro assemblers have the capability of assembling source code conditionally based on a series of conditional assembly directives. These directives can prove useful when you want to have a program assemble differently under different circumstances. However, more to the point considering the thrust of this book, conditional assembly directives may be used within macros. It is for this reason that the ones germane to CHUCK are mentioned here.

IFB (If Parameter Is Blank)

The conditional expression IFB is used in CHUCK to determine whether a parameter has been passed. For example, look at the upcoming macro SET_STACK. The macro name comes in the first field, the MACRO directive comes next, followed by parameters separated by commas. In the case of SET_STACK there is only one parameter called stack_size:

```
SET_STACK MACRO stack_size
    IFB <stack_size>
        .STACK 100h
    ELSE
        .STACK stack_size
    ENDIF
    ENDM
```

If the programmer invokes the SET_STACK macro with SET_STACK then there is no value passed with stack_size; in other words, the stack_size parameter is blank. If the stack_size parameter is blank then the stack will be set to the default value of .STACK 100h.

If SET_STACK had been invoked with SET_STACK 250h then the stack_size parameter would not have been blank and .STACK 250h would have been assembled.

The use of IFB allows you to assemble one line of code if a parameter is not passed and take a different route if a parameter is actually passed. Later in the book you'll see how to code the well known (to C programmers, that is) ITOA procedure. The ITOA (Integer TO Ascii) procedure takes a 16-bit WORD and converts it to an ASCII string. The ITOA procedure puts the ASCII string in a buffer and returns the offset to the buffer in the AX register.

Later in Part I you'll find the code for a PUTS (ah, the aroma of C again) procedure, which prints a buffer to the screen. You can call PUTS like this:

```
PUTS text_buffer
```

or like this

```
ITOA value,text_buffer
puts
```

In the first case PUTS simply puts the ASCII values in text_buffer to the screen at the current cursor location. Whereas in the second case the ITOA procedure takes the 16-bit WORD and puts the ASCII conversion value offset in text_buffer. However, note that because ITOA returns the pointer to text_buffer in the AX register, PUTS automatically knows that an offset is in the AX register and handles things appropriately.

IFNB (If Not Blank)

The IFNB directive, If Not Blank, is the converse of If Blank. This conditional directive snaps into action if a parameter is actually passed. The IFNB directive takes the same form as IFB.

```
IFB     <argument>      If argument blank then . . .
        statement1
ENDIF

IFNB    <argument>      If argument not blank then . . .
        statement1
ENDIF
```

IFDIFI (If Values Are Different)

Like assembly, CHUCK is not a case sensitive language. All conditional macros used for CHUCK ignore case.

The IFDIFI conditional directive allows you to assemble when a comparison of two variables indicates that they are different. For example, let's say that you wish to load the X register, which has a 16-bit value, with your procedure, but the programmer decided to pass the value to the procedure directly in the AX register. This is of particular interest to CHUCK programmers because of the return value rules for CHUCK: all 16-bit values come back in AX. The code

```
IFDIFI <AX>,<value>
        mov   AX,value
ENDIF
```

assembles

```
mov   AX,value
```

if value is not AX. The IFDIFI conditional directive along with IFB prove extremely useful when we wish to use a returned value from one procedure with the following procedure.

IFIDNI (If Values Are the Same)

The IFIDNI conditional directive (not case sensitive) is used to test if macro parameters are identical. IFIDNI is the opposite of IFDIFI.

ELSEIF (Family of Directives)

The ELSEIF family of directives allow you to filter many different parameter values. Here's an example of ELSEIF:

```
IFB <argv1>
      mov   AX,1
ELSEIFIDNI  <AX>,<argv1>
      mov   BX,AX
ELSE
      mov   AX,2
ENDIF
```

In the previous example if the parameter argv1 is blank then AX receives the value of 1. If argv1 is not blank and equal to AX then move the AX register to the BX register. Finally, if argv1 is not blank and not equal to AX then move the value of 2 to the AX register.

You can see that these conditional assembly directives add quite a bit of clout to the process of parameter analysis. The structural tendencies of CHUCK do not come from the conditional assembly directives, though, they do come from the ability of one macro to communicate with another. That facet of macro expansion is discussed in Part II.

SPECIALIZED EXE MACROS

Let's demonstrate specifically what a macro looks like and how it is invoked in a program. CODE1.ASM started with the following assembly directives:

```
DOSSEG
.MODEL SMALL
.STACK 100h
```

It is very easy to create a macro which can replace those three directives. It can be called PROG_EXE:

```
PROG_EXE MACRO
        DOSSEG
        .MODEL SMALL
        .STACK 100h
        ENDM
```

When PROG_EXE is invoked by PROG_EXE then:

```
DOSSEG
.MODEL SMALL
.STACK 100h
```

is assembled.

Using the PROG_EXE macro you could start an EXE assembly program with:

```
PROG_EXE
.CODE
```

The macro PROG_EXE replaces three lines of code with one line of code. Continuing, you could replace the .CODE directive with one called PROG_CODE, and the .DATA directive with PROG_DATA.

Figure 2-1 presents the source code listing for the PROG_EXE macro. Note that there is a conditional expression now included in the macro.

```
PROG_EXE MACRO stk
      .
      .
    IFB  <stk>
        .STACK 100h
    ELSE
        .STACK stk
    ENDIF
      .
      .
```

The letters stk following the MACRO declaration indicate that one parameter is being passed to the macro. If the parameter stk is not present (blank) then the text .STACK 100h will be written ELSE if stk has a value then that value will be used as the new stack.

Fig. 2-1. The EXE macro listing to PROG_EXE.

```
;;----------------------------------------
;; Macro: PROG_EXE
;;
;; Description: Make the
;;    program an .EXE file
;;
PROG_EXE MACRO stk
        DOSSEG
        .MODEL SMALL
    IFB <stk>
        .STACK 100h
    ELSE
        .STACK stk
    ENDIF
        ENDM
;;----------------------------------------
```

PROG_EXE

PROG_EXE is the start of a program with an EXE file structure. The PROG_EXE macro is placed immediately after the INCLUDE files in the main program module. Using simplified directives, PROG_EXE sets the file segment ordering as fitting to the MicroSoft standard, declares the memory model, and sets the stack size. If no stack parameter is passed then a default stack size of 100h is set. Figure 2-1 presents the source listing to PROG_EXE. Place the PROG_EXE macro in a file named CHUCK.MAC. For example:

```
; FILE.ASM
;
INCLUDE CHUCK.MAC   ; Include macro script
PROG_EXE 200h       ; Declare EXE file structure with
                    ; a stack size of 200h
PROG_CODE           ; Begin Code segment
.
.
.
END_EXE             ; Return to DOS
END                 ; End of source file listing
```

END_EXE

END_EXE returns an EXE program to DOS via the BIOS. The END_EXE macro uses interrupt 21h, function 4Ch, to return the program to DOS. Figure 2-2 presents the source code listing for END_EXE. Add the END_EXE macro to your CHUCK.MAC file. Here is an example of a program using the END_EXE macro:

```
; FILE.ASM
;
INCLUDE CHUCK.MAC   ; Include macro script
PROG_EXE 200h       ; Declare EXE file structure with
                    ; a stack size of 200h
PROG_CODE           ; Begin Code segment
.
.
.
END_EXE             ; Return to DOS
END                 ; End of source file listing
```

Fig. 2-2. The EXE macro listing to END_EXE.

```
;;----------------------------------------
;; Macro: END_EXE
;;
;; Description: End the program
;;    and exit to caller
;;
END_EXE MACRO
        mov     AH,4ch
        int     21h
        ENDM
;;----------------------------------------
```

PROG_CODE

PROG_CODE begins the .CODE segment. It uses the simplified .CODE directive to declare the start of a code segment. Figure 2-3 presents the source code listing to the PROG_CODE macro. Add the PROG_CODE macro to your CHUCK.MAC file. Here is an example of a program that uses the PROG_CODE macro:

```
; FILE.ASM
;
INCLUDE CHUCK.MAC    ; Include macro script
PROG_EXE 200h        ; Declare EXE file structure with
                     ; a stack size of 200h
PROG_DATA            ; Begin Date segment
; data here
PROG_CODE            ; Begin Code segment
; code here
.

.
END_EXE              ; Return to DOS
END                  ; End of source file listing
```

Fig. 2-3. The EXE macro listing to PROG_CODE.

```
;;----------------------------------------
;; Macro: PROG_CODE
;;
;; Description: Declare CODE segment
;;
PROG_CODE MACRO
        .CODE
        ENDM
;;----------------------------------------
```

PROG_DATA

PROG_DATA begins a .DATA segment. It uses the simplified .DATA directive to declare the start of a data segment. Figure 2-4 presents the source code listing to the PROG_DATA macro. Add the PROG_DATA macro to your CHUCK.MAC file. Here is an example of a program that uses PROG_DATA:

```
; FILE.ASM
;
INCLUDE CHUCK.MAC    ; Include macro script
PROG_EXE 200h        ; Declare EXE file structure with
                     ; a stack size of 200h
PROG_DATA            ; Begin Date segment
; data here
```

```
PROG_CODE                  ; Begin Code segment
; code here

   .

END_EXE                    ; Return to DOS
END                        ; End of source file listing
```

Fig. 2-4. The EXE macro listing to PROG_DATA.

```
;;-------------------------------------
;;
;; Macro: PROG_DATA
;;
;; Description: Declare CODE segment
;;
PROG_DATA MACRO
        .DATA
        ENDM
;;-------------------------------------
```

Now let's rewrite COND1.ASM using the new macros. This rewritten assembly file is called COND1A.ASM and is presented in Fig. 2-5. Of course the file sizes of COND1.EXE and COND1A.EXE are the same: 525 bytes.

Fig. 2-5. The source code listing to COND1A.ASM.

```
;-------------------------------------
; Source Listing Start
;
; File Name: COND1A.ASM
;
; Description:
;   Uses BIOS int 17h function 0h
;   to send a byte to printer number
;   0.
;


;
; Include Macro file
;

INCLUDE CHUCK.MAC

        PROG_EXE
        PROG_CODE

        mov     DX,0     ; send 0Fh to printer 0
        mov     AH,0
        mov     AL,0fh
        int     17h

        END_EXE
        END


;
; End of Source Listing
;-------------------------------------
```

Note that I've pulled the comments from the file to enhance file reading clarity. Figure 2-5 shows that you always begin a program listing including the appropriate macro files. At this time you have one macro file named CHUCK-.MAC with four macros for use with EXE files. That will change soon.

Once the CHUCK.MAC has been included you are free to use the macros:

- PROG_EXE   This is an EXE file
- PROG_CODE   Start the code segment here
- END_EXE   Use DOS terminate function

The assembly program COND1A.ASM if Fig. 2-5 is still looking like an assembly program. You're still moving values into registers and calling the printer BIOS interrupt. Not for long though. However, before we present PRCHAR, the send a byte to the printer procedure, let's look at a modified listing of COND1A which the Borland Macro Assembler gladly provides when you type:

TASM COND1A,,COND1A.LST

Figure 2-6 presents the listing to COND1A.LST. See how the macros that were contained in CHUCK.MAC were expanded into the appropriate assembly code.

I hope you now have a better understanding of how the macros are expanded in the source listing by the macro assembler during assembly. However, let's not stop here, there is more that we can do to this file to make it look more like a full-fledged CHUCK program.

Fig. 2-6. The disassembled code listing to COND1A.

```
;------------------------------------
; Source Listing Start
;
; File Name: COND1A
;
; Description:
;   Uses BIOS int 17h function 0h
;   to send a byte to printer number
;   0.
;


;
; Include macro files first
;

PROG_EXE        ; macro expands to...

        DOSSEG
        .MODEL SMALL
        .STACK  100h

PROG_CODE       ; macro expands to ...

        .CODE
```

```
            mov     DX,0
            mov     AH,0
            mov     AL,0fh
            int     17h

END_EXE         ; macro expands to ...

            mov     AH,4Ch
            int     21h

            END

;
; End of Listing
;------------------------------------
```

Fig. 2-6 ends.

CHUCK'S CALLING CONVENTIONS

As the first Macro-generated procedure, PRCHAR receives two parameters and returns an 8-bit value, it is important to clarify CHUCK's calling conventions at this time.

Calling conventions simply define what registers will hold which parameters. First you should learn the rules concerning how parameters are passed.

- *Rule 1* Only 16-bit values (WORDS) may be passed to a MACRO defined procedure. Any number of 16-bit values may be passed to a MACRO defined procedure.
- *Rule 2* No more than four parameters may be passed to a subroutine called within a MACRO.
- *Rule 3* The 16-bit values are passed in the AX, DX, BX, CX registers (in that order) to subroutines called within a MACRO, unless there is a special reason to do otherwise. Any calling convention variations should be amply commented.
- *Rule 4* All register values, with the exception of registers that hold a return value (AX or DX:AX) should be unaltered from the state before the procedure was called.

Next I'll present the rules for values returned from procedures.

- *Rule 1* The 8-bit values are returned in AL.
- *Rule 2* The 16-bit values are returned in AX.
- *Rule 3* The 32-bit values are returned in DX:AX.

CHUCK's calling conventions are often discussed as MACRO defined procedures and subroutines in this text. If you are not familiar with the notion of calling conventions, the following discussions should prove helpful in deepening your understanding.

A PROCEDURE TO SEND A BYTE TO THE PRINTER

PRCHAR, the first MACRO-defined procedure, is slightly more compli-
cated than the macros previously presented in the text. PRCHAR is designed
to replace the following code:

```
mov    DX,0
mov    AH,0
mov    AL,0fh
int    17h
```

The previous code sends the byte 0Fh to printer 0. Of course, most of the time
you will want to send bytes to the printer other than the Epson CONDENSE
ON (0Fh) code. Let's look into what parameters you need to pass MACRO
PRCHAR.

The first parameter could be the printer number and the second parameter could be the character sent to the printer. Once interrupt 17h is invoked in
the above code a printer status value is returned in the AH register.

For the time being, this macro procedure is coded without calling a subroutine from within it. When the MACRO-defined procedure is only a few
bytes, there are times when it doesn't pay to write a subroutine that will be
called from with the MACRO-defined procedure.

Let's explore the approach to take in figuring out how to apply the calling
convention rules to the creation of the macro. First, you don't have to worry
about passing 16-bit values to a subroutine called from within the macro procedure because PRCHAR will not call any subroutines. Because there is an
8-bit value returned, all registers other than AX should remain unchanged.
Sounds simple.

Because interrupt 17h returns the printer status code in AH, you need to
transfer the value in AH to AL before exiting the procedure. This conforms to
the calling conventions rules for values returned from procedures.

Yes, there is some overhead by using macro-defined procedures and preserving registers, but the code overhead is quite small when compared to compiled high-level languages. The procedure PRCHAR should be placed in a
newly created file called PRINT.MAC.

PRCHAR

PRCHAR sends a byte to the printer. The syntax for PRCHAR is:

```
PRCHAR    printer, cval
```

where *printer* = memory|register
     cval = memory|register

PRCHAR uses BIOS interrupt 17h, function 0, to send a byte to the printer.
The printer status value is returned in the AL register. The values for the

printer status are as follows:

Meaning	Bit							
Timeout	0	0	0	0	0	0	0	1
I/O Error	0	0	0	0	1	0	0	0
Printer Selected	0	0	0	1	0	0	0	0
Out of Paper	0	0	1	0	0	0	0	0
Acknowledged	0	1	0	0	0	0	0	0
Printer Not Busy	1	0	0	0	0	0	0	0

The source code listing for PRCHAR is presented in Fig. 2-7. The following is an example of a program using the PRCHAR macro:

```
; FILE.ASM
;
INCLUDE CHUCK.MAC        ; Include macro files
INCLUDE PRINT.MAC
;
; Send 'A' to printer 0
        PROG_EXE         ; Make EXE file
        PROG_DATA        ; Declare data segment
val     DW      'A'      ; DW val contains 'A'
        PROG_CODE        ; Declare code segment
        prchar     0,val ; Send 'A' to printer 0
        END_EXE          ; return to DOS
        END              ; End of source file listing
```

Fig. 2-7. The EXE and COM macro listing to PRCHAR.

```
;-------------------------------------
;
; Macro: PRCHAR number,cval
;
; Description:
;   Send a byte to printer where:
;     number is the printer number
;     cval's LSB is char to be printed
;

PRCHAR MACRO number,cval

; save DX

        push    DX

; move printer number to DX

        mov     DX,number

; move cval to AX (AL holds char to be printed)
```

```
        mov     AX,cval

; move 0 to AH (function 0)

        xor     AH,AH

; invoke interrupt 17h

        int     17h

; move printer status value to AL

        mov     AL,AH

; move 0 to AH for safety

        xor     AH,AH

; restore DX

        pop     DX

; End macro

        ENDM

;-------------------------------------

;
```

Fig. 2-7 ends.

Now that you've created a macro file called PRINT.MAC, let's create another MAC file that will load both CHUCK.MAC and PRINT.MAC. Because INCLUDE files may be nested, there will be no problems in creating a file called SMALL.MAC. SMALL.MAC looks like this:

```
INCLUDE CHUCK.MAC
INCLUDE PRINT.MAC
```

Figure 2-8 is the source code to COND1B.ASM. This thrice-revised file now appears as a full-fledged CHUCK program.

Note that the only standard assembly directive is END. COND1B.ASM's EXE file size is 532 bytes as compared to the 525 bytes before the PRCHAR procedure was added to the source code. I say that the seven bytes added to the EXE file is a small price to pay for code readability.

To be properly fair, though, PRCHAR is also a function in the 'C'erious library. Figure 2-9 is the source code listing for C-COND1B.C, which uses the prChar(. . .) function from the 'C'erious Library to send a byte to the printer.

Figure 2-10 presents a segment of the CHUCK source code side-by-side with the C source code.

Of course, C programmers will be more familiar with the look of the C source presented in Fig. 2-10 than the CHUCK source. As for the procedure call

Fig. 2-8. The source code listing to COND1B.ASM.

```
;-------------------------------------
; Source Listing Start
;
; File Name: COND1B.ASM
;
; Description:
;   Uses BIOS int 17h function 0h
;   to send a byte to printer number
;   0.
;


;
; Include Macro file
;

INCLUDE SMALL.MAC

        PROG_EXE
        PROG_CODE

        prchar  0,0Fh    ; 0Fh => printer 0

        END_EXE
        END


;
; End of Source Listing
;-------------------------------------
```

Fig. 2-9. The source code listing to C-COND1B.C.

```
/*-------------------------------------
 * Source Listing Start
 *
 * File Name: C-COND1B.C
 *
 * Description:
 *   Uses BIOS int 17h function 0h
 *   to send a byte to printer number
 *   0.
 *
 */

#include <tproto.h>

void main(void);

void
main()
{
prChar(0,15);
}

/*
 * End of Source Listing
 *-------------------------------------*/
```

Fig. 2-10. A comparison of CHUCK source code and C source code.

```
CHUCK SOURCE              C SOURCE

INCLUDE SMALL.MAC        #include <tproto.h>

PROG_EXE                 main()
PROG_CODE                {
prchar      0,0Fh        prChar(0,15);
END_EXE                  }
END
```

PRCHAR, notice that the CHUCK procedure lacks the parenthesis and semi-colon of the C syntax. Let's compare the EXE files:

```
COND1B.EXE     532 bytes
C-COND1B.EXE   2342 bytes
```

As you progress through the text you'll find dozens of procedures and program flow keywords to add, and continue looking at C executable files versus CHUCK executable files. Most of the time CHUCK will win out, no contest!

SPECIALIZED COM MACROS

In Chapter 1 there was a COM program generated by COND2.ASM. COND2.ASM started with:

```
DOSSEG
.MODEL SMALL
.CODE
ORG    100h
ProgramStart:
```

Writing a macro to start that beginning would be very simple. What you could do, though, would be to set the DS equal to the CS and then prepare a jump over the data portion of the code segment.

Terminating a COM program is slightly different from the method used to terminate an EXE program. As with END_EXE, you could create a COM_TO_DOS macro.

Finally, the END_COM macro is needed because the field after the END directive tells the COM program where to start execution after it has been loaded.

PROG_COM

PROG_COM is the start of a program with a COM file structure. The syntax is:

```
PROG_COM
```

Fig. 2-11. The COM macro listing to PROG_COM.

```
;;----------------------------------------
;; Macro: PROG_COM
;;
;; Description: Make the
;;    program an .COM file
;;
PROG_COM MACRO
         DOSSEG
         .MODEL SMALL
         .CODE
         ORG 100H
Start:
         push    CS
         pop     DS
         jmp     program
quotient  DD     0
remainder DD     0
dividend  DD     0
divisor   DD     0
         ENDM
;;----------------------------------------
```

The PROG_COM macro, listed in Fig. 2-11, is placed immediately after the include macro files. Using the simplified directives is handily taken care of:

DOSSEG		sets MicroSoft standard segment ordering
.MODEL	SMALL	enables the small model
.CODE		starts the code segment
ORG	100h	starts code at CS:100h

Start:

push	CS	
pop	DS	CS = > DS
jmp	program	jump over data in CS to program label
		default names used in long division routines

Here is an example of how a program uses the PROG_COM macro:

```
        PROG_COM
program:
; program here
; return to DOS
        END Start
```

COM_TO_DOS

COM_TO_DOS terminates the COM program. The syntax is:

COM_TO_DOS

The COM_TO_DOS macro, listed in Fig. 2-12, uses DOS interrupt 20h to terminate and return to DOS or a calling DOS program.

Fig. 2-12. The COM macro listing to COM_TO_DOS.

```
;;------------------------------------
;; Macro: COM_TO_DOS
;;
;; Description: Terminate the
;;    com program and return to
;;    DOS
;;
COM_TO_DOS MACRO
        int     20h
        ENDM
;;------------------------------------
```

Here is an example of how a program uses the COM_TO_DOS macro:

```
        PROG_COM
program:
;program here
        COM_TO_DOS
        END start
```

END_COM

END_COM ends the COM file listing and exits to the caller. The syntax is:

```
END_COM
```

END_COM, listed in Fig. 2-13, appends the default name of Start to the END directive. The following is an example of how a program uses the END_COM macro:

```
        PROG_COM
program:
; program here
        COM_TO_DOS
; program procedures here
        END_COM
```

Now that the three COM macros have been presented, it's time to write a COM program combining them with the PRCHAR procedure. The demonstration program, COND2A.ASM is presented in Fig. 2-14.

Now it's time to compare file sizes for the CHUCK EXE, CHUCK COM and the Turbo C EXE Epson condense mode programs.

```
COND2A.COM        39 bytes
COND1B.EXE       532 bytes
C-COND1B.EXE    2342 bytes
```

Fig. 2-13. The COM macro listing to END_COM.

```
;;--------------------------------------------
;;
;; Macro: END_COM
;;
;; Description: End the program
;;   and exit to caller
;;
END_COM MACRO
        END   Start
        ENDM
;;--------------------------------------------
```

Fig. 2-14. The source code listing to COND2A.ASM.

```
;--------------------------------------------
; Source Listing Start
;
; File Name: COND2A.ASM
;
; Description:
;   Uses BIOS int 17h function 0h
;   to send a byte to printer number
;   0.
;
;
; Include Macro file
;
INCLUDE SMALL.MAC

        PROG_COM
program:
        prchar 0,0Fh    ; 0Fh => printer 0
        COM_TO_DOS
        END_COM

; End of Source Listing
;--------------------------------------------
```

As you can see there is a considerable savings using either the CHUCK generated EXE or the CHUCK generated COM files over the C generated file. Here, I cannot resist using my disassembler to look at the code generated by each of the three programs. I have a suspicion that you might feel I'm being a tad heavy-handed when making the point that CHUCK should receive a serious look from all programmers interested in improving coding efficiency. However, the only way I think I'm ever going to get programmers to take a serious look at CHUCK is to be heavy-handed.

When you peruse the two CHUCK disassemblies try to trace how the PRCHAR macro expands. Later in the book when subroutines are called you'll get a feel for how the procedure-calling conventions work. Figure 2-15 presents the disassembly to COND2A.COM, Fig. 2-16 presents the disassembly to C-COND1B.EXE and Fig. 2-17 presents the disassembly to C-COND1B.EXE. OK. I'm done comparing CHUCK to the C compiler, for now.

Fig. 2-15. The disassembled source to COND2A.COM.

```
PAGE  60,132
.286c

code_seg_a    segment
        assume   cs:code_seg_a, ds:code_seg_a

        org    100h

cond2a      proc    far

start:
        push   cs
        pop    ds
        jmp    short loc_1
        db     90h
        db     16 dup (0)
loc_1:
        push   dx
        mov    dx,0
        mov    ax,0Fh
        xor    ah,ah
        int    17h

        mov    al,ah
        xor    ah,ah
        pop    dx
        int    20h

cond2a      endp

code_seg_a    ends

        end    start
```

Fig. 2-16. The disassembled source to COND1B.EXE.

```
PAGE  60,132

.286c

seg_a      segment    para public
        assume cs:seg_a, ds:seg_a, ss:stack_seg_b

cond1b      proc    far

start:
        push   dx
        mov    dx,0
        mov    ax,0Fh
        xor    ah,ah
```

```
        int    17h

        mov    al,ah
        xor    ah,ah
        pop    dx
        mov    ah,4Ch
        int    21h

        db     12 dup (0)

cond1b      endp

seg_a       ends

stack_seg_b    segment    para stack

        db     256 dup (0)

stack_seg_b    ends

        end    start
```

Fig. 2-16 ends.

Fig. 2-17. The disassembled source to C generated C-COND1B.EXE.

```
PAGE   60,132

.286c

data_1e     equ    74h
data_2e     equ    78h
data_3e     equ    7Ch
data_4e     equ    80h
data_5e     equ    84h
data_6e     equ    86h
data_7e     equ    88h
data_8e     equ    8Ah
data_9e     equ    8Ch
data_10e    equ    8Eh
data_11e    equ    98h
data_12e    equ    9Ah
data_13e    equ    194h
data_14e    equ    196h
data_15e    equ    198h
data_16e    equ    19Eh
data_17e    equ    1A2h
data_18e    equ    1A4h
data_19e    equ    1A6h
data_20e    equ    1E8h
data_21e    equ    1EAh
data_22e    equ    2
data_23e    equ    2Ch
data_24e    equ    72h
data_25e    equ    94h
data_26e    equ    9Eh
data_27e    equ    19Eh
data_28e    equ    1A6h
```

Fig. 2-17 continued.

```
seg_a        segment    para public
      assume cs:seg_a, ds:seg_a, ss:stack_seg_c


c-cond1b    proc    far

start:
      mov    dx,seg_b
      mov    cs:data_29,dx
      mov    ah,30h
      int    21h

      mov    bp,ds:data_22e
      mov    bx,ds:data_23e
      mov    ds,dx
      mov    data_45,ax
      mov    data_44,es
      mov    data_42,bx
      mov    data_52,bp
      mov    data_47,0FFFFh
      call   sub_2
      les    di,data_41
      mov    ax,di
      mov    bx,ax
      mov    cx,7FFFh
loc_1:
      cmp    word ptr es:[di],3738h
      jne    loc_2
      mov    dx,es:[di+2]
      cmp    dl,3Dh
      jne    loc_2
      and    dh,0DFh
      inc    data_47
      cmp    dh,59h
      jne    loc_2
      inc    data_47
loc_2:
      repne  scasb
      jcxz   loc_5
      inc    bx
      cmp    es:[di],al
      jne    loc_1
      or     ch,80h
      neg    cx
      mov    word ptr data_41,cx
      mov    cx,1
      shl    bx,cl
      add    bx,8
      and    bx,0FFF8h
      mov    data_43,bx
      mov    dx,ds
      sub    bp,dx
      mov    di,data_54
      cmp    di,200h
      jae    loc_3
      mov    di,200h
      mov    data_54,di
loc_3:
      add    di,1ECh
      jc     loc_5
```

Fig. 2-17 continued.

```
        add    di,data_53
        jc     loc_5
        mov    cl,4
        shr    di,cl
        inc    di
        cmp    bp,di
        jb     loc_5
        cmp    data_54,0
        je     loc_4
        cmp    data_53,0
        jne    loc_6
loc_4:
        mov    di,1000h
        cmp    bp,di
        ja     loc_6
        mov    di,bp
        jmp    short loc_6
loc_5:
        jmp    loc_9
loc_6:
        mov    bx,di
        add    bx,dx
        mov    data_50,bx
        mov    data_51,bx
        mov    ax,data_44
        sub    bx,ax
        mov    es,ax
        mov    ah,4Ah
        push   di
        int    21h

        pop    di
        shl    di,cl
        cli
        mov    ss,dx
        mov    sp,di
        sti
        xor    ax,ax
        mov    es,cs:data_29
        mov    di,1A6h
        mov    cx,1ECh
        sub    cx,di
        rep    stosb
        push   cs
        call   data_55
        call   sub_8
        call   sub_10
        mov    ah,0
        int    1Ah

        mov    ds:data_11e,dx
        mov    ds:data_12e,cx
        call   word ptr ds:data_18e
        push   word ptr ds:data_7e
        push   word ptr ds:data_6e
        push   word ptr ds:data_5e
        call   sub_5
        push   ax
        call   sub_7
```

Fig. 2-17 continued.

```
c-cond1b    endp

sub_1       proc   near
       mov   ds,cs:data_29
       call  sub_3
       push  cs
       call  word ptr ds:data_17e
       xor   ax,ax
       mov   si,ax
       mov   cx,2Fh
       nop
       cld

locloop_7:
       add   al,[si]
       adc   ah,0
       inc   si
       loop  locloop_7

       sub   ax,0D37h
       nop
       jz    loc_8
       mov   cx,19h
       nop
       mov   dx,2Fh
       call  sub_4
loc_8:
       mov   bp,sp
       mov   ah,4Ch
       mov   al,[bp+2]
       int   21h

sub_1       endp


int_00h_entry   proc   far
       mov   cx,0Eh
       nop
       mov   dx,48h
       jmp   loc_10
int_00h_entry   endp

sub_2       proc   near
       push  ds
       mov   ax,3500h
       int   21h

       mov   data_33,bx
       mov   data_34,es
       mov   ax,3504h
       int   21h

       mov   data_35,bx
       mov   data_36,es
       mov   ax,3505h
       int   21h

       mov   data_37,bx
       mov   data_38,es
```

Fig. 2-17 continued.

```
            mov     ax,3506h
            int     21h

            mov     data_39,bx
            mov     data_40,es
            mov     ax,2500h
            mov     dx,cs
            mov     ds,dx
            mov     dx,158h
            int     21h

            pop     ds
            ret
sub_2       endp


sub_3       proc    near
            push    ds
            mov     ax,2500h
            lds     dx,dword ptr ds:data_1e
            int     21h

            pop     ds
            push    ds
            mov     ax,2504h
            lds     dx,dword ptr ds:data_2e
            int     21h
            pop     ds
            push    ds
            mov     ax,2505h
            lds     dx,dword ptr ds:data_3e
            int     21h

            pop     ds
            push    ds
            mov     ax,2506h
            lds     dx,dword ptr ds:data_4e
            int     21h

            pop     ds
            ret
sub_3       endp

            db      0C7h, 6, 96h, 0, 0, 0
            db      0CBh, 0C3h


sub_4       proc    near
            mov     ah,40h
            mov     bx,2
            int     21h

            ret
sub_4       endp

loc_9:
            mov     cx,1Eh
            nop
            mov     dx,56h
```

Fig. 2-17 continued.

```
loc_10:
        mov     ds,cs:data_29
        call    sub_4
        mov     ax,3
        push    ax
        call    sub_1
data_29         dw      0

sub_5           proc    near
        mov     ax,0Fh
        push    ax
        xor     ax,ax
        push    ax
        call    sub_6
        pop     cx
        pop     cx
        ret
sub_5           endp

        db      0

sub_6           proc    near
        push    si
        push    di
        push    bp
        mov     bp,sp
        mov     dx,[bp+8]
        mov     ax,[bp+0Ah]
        mov     ah,0
        int     17h

        mov     al,ah
        xor     ah,ah
        mov     sp,bp
        pop     bp
        pop     di
        pop     si
        ret
sub_6           endp

        db      0C3h

sub_7           proc    near
        push    bp
        mov     bp,sp
        jmp     short loc_12
loc_11:
        mov     bx,ds:data_16e
        shl     bx,1
        call    word ptr ds:data_19e[bx]
loc_12:
        mov     ax,ds:data_16e
        dec     word ptr ds:data_16e
        or      ax,ax
        jnz     loc_11
        call    word ptr ds:data_13e
        call    word ptr ds:data_14e
        call    word ptr ds:data_15e
        push    word ptr [bp+4]
```

Fig. 2-17 continued.

```
            call    sub_1
            pop     cx
            pop     bp
            ret
sub_7       endp

data_30     dw      0
data_31     dw      0
            db      0, 0

sub_8       proc    near
            pop     cs:data_30
            mov     cs:data_31,ds
            cld
            mov     es,data_44
            mov     si,80h
            xor     ah,ah
            lods    byte ptr es:[si]
            inc     ax
            mov     bp,es
            xchg    dx,si
            xchg    ax,bx
            mov     si,word ptr data_41
            add     si,2
            mov     cx,1
            cmp     byte ptr data_45,3
            jb      loc_13
            mov     es,data_42
            mov     di,si
            mov     cl,7Fh
            xor     al,al
            repne   scasb
            jcxz    loc_21
            xor     cl,7Fh
loc_13:
            sub     sp,2
            mov     ax,1
            add     ax,bx
            add     ax,cx
            and     ax,0FFFEh
            mov     di,sp
            sub     di,ax
            jc      loc_21
            mov     sp,di
            mov     ax,es
            mov     ds,ax
            mov     ax,ss
            mov     es,ax
            push    cx
            dec     cx
            rep     movsb
            xor     al,al
            stosb
            mov     ds,bp
            xchg    si,dx
            xchg    bx,cx
            mov     ax,bx
            mov     dx,ax
            inc     bx
```

Fig. 2-17 continued.

```
loc_14:
      call    sub_9
      ja    loc_16
loc_15:
      jc    loc_22
      call    sub_9
      ja    loc_15
loc_16:
      cmp    al,20h

      je    loc_17
      cmp    al,0Dh
      je    loc_17
      cmp    al,9
      jne    loc_14
loc_17:
      xor    al,al
      jmp    short loc_14


sub_9:
      or    ax,ax
      jz    loc_18
      inc    dx
      stosb
      or    al,al
      jnz    loc_18
      inc    bx
loc_18:
      xchg    ah,al
      xor    al,al
      stc
      jcxz    loc_ret_20
      lodsb
      dec    cx
      sub    al,22h
      jz    loc_ret_20
      add    al,22h
      cmp    al,5Ch
      jne    loc_19
      cmp    byte ptr [si],22h
      jne    loc_19
      lodsb
      dec    cx
loc_19:
      or    si,si

loc_ret_20:
      ret
loc_21:
      jmp    loc_9
loc_22:
      pop    cx
      add    cx,dx
      mov    ds,cs:data_31
      mov    ds:data_5e,bx
      inc    bx
      add    bx,bx
      mov    si,sp
      mov    bp,sp
      sub    bp,bx
```

Fig. 2-17 continued.

```
        jc    loc_21
        mov   sp,bp
        mov   ds:data_6e,bp
loc_23:
        jcxz  loc_25
        mov   [bp],si
        add   bp,2

locloop_24:
        lods   byte ptr ss:[si]
        or    al,al
        loopnz  locloop_24

        jz    loc_23
loc_25:
        xor   ax,ax
        mov   [bp],ax
        jmp   cs:data_30
sub_8   endp


sub_10     proc   near
        mov   cx,ds:data_8e
        push  cx
        call  sub_15
        pop   cx
        mov   di,ax
        or    ax,ax
        jz    loc_26
        push  ds
        push  ds
        pop   es
        mov   ds,ds:data_9e
        xor   si,si
        cld
        rep   movsb
        pop   ds
        mov   di,ax
        push  es
        push  word ptr ds:data_10e
        call  sub_15
        add   sp,2
        mov   bx,ax
        pop   es
        mov   ds:data_7e,ax
        or    ax,ax
        jnz   loc_27
loc_26:
        jmp   loc_9
loc_27:
        xor   ax,ax
        mov   cx,0FFFFh
loc_28:
        mov   [bx],di
        add   bx,2
        repne   scasb
        cmp   es:[di],al
        jne   loc_28
        mov   [bx],ax
        ret
```

Fig. 2-17 continued.

```
sub_10       endp

       db    55h, 8Bh, 0ECh, 83h, 3Eh, 9Eh
       db    1, 20h, 75h, 5, 0B8h, 1
       db    0, 0EBh, 15h, 8Bh, 46h, 4
       db    8Bh, 1Eh, 9Eh, 1, 0D1h, 0E3h
       db    89h, 87h, 0A6h, 1, 0FFh, 6
       db    9Eh, 1, 33h, 0C0h, 0EBh, 0
loc_29:
       pop   bp
       ret


sub_11       proc   near
       push  bp
       mov   bp,sp
       push  si
       push  di
       mov   di,[bp+4]
       mov   ax,[di+6]
       mov   ds:data_20e,ax
       cmp   ax,di
       jne   loc_30
       mov   word ptr ds:data_20e,0
       jmp   short loc_31
loc_30:
       mov   si,[di+4]
       mov   bx,ds:data_20e
       mov   [bx+4],si
       mov   ax,ds:data_20e
       mov   [si+6],ax
loc_31:
       pop   di
       pop   si
       pop   bp
       ret
sub_11       endp


sub_12       proc   near
       push  bp
       mov   bp,sp
       push  si
       push  di
       mov   di,[bp+4]
       mov   ax,[bp+6]
       sub   [di],ax
       mov   si,[di]
       add   si,di
       mov   ax,[bp+6]
       inc   ax
       mov   [si],ax
       mov   [si+2],di
       mov   ax,data_62
       cmp   ax,di
       jne   loc_32
       mov   data_62,si
       jmp   short loc_33
```

Fig. 2-17 continued.

```
loc_32:
     mov   di,si
     add   di,[bp+6]
     mov   [di+2],si
loc_33:
     mov   ax,si
     add   ax,4
     jmp   short loc_34
loc_34:
     pop   di
     pop   si
     pop   bp
     ret
sub_12     endp

sub_13     proc   near
     push  bp
     mov   bp,sp
     push  si
     mov   ax,[bp+4]
     xor   dx,dx
     and   ax,0FFFFh
     and   dx,0
     push  dx
     push  ax
     call  sub_16
     pop   cx
     pop   cx
     mov   si,ax
     cmp   si,0FFFFh
     jne   loc_35
     xor   ax,ax
     jmp   short loc_36
loc_35:
     mov   ax,data_62
     mov   [si+2],ax
     mov   ax,[bp+4]
     inc   ax
     mov   [si],ax
     mov   data_62,si
     mov   ax,data_62
     add   ax,4
     jmp   short loc_36
loc_36:
     pop   si
     pop   bp
     ret
sub_13     endp

sub_14     proc   near
     push  bp
     mov   bp,sp
     push  si
     mov   ax,[bp+4]
     xor   dx,dx
     and   ax,0FFFFh
     and   dx,0
     push  dx
     push  ax
```

Fig. 2-17 continued.

```
        call    sub_16
        pop     cx
        pop     cx
        mov     si,ax
        cmp     si,0FFFFh
        jne     loc_37
        xor     ax,ax
        jmp     short loc_38
loc_37:
        mov     ds:data_21e,si
        mov     data_62,si
        mov     ax,[bp+4]
        inc     ax
        mov     [si],ax
        mov     ax,si
        add     ax,4
        jmp     short loc_38
loc_38:
        pop     si
        pop     bp
        ret
sub_14          endp

sub_15          proc    near
        push    bp
        mov     bp,sp
        push    si
        push    di
        mov     di,[bp+4]
        or      di,di
        jnz     loc_39
        xor     ax,ax
        jmp     short loc_45
loc_39:
        mov     ax,di
        add     ax,0Bh
        and     ax,0FFF8h
        mov     di,ax
        cmp     word ptr ds:data_21e,0
        jne     loc_40
        push    di
        call    sub_14
        pop     cx
        jmp     short loc_45
loc_40:
        mov     si,ds:data_20e
        mov     ax,si
        or      ax,ax
        jz      loc_44
loc_41:
        mov     ax,[si]
        mov     dx,di
        add     dx,28h
        cmp     ax,dx
        jb      loc_42
        push    di
        push    si
        call    sub_12
        pop     cx
        pop     cx
```

Fig. 2-17 continued.

```
        jmp     short loc_45
loc_42:
        mov     ax,[si]
        cmp     ax,di
        jb      loc_43
        push    si
        call    sub_11
        pop     cx
        inc     word ptr [si]
        mov     ax,si
        add     ax,4
        jmp     short loc_45
loc_43:
        mov     si,[si+6]
        cmp     si,ds:data_20e
        jne     loc_41
loc_44:
        push    di
        call    sub_13
        pop     cx
        jmp     short loc_45
loc_45:
        pop     di
        pop     si
        pop     bp
        ret
sub_15          endp

        db      55h, 8Bh, 0ECh, 8Bh, 46h, 4
        db      8Bh, 0D4h, 81h, 0EAh, 0, 1
        db      3Bh, 0C2h, 73h, 7, 0A3h, 9Eh
        db      0, 33h, 0C0h, 0EBh, 0Bh
loc_46:
        mov     word ptr ds:data_25e,8
        mov     ax,0FFFFh
        jmp     short loc_47
loc_47:
        pop     bp
        ret

sub_16          proc    near
        push    bp
        mov     bp,sp
        mov     ax,[bp+4]
        mov     dx,[bp+6]
        add     ax,data_63
        adc     dx,0
        mov     cx,ax
        add     cx,100h
        adc     dx,0
        or      dx,dx
        jnz     loc_48
        cmp     cx,sp
        jae     loc_48
        xchg    ax,data_63
        jmp     short loc_49
loc_48:
        mov     data_64,8
        mov     ax,0FFFFh
```

Fig. 2-17 continued.

```
        jmp     short loc_49
loc_49:
        pop     bp
        ret
sub_16      endp

        db      55h, 8Bh, 0ECh, 0FFh, 76h, 4
        db      0E8h, 9Fh, 0FFh, 59h, 0EBh, 0
        db      5Dh, 0C3h, 55h, 8Bh, 0ECh, 8Bh
        db      46h, 4, 99h, 52h, 50h, 0E8h
        db      0B2h, 0FFh, 8Bh, 0E5h, 0EBh, 0
        db      5Dh, 0C3h
        db      9 dup (0)


seg_a       ends

seg_b       segment   para public
        assume cs:seg_b, ds:seg_b, ss:stack_seg_c

        db      0, 0, 0, 0
        db      'Turbo-C - Copyright (c) 1988 Bor'
        db      'land Intl.'
        db      0
        db      'Null pointer assignment', 0Dh, 0Ah
        db      'Divide error', 0Dh, 0Ah, 'Abnorm'
        db      'al program termination', 0Dh, 0Ah
data_33     dw      0
data_34     dw      0
data_35     dw      0
data_36     dw      0
data_37     dw      0
data_38     dw      0
data_39     dw      0
data_40     dw      0
        db      0, 0, 0, 0, 0, 0
data_41     dw      0
data_42     dw      0
data_43     dw      0
data_44     dw      0
data_45     dw      0
data_46     dw      0
data_47     dw      0
        db      4 dup (0)
        db      0ECh, 1
data_48     dw      1ECh
        db      0ECh, 1, 0
        db      0
data_50     dw      0
        dw      0
data_51     dw      0
        dw      0
data_52     dw      0
        db      230 dup (0)
        db      21h, 2, 21h, 2, 21h, 2
data_53     dw      0
data_54     dw      1000h
        db      0, 0
data_55     dw      1D2h
        db      0D2h, 1, 0D9h, 1, 0, 0
```

```
        db      62 dup (0)
data_57         dw      0
data_58         dw      0
data_59         dw      0
        db      4 dup (0)

seg_b           ends


stack_seg_c     segment    para stack

        db      111 dup (0)
data_61         dw      0, 0
        db      13 dup (0)

stack_seg_c     ends


        end     start
```

Fig. 2-17 ends.

3

Simulated Extensions to Assembler Instruction Set

Ah, the question: "Why do you need extensions to the standard assembly mnemonics?"

Answer: For two reasons. The sales/marketing force at TSR Systems Ltd, the company that will be marketing a commercial version of CHUCK under the ASMplus™ name, complained whenever he saw a standard assembly instruction in an ASMplus demonstration program. Although seeing a 'mov' instruction in a CHUCK program didn't bother me one whit, I'm a compromising sort and added a few macros to reduce the presence of those mnemonics that offended.

The second reason is that there are certain operations which I occasionally need to do where a macro extension to the standard assembly mnemonics come in very handy. For example, there are times when I wish to move word-sized data in one memory location to another memory location. Because the 'mov' instruction does not allow memory to memory moves, writing a simple macro proves to be a convenience. There are other macros of convenience which I've included in CHUCK's list of macro extensions.

REGSEXT.MAC

REGSEXT.MAC, presented in Fig. 3-1, is the file containing all the macro definitions for extended instruction operations.

Fig. 3-1. The source code listing to REGSEXT.MAC.

```
;;-------------------------------------
;;
;;
;; File Name: REGSEXT.MAC
```

Fig. 3-1 continued.

```
;;
;;------------------------------------;;
;;                                    ;;
;; CHUCK Instruction Set Extensions   ;;
;;                                    ;;
;;------------------------------------;;
;; ADD1      Add 1 to reg or memory   ;;
;; ADD2      Add 2 to reg or memory   ;;
;; DIV2      Divide register by two   ;;
;; GETPTR    Get PTR from table of PTRs;;
;; MUL2      Multiply register by 2   ;;
;; PUSHAA    Push AX,BX,CX,CD,SI,DI,ES ;;
;; POPAA     Pop AX,BX,CX,CD,SI,DI,ES  ;;
;; PUSHX     Push AX,BX,CX,DX         ;;
;; POPX      Pop AX,BX,CX,DX          ;;
;; PUSHAD    Push AX,DX               ;;
;; POPAD     Pop AX,DX                ;;
;; PUSHABD   Push AX,BX,DX            ;;
;; POPABD    Pop AX,BX,DX             ;;
;; PUSHBCD   Push BX,CX,DX            ;;
;; POPBCD    Pop BX,CX,DX             ;;
;; PUSHAB    Push AX,BX               ;;
;; POPAB     Pop AX,BX                ;;
;; SUB1      Sub 1 from reg or mem    ;;
;; SUB2      Sub 2 from reg or mem    ;;
;; SETPTR    Moves offset to PTR reg  ;;
;; SETV      Set reg or mem to value  ;;
;; SETMV     Set mem to mem           ;;
;; SETVO     Set reg or mem to 0      ;;
;;------------------------------------;;


;;-------------------------------------
;;
;; Macro: ADD1 val
;;
;; Description: Add 1 to a register
;;    or memory

ADD1 MACRO val
        inc     val
        ENDM

;;-------------------------------------

;;-------------------------------------
;;
;; Macro: ADD2 val
;;
;; Description: Add 2 to a register
;;    or memory

ADD2 MACRO val
        inc     val
        inc     val
        ENDM

;;-------------------------------------

;;-------------------------------------
;;
```

Fig. 3-1 continued.

```
;; Macro: DIV2 val
;;
;; Description: Divide val by 2
;;   (remainder lost)

DIV2 MACRO val
        ror     val,1
        ENDM

;;-------------------------------------

;;-------------------------------------
;;
;; Macro: GETPTR         pointer,ptr_table
;;
;; Description: Get pointer from table
;;   of pointer and move into Index
;;   register Pointer

GETPTR  MACRO pointer,ptr_table
        push    AX
        mov     AX,WORD PTR [ptr_table]
        mov     pointer,AX
        pop     AX
        ENDM

;;-------------------------------------

;;-------------------------------------
;;
;; Macro: JUMP label
;;
;; Description: jmp to label

JUMP MACRO label
        jmp     label
        ENDM

;;-------------------------------------

;;-------------------------------------
;;
;; Macro: MUL2 val
;;
;; Description: Multiply val by 2
;;   or memory

MUL2 MACRO val
        rol     val,1
        ENDM

;;-------------------------------------

;;-------------------------------------
;;
;; Macro: PUSHAA
;;
;; Description: Push regs
```

Fig. 3-1 continued.

```
PUSHAA MACRO
        push    AX
        push    BX
        push    CX
        push    DX
        push    SI
        push    DI
        push    ES
        ENDM

;;--------------------------------------

;;--------------------------------------
;;
;; Macro: POPAA
;;
;; Description: Pop regs

POPAA MACRO
        pop     ES
        pop     DI
        pop     SI
        pop     DX
        pop     CX
        pop     BX
        pop     AX
        ENDM

;;--------------------------------------

;;--------------------------------------
;;
;; Macro: PUSHX
;;
;; Description: Push all general
;;   purpose registers

PUSHX MACRO
        push    AX
        push    BX
        push    CX
        push    DX
        ENDM

;;--------------------------------------

;;--------------------------------------
;;
;; Macro: POPX
;;
;; Description: Pop all general
;;   purpose registers

POPX MACRO
        pop     DX
        pop     CX
        pop     BX
        pop     AX
        ENDM
```

Fig. 3-1 continued.

```
;;--------------------------------------

;;--------------------------------------
;;
;; Macro: PUSHAD
;;
;; Description: Push AX,DX

PUSHABD MACRO
        push    AX
        push    DX
        ENDM

;;--------------------------------------

;;--------------------------------------
;;
;; Macro: POPAD
;;
;; Description: Push AX,DX

POPABD MACRO
        pop     DX
        pop     AX
        ENDM

;;--------------------------------------

;;--------------------------------------
;;
;; Macro: PUSHABD
;;
;; Description: Push AX,BX,DX

PUSHABD MACRO
        push    AX
        push    BX
        push    DX
        ENDM

;;--------------------------------------

;;--------------------------------------
;;
;; Macro: POPABD
;;
;; Description: Push AX,BX,DX

POPABD MACRO
        pop     DX
        pop     BX
        pop     AX
        ENDM

;;--------------------------------------

;;--------------------------------------
;;
;; Macro: PUSHBCD
```

Fig. 3-1. continued.

```
;;
;; Description: Push BX,CX,DX

PUSHBCD MACRO
        push    BX
        push    CX
        push    DX
        ENDM

;;------------------------------------

;;------------------------------------
;;
;; Macro: POPBCD
;;
;; Description: POp BX,CX,DX

POPBCD MACRO
        pop     DX
        pop     CX
        pop     BX
        ENDM

;;------------------------------------

;;------------------------------------
;;
;; Macro: PUSHAB
;;
;; Description: Push AX,BX

PUSHAB MACRO
        push    AX
        push    BX
        ENDM

;;------------------------------------

;;------------------------------------
;;
;; Macro: POPAB
;;
;; Description: POP AX,BX

POPAB MACRO
        pop     BX
        pop     AX
        ENDM

;;------------------------------------

;;------------------------------------
;;
;; Macro: SETVO val
;;
;; Description: Set val to 0

SETVO MACRO val
        mov     val,0
        ENDM
```

Fig. 3-1 continued.

```
;;--------------------------------------

;;--------------------------------------
;; Macro: SETV loc,val
;;
;; Description: Set val

SETV MACRO loc,val
        mov      loc,val
        ENDM

;;--------------------------------------

;;--------------------------------------
;;
;; Macro: SUB1 val
;;
;; Description: Subtract 1 from register
;;   or memory

SUB1 MACRO val
        dec      val
        ENDM

;;--------------------------------------

;;--------------------------------------
;;
;; Macro: SUB2 val
;;
;; Description: Subtract 2 from register
;;   or memory

SUB2 MACRO val
        dec      val
        dec      val
        ENDM

;;--------------------------------------

;;--------------------------------------
;;
;; Macro: SETPTR reg,name
;;
;; Description: Loads the effective
;;              offset of label into
;;              the named register

SETPTR MACRO regis,name
        lea      regis,name
        ENDM

;;--------------------------------------

;;--------------------------------------
;;
;; Macro: SETMV mem1, mem2
;;
;; Description: set memory to memory
```

```
;;  (dest,src)

SETMV MACRO mem1,mem2
        push    AX
        mov     AX,DS:[mem2]
        mov     DS:[mem1],AX
        pop     AX
        ENDM

;;-------------------------------------------
```

Fig. 3-1 ends

STANDARD ASSEMBLY MNEMONICS/CHUCK EXTENSIONS

The following table lists the standard Assembly Mnemonics and CHUCK Extensions.

Mnemonic/Extension	Description
(CHUCK Extensions denoted by *)	
AAA	ASCII adjust after addition
AAS	ASCII adjust after subtraction
AAM	ASCII adjust after multiplication
AAD	ASCII adjust after division
DAA	Packed BCD adjust for addition
DAS	Packed BCD adjust for subtraction
ADC	Add with carry
ADD	Add without carry
*ADD1	Add one by increment
*ADD2	Add two by incrementing twice
DEC	Decrement destination by one
INC	Increment destination by one
DIV	Unsigned divide
*DIV2	Divide by two using shift right
IDIV	Signed integer divide
MUL	Unsigned multiply
*MUL2	Multiply by two using shift left
IMUL	Signed integer multiply
SBB	Subtract with borrow
SUB	Subtract without borrow
*SUB1	Subtract one by increment
*SUB2	Subtract two by increment

Continues.

Mnemonic/Extension	Description
(CHUCK Extensions denoted by *)	
AND	Logical AND
NOT	Logical NOT
OR	Logical inclusive OR
XOR	Logical exclusive OR
NEG	Negate (two's complement)
NOP	No operation
TEST	Logically AND operands (affects flags only)
CALL	Call a procedure
*CPROC	Call a procedure with PUSHX prior and POPX after (CPROC located in CHUCK.MAC)
CLC	Clear the carry flag
CLD	Clear direction flag
CLI	Clear interrupt flag
CMC	Complement carry flag
STC	Set carry flag
STD	Set direction flag
STI	Set interrupt enable flag
CMP	Compare
CWD	Convert (extended) qword to double word
CBW	Convert byte to word
ESC	Escape
HLT	Halt the processor
IN	Input byte or word
OUT	Output byte or word
INT	Invoke interrupt
INTO	Interrupt if zero
J(xx)	Conditional and unconditional Jump
LAHF	Load AH from flags
SAHF	Store AH in flags
LDS	Load pointer using DS
LEA	Load effective address (offset)
LES	Load pointer using ES
LOD(x)	Load byte, word, or string
LOCK	Lock the Bus

Continues.

Mnemonic/Extension	Description
(CHUCK Extensions denoted by *)	
LOOP	Loop until CX is zero
LOOP(x)	Conditional loops
MOV	Move byte or word
MOV(x)	Move byte or word string
*GETPTR	Relocates pointer from table of pointers to a pointer
*SETV	Operates as MOV mnemonic
*SETMV	Permits MOV from memory to memory locations
*SETV0	Set variable or register to 0
*SETPTR	Moves offset of symbol to PTR register
POP	Pop word off stack
POPF	Pop flags off stack
*POPAA	Pop AX, BX, CX, DX, SI, DI, ES off stack
*POPX	Pop AX, BX, CX, DX off stack
*POPABD	Pop AX, BX, DX off stack
*POPAD	POP AX, DX, off stack
*POPBCD	Pop BX, CX, DX off stack
*POPAB	Pop AX, BX, off stack
PUSH	Push word on stack
PUSHF	Push flags on stack
*PUSHAA	Push AX, BX, CX, DX, SI, DI, ES on stack
*PUSHX	Push AX, BX, CX, DX on stack
*PUSHABD	Push AX, BX, DX on stack
*PUSHAD	Push AX, DX, on stack
*PUSHBCD	Push BX, CX, DX on stack
*PUSHAB	Push AX, BX on stack
RCL	Rotate left through carry
RCR	Rotate right through carry
ROL	Rotate left
ROR	Rotate right
SAL/SHL	Shift arithmetic left/Shift logical left
SAR	Shift arithmetic right
SHR	Shift logical right
REP(x)	Repeat string operation
IRET	Return from interrupt
RET	Return from subroutine

Continues.

Mnemonic/Extension	**Description**
(CHUCK Extensions denoted by *)	
SCA(xx)	Scan byte or word string
STO(xx)	Store byte word or string
WAIT	Wait
XCHG	Exchange two operands
XLAT	Translate

A DETAILED LOOK AT CHUCK EXTENSIONS

The following sections give an indepth discussion of the CHUCK extensions to the instruction set.

ADD1

The ADD1 macro uses the INC instruction to add one to a register or memory location. The INC instruction is used as it uses less memory than the ADD instruction. ADD1 is useful for incrementing BYTE PTRs and counters. The syntax for ADD1 is:

```
ADD1 {register|memory}
```

Here is an example:

```
    .
    .
    .
add1 BX
mov  AL,BYTE PTR [BX]
    .
    .
```

ADD2

The ADD2 macro uses the INC instruction twice to add two to a register or memory location. The INC instruction is used as it uses less memory than the ADD instruction. ADD2 is useful for incrementing WORD PTRs. The syntax for ADD2 is:

```
ADD2 {register|memory}
```

Here is an example:

```
    .
    .
    .
add2 BX
mov  AX,WORD PTR [BX]
    .
    .
```

DIV2

The DIV2 macro uses ROR to shift right one bit. Note that the remainder will be lost during the divide and only the quotient will remain. The syntax for DIV2 is:

DIV2 {*register* | *memory*}

Here is an example:

```
    .
    .
    div2 count ; divide variable in memory by 2
    .
    .
```

GETPTR

GETPTR moves a pointer to a label from a table of pointers to another pointer register. The syntax of GETPTR is:

getptr   {BX|SI|DI},{BX|SI|DI}

Here is an example:

```
; get the 11th near pointer from array named 'table' of pointers
    setptr    DBASE_PTR, table   ; offset of table to BASE_PTR
    add       DBASE_PTR,22       ; get 11th element (offset = 11*2)
    getptr    SRCE_PTR,DBASE_PTR ; pointer from table = > SRCE_PTR
; SRCE_PTR holds pointer to array
```

MUL2

The MUL2 macro uses ROL to shift left one bit. Note that the product may not be greater than 16 bits. The syntax for MUL2 is:

MUL2 {*register* | *memory*}

Here is an example:

```
    .
    .
    mul2 count ; multiply variable in memory by 2
    .
    .
```

PUSHAA
POPAA

The PUSHAA macro is always used in conjunction with POPAA and is used to save and restore the following registers: AX, BX, CX, DX, SI, DI, ES. The syntax for PUSHAA and POPAA is:

```
PUSHAA
POPAA
```

Here is an example:

```
    .
    .
    pushaa
    call your_procedure
    popaa
    .
    .
```

PUSHX
POPX

The PUSHX macro is always used in conjunction with POPX and is used to save and restore the following registers: AX, BX, CX, DX. The syntax for PUSHX and POPX is:

```
PUSHX
POPX
```

Here is an example:

```
    .
    .
    pushx
    call your_procedure
    popx
    .
    .
```

PUSHAD
POPAD

The PUSHAD macro is always used in conjunction with POPAD and is used to save and restore the following registers: AX, DX. The syntax for PUSHAD and POPAD is:

```
PUSHAD
POPAD
```

Here is an example:

-
-

```
pushad
call your_procedure
popad
```

-
-

PUSHABD
POPABD

The PUSHABD macro is always used in conjunction with POPABD and is used to save and restore the following registers: AX, BX, DX. The syntax for PUSHABD and POPABD is:

```
PUSHABD
POPABD
```

Here is an example:

-
-

```
pushabd
call your_procedure
popabd
```

-
-

PUSHBCD
POPBCD

The PUSHBCD macro is always used in conjunction with POPBCD and is used to save and restore the following registers: BX, CX, DX. The syntax for PUSHBCD and POPBCD is:

```
PUSHBCD
POPBCD
```

Here is an example:

-
-

```
pushbcd
call your_procedure
popbcd
```

-
-

PUSHAB
POPAB

The PUSHAB macro is always used in conjunction with POPAB and is used to save and restore the following registers: AX, BX. The syntax for PUSHAB and POPAB is:

```
PUSHAB
POPAB
```

Here is an example:

```
    .
    .
pushab
call your_procedure
popab
    .
    .
```

SETV0

The SETV0 macro sets a register or memory location to 0. There are more efficient ways to set a register to 0 than by using MOV to set a value of 0 to a register, but SETV0 needs to operate on both registers and memory. The syntax for SETV0 is:

```
SETV0 {register|memory}
```

Here is an example:

```
    .
    .
setv0   counter ; 0 => variable counter in memory
    .
    .
```

SETV

The SETV macro is identical to the standard MOV instruction. Consult your assembler's manual for the appropriate MOV mnemonic syntax. Here is an example:

```
    .
    .
setv   counter,5 ; 5 => variable counter in memory
    .
    .
```

SETMV

The SETMV macro is a special case MOV instruction which moves a 16-bit value from one memory location to another memory location. All register values are preserved. The syntax for SETMV is:

SETMV {memory},{memory}

Here is an example:

```
        •
counter   DW   ?
index     DW   10

        •
        setmv counter,index ; 10 in index to counter
        •
        •
```

SUB1

The SUB1 macro uses the DEC instruction to subtract one from a register or memory location. The DEC instruction is used because it uses less memory than the SUB instruction. SUB1 is useful for decrementing BYTE PTRs and counters. The syntax for SUB1 is:

SUB1 {register|memory}

Here is an example:

```
        •
        •
        sub1 BX
        mov  AL,BYTE PTR [BX]
        •
        •
```

SUB2

The SUB2 macro uses the DEC instruction twice to subtract two from a register or memory location. The DEC instruction is used because it uses less memory than the SUB instruction. SUB2 is useful for decrementing WORD PTRs and counters. The syntax for SUB2 is:

SUB2 {register|memory}

Here is an example:

```
    .
    .
sub2 BX
mov  AX,WORD PTR [BX]
    .
    .
```

SETPTR

The SETPTR macro is used to load a register with the offset of a symbol and identical to the standard LEA (Load Effective Address) mnemonic. Consult your assembler's manual for LEA's usage syntax. Here is an example:

```
       .
buffer    DB   25 DUP(0)
       .
    setptr  DBASE_PTR,buffer ; offset buffer => DBASE_PTR
       .
       .
```

CHUCK DEFINES AND STRUCTURES

As you can see some of the register extensions are simply new names for old mnemonics while others are programming convenience macros. Chapter 3 ends with the listing of DEFINES.MAC. This file holds many keyboard equates and a few structures and is to be included before all CHUCK macro files.

The order of inclusion for CHUCK macro scripts is:

```
DEFINES.MAC
REGSEXT.MAC
CHUCK.MAC
... specific macro files here ...
```

DEFINES.MAC

Figure 3-2 presents the code listing for DEFINES.MAC.

Fig. 3-2. The source code listing to DEFINES.MAC.

```
;;----------------------------------------
;;
;; File Name: DEFINES.MAC
;;
;;----------------------------------------
;;
;; FSEEK equates
;;

SEEK_SET          equ    0
```

Fig. 3-2 continued.

```
SEEK_CUR          equ    1
SEEK_END          equ    2


;;------------------------------------
;; Equates: These simplified equates
;;          may be used along with the
;;          assembler assigned register
;;          names

SRCE_PTR   equ   SI
DEST_PTR   equ   DI
DBASE_PTR  equ   BX
RET_VAL    equ   AX

;;------------------------------------
;; Disk IO equates
;;

O_RDONLY   equ   0
O_WRONLY   equ   1
O_RDWR     equ   2
F_NORMAL   equ   0
F_HIDDEN   equ   2
F_SYS      equ   4
F_HIDSYS   equ   6

;;------------------------------------;;
;; WINDOW    Screen Window Structure  ;;
;;------------------------------------;;

WINDOW    STRUC
    ulrow    DB    ?   ;; upper left row
    ulcol    DB    ?   ;; upper left col
    lrrow    DB    ?   ;; lower right row
    lrcol    DB    ?   ;; lower right col
    attr     DB    ?   ;; window attribute
    scrnimg DW    ?   ;; pointer to screen image
    windimg DW    ?   ;; pointer to rect image
WINDOW    ENDS

;;------------------------------------;;
;; DRIVE_STAT Drive status Structure  ;;
;;------------------------------------;;

DFREE    STRUC
    clust_avail   DW   ?   ;; available clusters
    total_clust   DW   ?   ;; total clusters
    byte_per_sec  DW   ?   ;; bytes per sector
    sec_per_clust DW   ?   ;; sectors per cluster
    free_bytes    DW   ?,? ;; Free bytes on disk
DFREE    ENDS

;;------------------------------------;;
;; Defines for MAKEATTR                ;;
;;------------------------------------;;

ON_INTEN  equ   8
OFF_INTEN equ   0
```

Fig. 3-2 continued.

```
ON_BLINK    equ  128
OFF_BLINK   equ  0

BLACK       equ  0
BLUE        equ  1
GREEN       equ  2
CYAN        equ  3
RED         equ  4
MAGENTA     equ  5
BROWN       equ  6
WHITE       equ  7
NORMAL      equ  7
REVERSE     equ  112


S_S_S_S     equ  0
S_S_D_D     equ  1
D_D_S_S     equ  2
D_D_D_D     equ  3


;;----------------------------------------
;; Keys
;;

;; INSERT        equ 5200
;; DELETE        equ 5300
;; SPACE         equ 3920

E_CR          equ 1C0Dh

ESCAPE        equ 011Bh
PGDN          equ 5100h
PGUP          equ 4900h
PERIOD        equ 342Eh
TAB           equ 0F09h
RT_SQUARE     equ 1B5Dh
LT_SQUARE     equ 1A5Bh
RT_BRACKET    equ 1B7Dh
LT_BRACKET    equ 1A7Bh
CNTL_HOME     equ 7700h
CNTL_END      equ 7500h
HOME          equ 4700h
END_KEY       equ 4F00h
s_BS          equ 0008h
BS            equ 0E08h
BACKSPACE     equ 0E08h
s_CR          equ 000Dh
CR            equ 1C0Dh
ENTER_KEY     equ 1C0Dh
UP_ARROW      equ 4800h
RIGHT_ARROW   equ 4D00h
LEFT_ARROW    equ 4B00h
DOWN_ARROW    equ 5000h
F1            equ 3B00h
F2            equ 3C00h
F3            equ 3D00h
F4            equ 3E00h
F5            equ 3F00h
F6            equ 4000h
F7            equ 4100h
```

Fig. 3-2 continued.

```
F8              equ 4200h
F9              equ 4300h
F10             equ 4400h


SHIFT_TAB       equ 0F00h
SHIFT_HOME      equ 4737h
SHIFT_END       equ 4F31h
SHIFT_INSERT    equ 5230h
SHIFT_DELETE    equ 532Eh
SHFT_INSERT     equ 5230h
SHFT_F1         equ 5400h
SHFT_F2         equ 5500h
SHFT_F3         equ 5600h
SHFT_F4         equ 5700h
SHFT_F5         equ 5800h
SHFT_F6         equ 5900h
SHFT_F7         equ 5A00h
SHFT_F8         equ 5B00h
SHFT_F9         equ 5C00h
SHFT_F10        equ 5D00h
SH_R_ARROW      equ 4D36h
SH_L_ARROW      equ 4B34h
SH_U_ARROW      equ 4838h
SH_D_ARROW      equ 5032h


CNTL_F1         equ 5E00h
CNTL_F2         equ 5F00h
CNTL_F3         equ 6000h
CNTL_F4         equ 6100h
CNTL_F5         equ 6200h
CNTL_F6         equ 6300h
CNTL_F7         equ 6400h
CNTL_F8         equ 6500h
CNTL_F9         equ 6600h
CNTL_F10        equ 6700h
CNTL_LEFTA      equ 7300h
CNTL_RIGHTA     equ 7400h

ALT_F1          equ 6800h
ALT_F2          equ 6900h
ALT_F3          equ 6A00h
ALT_F4          equ 6B00h
ALT_F5          equ 6C00h
ALT_F6          equ 6D00h
ALT_F7          equ 6E00h
ALT_F8          equ 6F00h
ALT_F9          equ 7000h
ALT_F10         equ 7100h

ALT_A           equ 1E00h
ALT_B           equ 3000h
ALT_C           equ 2E00h
ALT_D           equ 2000h
ALT_E           equ 1200h
ALT_F           equ 2100h
ALT_G           equ 2200h
ALT_H           equ 2300h
```

Fig. 3-2 continued.

```
ALT_I        equ 1700h
ALT_J        equ 2400h
ALT_K        equ 2500h
ALT_L        equ 2600h
ALT_M        equ 3200h
ALT_N        equ 3100h
ALT_O        equ 1800h
ALT_P        equ 1900h
ALT_Q        equ 1000h
ALT_R        equ 1300h
ALT_S        equ 1F00h
ALT_T        equ 1400h
ALT_U        equ 1600h
ALT_V        equ 2F00h
ALT_W        equ 1100h
ALT_X        equ 2D00h
ALT_Y        equ 1500h
ALT_Z        equ 2C00h

CNTL_A       equ 1E01h
CNTL_B       equ 3002h
CNTL_C       equ 2E03h
CNTL_D       equ 2004h
CNTL_E       equ 1205h
CNTL_F       equ 2106h
CNTL_G       equ 2207h
CNTL_H       equ 2308h
CNTL_I       equ 1709h
CNTL_J       equ 240Ah
CNTL_K       equ 250Bh
CNTL_L       equ 260Ch
CNTL_M       equ 320Dh
CNTL_N       equ 310Eh
CNTL_O       equ 180Fh
CNTL_P       equ 1910h
CNTL_Q       equ 1011h
CNTL_R       equ 1312h
CNTL_S       equ 1F13h
CNTL_T       equ 1414h
CNTL_U       equ 1615h
CNTL_V       equ 2F16h
CNTL_W       equ 1117h
CNTL_X       equ 2D18h
CNTL_Y       equ 1519h
CNTL_Z       equ 2C1Ah

K_0          equ 0B30h
K_1          equ 0231h
K_2          equ 0332h
K_3          equ 0433h
K_4          equ 0534h
K_5          equ 0635h
K_6          equ 0736h
K_7          equ 0837h
K_8          equ 0938h
K_9          equ 0A39h

ALT_0        equ 8100h
ALT_1        equ 7800h
```

Fig. 3-2 continued.

```
ALT_2        equ 7900h
ALT_3        equ 7A00h
ALT_4        equ 7B00h
ALT_5        equ 7C00h
ALT_6        equ 7D00h
ALT_7        equ 7E00h
ALT_8        equ 7F00h
ALT_9        equ 8000h

K_SPACE      equ 3920h
K_EXCLAM     equ 0221h
K_QUOTE      equ 2822h
K_POUND      equ 0423h
K_DOLLAR     equ 0524h
K_PERCENT    equ 0625h
K_AND        equ 0826h
K_APOST      equ 2827h
K_LPAREN     equ 0A28h
K_RPAREN     equ 0B29h
K_STAR       equ 092Ah
K_PLUS       equ 0D2Bh
K_COMMA      equ 332Ch
K_MINUS      equ 0C2Dh
K_PERIOD     equ 342Eh
K_FSLASH     equ 352Fh

K_COLON      equ 273Ah
K_SCOLON     equ 273Bh
K_LESS       equ 333Ch
K_EQUAL      equ 0D3Dh
K_GREAT      equ 343Eh
K_QUEST      equ 353Fh
K_AMPER      equ 0340h

K_A          equ 1E61h - 20h
K_B          equ 3062h - 20h
K_C          equ 2E63h - 20h
K_D          equ 2064h - 20h
K_E          equ 1265h - 20h
K_F          equ 2166h - 20h
K_G          equ 2267h - 20h
K_H          equ 2368h - 20h
K_I          equ 1769h - 20h
K_J          equ 246Ah - 20h
K_K          equ 256Bh - 20h
K_L          equ 266Ch - 20h
K_M          equ 326Dh - 20h
K_N          equ 316Eh - 20h
K_O          equ 186Fh - 20h
K_P          equ 1970h - 20h
K_Q          equ 1071h - 20h
K_R          equ 1372h - 20h
K_S          equ 1F73h - 20h
K_T          equ 1474h - 20h
K_U          equ 1675h - 20h
K_V          equ 2F76h - 20h
K_W          equ 1177h - 20h
K_X          equ 2D78h - 20h
```

```
K_Y              equ 1579h - 20h
K_Z              equ 2C7Ah - 20h

K_LBRACK         equ 1A5Bh
K_BSLASH         equ 2B5Ch
K_RBRACK         equ 1B5Dh
K_KARAT          equ 075Eh
K_UNDER          equ 0C5Ch

K_LC_a           equ 1E61h
K_LC_b           equ 3062h
K_LC_c           equ 2E63h
K_LC_d           equ 2064h
K_LC_e           equ 1265h
K_LC_f           equ 2166h
K_LC_g           equ 2267h
K_LC_h           equ 2368h
K_LC_i           equ 1769h
K_LC_j           equ 246Ah
K_LC_k           equ 256Bh
K_LC_l           equ 266Ch
K_LC_m           equ 326Dh
K_LC_n           equ 316Eh
K_LC_o           equ 186Fh
K_LC_p           equ 1970h
K_LC_q           equ 1071h
K_LC_r           equ 1372h
K_LC_s           equ 1F73h
K_LC_t           equ 1474h
K_LC_u           equ 1675h
K_LC_v           equ 2F76h
K_LC_w           equ 1177h
K_LC_x           equ 2D78h
K_LC_y           equ 1579h
K_LC_z           equ 2C7Ah
```

Fig. 3-2 ends.

4

BIOS Video Procedures

There are a variety of ways for a programmer to send information to the screen. In this book two ways are presented. The first way is to use the computer's BIOS (Basic Input Output System) to write to the screen. This is a very safe method to use because most IBM PCs and PC Clones have a very similar BIOS. You can be fairly certain that the BIOS video routines presented in this chapter will work on virtually every PC or Clone made.

Later in the book a method of writing directly to screen memory will be presented. This method of writing is the very fastest, but is a bit more risky to use. In my opinion, though, the risks are very small. More on direct video access later.

The reason I decided to present the BIOS video procedures before the CHUCK program flow control macros is that they will prove very convenient in demonstrating CHUCK program flow patterns. These routines will be placed in a library for EXE programs, and presented as subroutines for COM programs. The BIOS video procedures will signal the end of Part I. Part II will start with a global look at the CHUCK Programming Language and Library and follow by building many more library routines and procedures.

PROCEDURES FOR WRITING TEXT TO SCREEN

As this section of the book introduces the technique of placing subroutines within macros, I must make a small point as to how this is accomplished. The subroutines for EXE modules are declared as EXTRN proc_name:NEAR directly before the call. Originally I had a file filled with EXTRNs and that seemed to work just fine with one exception. And it was a terrible exception. It was that the linker linked every object file into the main program that was declared as an EXTRN, whether it was used in the program or not. As there was an EXTRN for every subroutine in the CHUCK library, every subroutine was included in every program. Not very efficient, indeed.

However, when the EXTRN is declared within the macro, it becomes visible to the linker only if the macro had been expanded in the assembly file. This method of declaring subroutines as EXTRN ensures that only those routines that are needed by the program will in fact be linked into the final executable file. And the executable programs will be used as they were intended to be.

The CHUCK COM program development procedure is different. There is no COM library and each of the subroutines are held in source form with the subroutine names declared as PUBLIC. The source for the subroutines is included using subroutine loader macros placed in a designated spot in the source code. This method is a tad cumbersome but produces orderly and tight code.

The procedure wish list presented in Fig. 4-1 lists procedures that have been designed to write to the screen using the PC's BIOS. These procedures are a mix of a macro with a subroutine nested within the macro. Also, note that there will be a few additional procedures presented in Chapter 4. These additions will help to clarify BIOS video procedure usage.

Fig. 4-1. A list of BIOS video CHUCK macros and procedures.

Macro	Procedure
CLRSCREEN	Clear the screen
FLIPPAGE	Display new video page
GETMODE	Get video mode
NEWLINE	Carriage ret/Line feed
PRINTF	Put strings to screen
PUTCHAR	Put char to screen
PUTS	Put string to screen
READCHAR	Read Char & Attribute
SETMODE	Set video mode
SETPAGE	Set BIOS writes to Page
SWRITE	Write string at row,col
VIDINIT	Init Video Procedures

The method that will be used to describe each procedure listed in Fig. 4-1 will be to:

1. Discuss the EXE version:
   - Present EXE version procedure macro listing
   - Present EXE version of subroutine
   - Present EXE demonstration program

2. Discuss the COM version:
   - Present COM version procedure macro listing
   - Present COM version of subroutine
   - Present COM demonstration program

Procedure presentation will not be alphabetical. Because there is an interaction between procedures, the procedures that are most basic will be presented first.

VIDINIT

VIDINIT initializes CHUCK video variables. The syntax is:

vidinit

VIDINIT uses BIOS interrupt 10h to get the current display mode and report the display mode and active page to PUBLIC words. The VIDINIT call provides the basic information of active page and video mode for all of the BIOS video and direct memory access screen handling routines. VIDINIT must be called as the first procedure of every CHUCK program. Also note that the EXE version of VIDINIT loads the DS register with @DATA and the COM version sets the DS register with CS.

VIDINIT (EXE Version) Figure 4-2 presents the listing for the EXE VIDINIT macro. Create a file named VIDEO.MAC and place the VIDINIT macro in that file. Figure 4-3 presents the EXE version of the AVID subroutine which is called from the VIDINIT macro.

Fig. 4-2. The EXE macro listing to VIDINIT.

```
;;------------------------------------------
;;
;; Macro: VIDINIT
;;
;; Description: initialize A++ video structure
;;

VIDINIT MACRO

;; save general registers

        pushx

;; declare AVID as EXTRN

        EXTRN    AVID:NEAR

;; Call SCLR

        call    AVID

;; restore general registers
        popx

        ENDM
;;------------------------------------------
;;
```

If you go line by line in the VIDINIT macro you will see that the registers are not saved and restored in the AVID subroutine, rather, the registers are preserved in the macro itself.

The name of the subroutine called from within the VIDINIT macro is AVID. The source listing for VIDINIT.ASM, which holds the AVID subroutine listing, is shown in Fig. 4-3.

Fig. 4-3. The EXE source code listing to VIDINIT.ASM.

```
;******************
; Source Code Start
;
; File Name:   VIDINIT.ASM
;
; Synopsis:   AVID()
;
; Description: Calls gtMode to determine the
;             video mode and sets the
;             appropriate global video
;             addresses to there will
;             be a direct video write
;             to display ram.
;
;             EXE version - note that the
;             data is held in the .DATA segment,
;             as compared to the COM version
;             of vidinit where the data is held
;             in the .CODE segment
;
;             MONO SEG 0xB000 OFFSET 0x0000
;             COLR SEG 0xB800 OFFSET 0x0000 (PAGE 0)
;             COLR SEG 0xB900 OFFSET 0x0000 (PAGE 1)
;             COLR SEG 0xBA00 OFFSET 0x0000 (PAGE 2)
;             COLR SEG 0xBB00 OFFSET 0x0000 (PAGE 3)
;
;
; Returns:    Nothing
;


            DOSSEG
            .MODEL SMALL
            .DATA
            PUBLIC  PAG_NUM,SCRNSEG,VID_PORT

PAG_NUM DB      0               ; video page
VID_PORT DW     0               ; video controller status port
SCRNSEG DW      0               ; int holds scrn seg

            .CODE
            PUBLIC  AVID
AVID PROC NEAR
            mov     AX,@DATA        ; Set the DS register
            mov     DS,AX

            mov     AH,0fh          ; BIOS get mode
            int     10h             ; BIOS int
            mov     PAG_NUM,BH      ; page -> PUBLIC PAG_NUM
```

```
        cmp     AL,7            ; is mono?
        je      ismono          ; yes ->jump

        mov     VID_PORT,03dah  ; stat color controller port

;
; Set the SCRNSEG variable for direct screen memory access
; * Video pages not available in MONO
;
; The set SCRNSEG for direct video access to different
; pages
;
        cmp     [PAG_NUM],0
        jne     notpage0
        mov     SCRNSEG,0B800h  ; Page 0 scrn seg
        jmp     videxit

notpage0:
        cmp     [PAG_NUM],1
        jne     notpage1
        mov     SCRNSEG,0B900h  ; Page 1 scrn seg
        jmp     videxit

notpage1:
        cmp     [PAG_NUM],2
        jne     notpage2
        mov     SCRNSEG,0BA00h  ; Page 2 scrn seg
        jmp     videxit

notpage2:
        mov     SCRNSEG,0BB00h  ; Page 3 scrn seg
        jmp     videxit

ismono:

        mov     VID_PORT,03bah  ; stat mono controller port
        mov     SCRNSEG,0B000h  ; mono scrn seg

videxit:
        ret
AVID    ENDP
        END

; End of listing
;-------------------------------------
```

Fig. 4-3 ends.

Assemble VIDINIT.ASM into a .OBJ file using your assembler and then create a library named TAB.LIB by typing:

```
tlib tab + vidinit
```

TAB.LIB will hold all of the object modules for the EXE version of the subroutines that are called from within the macro procedures. Here is a VIDINIT EXE example:

```
; File
;
PROG_EXE 200h; EXE stack of 200h
PROG_CODE      ; Start code segment
vidinit            ; Initialize video
; program code here
END_EXE         ; EXE DOS terminate
; program subroutines here
END                ; End of file source listing
```

Now that the VIDEO.MAC file has been created you need a new SMALL.MAC file. The new SMALL.MAC file for EXE program development now looks like this:

```
INCLUDE DEFINES.MAC
INCLUDE REGSEXT.MAC
INCLUDE CHUCK.MAC
INCLUDE PRINT.MAC
INCLUDE VIDEO.MAC
```

VIDINIT (COM Version)   The macro to load VIDINIT.ASM is:

```
L_VIDINIT MACRO
        INCLUDE VIDINIT.ASM
        ENDM
```

Create a COM.MAC file and enter the L_VIDINIT macro. The new SMALL.MAC file for COM program development now looks like this:

```
INCLUDE DEFINES.MAC
INCLUDE REGSEXT.MAC
INCLUDE CHUCK.MAC
INCLUDE PRINT.MAC
INCLUDE VIDEO.MAC
INCLUDE COM.MAC
```

Figure 4-4 is a listing of the COM version of the VIDINIT macro. Note that the AVID call is declared as PUBLIC as opposed to being EXTRNed. That is because there will only be one object module used in the linking process.

The COM version of VIDINIT.ASM is not intended to be assembled into a separate object module, rather it will be included as the subroutine source proper after the COM_TO_DOS macro. The source code for the COM version of VIDINIT.ASM is listed in Fig. 4-5.

Fig. 4-4. The COM macro listing to VIDINIT.

```
;;-----------------------------------------
;;
;; Macro: VIDINIT
;;
;; Description: initialize A++ video structure
;;
VIDINIT MACRO

;; save general registers

        pushx

;; declare AVID as PUBLIC

        PUBLIC  AVID

;; Call SCLR

        call    AVID

;; restore general registers
        popx

        ENDM
;;-----------------------------------------
```

Fig. 4-5. The COM source code listing to VIDINIT.ASM.

```
;*******************
; Source Code Start
;
; File Name:   VIDINIT.ASM
;
; Synopsis:    AVID()
;
; Description: Calls gtMode to determine the
;              video mode and sets the
;              appropriate global video
;              addresses to there will
;              be a direct video write
;              to display ram.
;
;              COM version - note JMP over data
;              which is held in the code segment
;
;              MONO SEG 0xB000 OFFSET 0x0000
;              COLR SEG 0xB800 OFFSET 0x0000 (PAGE 0)
;              COLR SEG 0xB900 OFFSET 0x0000 (PAGE 1)
;              COLR SEG 0xBA00 OFFSET 0x0000 (PAGE 2)
;              COLR SEG 0xBB00 OFFSET 0x0000 (PAGE 3)
;
;
; Returns:     Nothing
;

        PUBLIC  AVID,PAG_NUM,SCRNSEG,VID_PORT
```

```
AVID PROC NEAR
        push    CS              ; CS => DS
        pop     DS
        jmp     avid1
PAG_NUM DB      0               ; video page
VID_PORT DW     0               ; video controller status port
SCRNSEG DW      0               ; int holds scrn seg
avid1:
        mov     AH,0fh          ; BIOS get mode
        int     10h             ; BIOS int
        mov     PAG_NUM,BH      ; page -> PUBLIC PAG_NUM

        cmp     AL,7            ; is mono?
        je      ismono          ; yes ->jump

        mov     VID_PORT,03dah  ; stat color controller port

;
; Set the SCRNSEG variable for direct screen memory access
; * Video pages not available in MONO
;
; The set SCRNSEG for direct video access to different
; pages
;

        cmp     [PAG_NUM],0
        jne     notpage0
        mov     SCRNSEG,0B800h  ; Page 0 scrn seg
        jmp     videxit

notpage0:
        cmp     [PAG_NUM],1
        jne     notpage1
        mov     SCRNSEG,0B900h  ; Page 1 scrn seg
        jmp     videxit

notpage1:
        cmp     [PAG_NUM],2
        jne     notpage2
        mov     SCRNSEG,0BA00h  ; Page 2 scrn seg
        jmp     videxit

notpage2:
        mov     SCRNSEG,0BB00h  ; Page 3 scrn seg
        jmp     videxit

ismono:
        mov     VID_PORT,03bah  ; stat mono controller port
        mov     SCRNSEG,0B000h  ; mono scrn seg

videxit:
        ret
AVID    ENDP

; End of listing
;------------------------------------
```

Fig. 4-5 ends.

Here is an example of how a program uses VIDINIT COM:

```
      ; File
      ;
      ;
      PROG_COM         ; Start COM program
Program:                 ; Program start label
      vidinit            ; Initialize video
; program code here
      COM_TO_DOS       ; COM DOS terminate
L_VIDINIT                ; Load VIDINIT.ASM subroutine
; program subroutines here
      END_COM          ; Set program execution point
```

CLRSCREEN

CLRSCREEN clears the active video page and moves the cursor to row 0, column 0. The syntax is:

```
clrscreen
```

CLRSCREEN clears the active video page using the BIOS scroll up function (interrupt 10h, function 6). The default background attribute is white foreground, black background, off intensity and off blink.

CLRSCREEN (EXE Version)   Figure 4-6 presents the EXE version of the CLRSCREEN macro. Figure 4-7 presents the source code listing to the EXE version of CLRSCRN.ASM.

The program EPROG1.ASM (Fig. 4-8) is a program that demonstrates both the VIDINIT macro and the CLRSCREEN macro. EPROG1 simply clears the screen and moves the cursor to row 0, column 0. EPROG1.EXE is 665 bytes.

After you've added CLRSCRN.OBJ to your TAB library your assemble and link batch file, AL.BAT, will look like this:

```
tasm %1
tlink %1,,,tab;
```

Once you've typed in the listing to EPROG.ASM assemble and link the program using the following command line:

```
al eprog1
```

CLRSCREEN (COM Version)   The L_CLRSCREEN loader macro is:

```
      L_CLRSCREEN MACRO
        INCLUDE CLRSCREEN.ASM
        ENDM
```

Fig. 4-6. The EXE macro listing to CLRSCREEN.

```
;;---------------------------------------
;;
;; Macro: CLRSCREEN
;;
;; Descritpion:
;;   Clears the screen using the
;;   normal attribute.
;;

CLRSCREEN MACRO

;; save general registers

        pushx

;; declare SCLR as EXTRN

        EXTRN    SCLR:NEAR

;; Call SCLR

        call     sclr

;; restore general registers

        popx

        ENDM
;;---------------------------------------
```

Fig. 4-7. The EXE source code listing to CLRSCRN.ASM.

```
;*******************
; Source Code Start
;
; File Name:   CLRSCRN.ASM
;
; Description: Clears the screen with
;                a white foreground and
;                black background if no
;                attribute received.
;                Otherwise the attribute
;                is used.  The cursor
;                is moved to row
;                0 and column 0.
;
; Returns:     Nothing
;

        DOSSEG

        .MODEL SMALL

        .CODE
        PUBLIC  SCLR

SCLR PROC NEAR
```

```
; AL holds the number of lines to scroll
; 0 => blank the video window

        mov     AL,0

; CH holds the row of the upper left corner

        mov     CH,0

; CL holds the column of the upper left corner

        mov     CL,0

; DH holds the row of the lower right corner

        mov     DH,24

; DL holds the column of the lower right corner

        mov     DL,79

; BH holds the new screen attribute ( 7 = normal )

        mov     BH,7

; Scroll Window Up via BIOS
; Function 6, interrupt 10h

        mov     AH,6
        int     10H

; Get the current display mode
; Function 15, interrupt 10h

        mov     AH,0fh
        int     10H

; Move the cursor to row 0, column 0
; Function 2, interrupt 10h

; DL & DH hold column and row of new cursor position

        xor     DX,DX  ; 0 => DL & DH
        mov     AH,2
        int     10H
        ret
SCLR ENDP
        END


;
; End of source
;**************
;
```

Fig. 4-7 ends.

Fig. 4-8. The source code listing to EPROG1.ASM.

```
;---------------------------------------
; Source Listing Start
;
; File Name: EPROG1.ASM
;
; Description:
;   Tests: VIDINIT & CLRSCREEN procedures
;

;
; Include Macro file
;

INCLUDE SMALL.MAC

        PROG_EXE
        PROG_CODE
        vidinit
        clrscreen
        END_EXE
        END

;
; End of Source Listing
;---------------------------------------
```

Add L_CLRSCREEN to your recently created COM.MAC file. Figure 4-9 represents the COM version of the CLRSCREEN macro. Figure 4-10 presents the source listing for the COM version of CLRSCRN.ASM and Fig. 4-11 presents the source code listing to the COM version of CPROG1.ASM.

CPROG1.COM and CPROG1.EXE function in an identical fashion but differ in size. As expected, CPROG1.COM is smaller at 181 bytes long and CPROG1.EXE is 665 bytes long.

Fig. 4-9. The COM macro listing to CLRSCREEN.

```
;;---------------------------------------
;;
;; Macro: CLRSCREEN
;;
;; Descritpion:
;;   Clears the screen using the
;;   normal attribute.
;;

CLRSCREEN MACRO

;; save general registers

        pushx

;; declare SCLR as PUBLIC

        PUBLIC   SCLR
```

```
;; Call SCLR

        call    sclr

;; restore general registers

        popx

        ENDM
;;--------------------------------------
```

Fig. 4-9 ends.

Fig. 4-10. The COM source code listing to CLRSCRN.ASM.

```
;********************
; Source Code Start
;
; File Name:    CLRSCRN.ASM
;
; Description: Clears the screen with
;                 a white foreground and
;                 black background if no
;                 attribute received.
;                 Otherwise the attribute
;                 is used.  The cursor
;                 is moved to row
;                 0 and column 0.
;
; Returns:      Nothing
;

SCLR PROC NEAR

; AL holds the number of lines to scroll
; 0 => blank the video window

        mov     AL,0

; CH holds the row of the upper left corner

        mov     CH,0

; CL holds the column of the upper left corner

        mov     CL,0

; DH holds the row of the lower right corner

        mov     DH,24

; DL holds the column of the lower right corner

        mov     DL,79

; BH holds the new screen attribute
; BH set in CLRSCREEN macro

; Scroll Window Up via BIOS
```

```
; Function 6, interrupt 10h

        mov     AH,6
        int     10H

; Get the current display mode
; Function 15, interrupt 10h

        mov     AH,0fh
        int     10H

; Move the cursor to row 0, column 0
; Function 2, interrupt 10h

; DL & DH hold column and row of new cursor position

        xor     DX,DX  ; 0 => DL & DH
        mov     AH,2
        int     10H
        ret
SCLR ENDP

;
; End of source
;**************
```

Fig. 4-10 ends.

Fig. 4-11. The source code listing to CPROG1.ASM.

```
;----------------------------------------
; Source Listing Start
;
; File Name: CPROG1.ASM
;
; Description:
;  Demonstrates use of VIDINIT and CLRSCREEN
;


;
; Include Macro file
;

INCLUDE SMALL.MAC

        PROG_COM
program:
        vidinit
        clrscreen
        COM_TO_DOS

;  Load subroutines

L_VIDINIT
L_CLRSCREEN

; COM DOS Terminate and end source file
```

```
        END_COM

;
; End of Source Listing
;-------------------------------------
```

Fig. 4-11 ends.

PUTCHAR

PUTCHAR puts a character to the screen. The syntax is:

putchar   *cval*

where *cval* = memory|register|immediate

PUTCHAR uses function 0Eh, interrupt 10h, to write the character to the screen. This function is the write text in teletype mode. The cursor is updated after the character is put to the screen.

PUTCHAR (EXE Version)   Figure 4-12 presents the PUTCHAR macro. This macro may be passed a 16-bit WORD which holds a printable character, a 16-bit register, or an immediate value. For example:

putchar 'A' ; immediate
putchar AX   ; register
putchar val ; memory

The subroutine called from the PUTCHAR macro is called APUTCH. That subroutine is located in PUTCHAR.ASM, which is presented in Fig. 4-13.

Fig. 4-12. The EXE macro listing to PUTCHAR.

```
;;-------------------------------------------
;;
;; Macro: PUTCHAR chval
;;
;; Description: Print a character at
;;   the current cursor location
;;
PUTCHAR MACRO chval
;; If parameters is not in AX then move
;; parameters to register
        pushab
    IFDIFI <AX>,<chval>
        mov     AX,chval
    ENDIF
        EXTRN   APUTCH:NEAR
        call    APUTCH
        popab
        ENDM
;;-------------------------------------------
```

Fig. 4-13. The EXE source code to PUTCHAR.ASM.

```
;******************
; Source Code Start
;
; File Name:    PUTCHAR.ASM
;
; Synopsis:    APUTCH ch
;
; int ch       Prints a character ch
;              to the screen at the
;              current cursor location
;
; Returns:     Nothing
;

;
; Enable DOS segment-ordering at link time
;

        DOSSEG

        .MODEL SMALL
        .DATA
        EXTRN PAG_NUM:BYTE

        .CODE
        PUBLIC  APUTCH

APUTCH PROC NEAR
;
; Prints a character to the screen
; via function 0Eh, interrupt 10h
;
; This is the Write Text in Teletype Mode
; function where the character to be
; printed comes in on the AX register.
;
; The display page to write text onto
; is held in the BH register. VIDINIT
; can set this value to the currently
; active page, although by changing
; this value you can write to a non-
; visible page.
;

; AX holds character on entry

        mov     BH,PAG_NUM

; Function 0Eh, interrupt 10h

        mov     AH,0Eh
        int     10h
        ret
APUTCH  ENDP
        END


;
; End of Assembly Source
;-------------------------------------
```

The PUTCHAR EXE demonstration program, EPROG2.ASM, clears the screen and prints an 'A' in the upper left-hand corner of the screen. EPROG2.EXE is 685 bytes. The source code to EPROG2.ASM is presented in Fig. 4-14.

Fig. 4-14. The source code listing to EPROG2.ASM.

```
;-------------------------------------
; Source Listing Start
;
; File Name: EPROG2.ASM
;
; Description:
;   Tests: VIDINIT & CLRSCREEN
;            & PUTCHAR
;
;
; Include Macro file
;

INCLUDE SMALL.MAC

        PROG_EXE
        PROG_CODE
        vidinit
        clrscreen
        putchar      'A'
        END_EXE
        END

;
; End of Source Listing
;-------------------------------------
```

PUTCHAR (COM Version)   The L_PUTCHAR macro subroutine loader is:

```
L_PUTCHAR MACRO
          INCLUDE PUTCHAR.ASM
          ENDM
```

The COM version PUTCHAR macro is presented in Fig. 4-15. The COM version of the source code to PUTCHAR.ASM is presented in Fig. 4-16.

The source code to CPROG2.ASM, the COM demonstration program for PUTCHAR is presented in Fig. 4-17.

Fig. 4-15. The COM macro listing to PUTCHAR.

```
;;-------------------------------------
;;
;; Macro: PUTCHAR chval
;;
;; Description: Print a character at
;;   the current cursor location
;;
```

```
PUTCHAR MACRO chval
;; If parameters is not in AX then move
;; parameters to register
        pushab
  IFDIFI <AX>,<chval>
        mov      AX,chval
  ENDIF
        PUBLIC  APUTCH
        call     APUTCH
        popab
        ENDM
;;-------------------------------------
```

Fig. 4-15 ends.

Fig. 4-16. The COM source code to PUTCHAR.ASM.

```
;********************
; Source Code Start
;
; File Name:    PUTCHAR.ASM
;
; Synopsis:     APUTCH ch
;
; int ch        Prints a character ch
;               to the screen at the
;               current cursor location
;
; Returns:      Nothing
;


;
; Enable DOS segment-ordering at link time
;

        PUBLIC  APUTCH

APUTCH PROC NEAR
;
; Prints a character to the screen
; via function OEh, interrupt 10h
;
; This is the Write Text in Teletype Mode
; function where the character to be
; printed comes in on the AX register.
;
; The display page to write text onto
; is held in the BH register. VIDINIT
; can set this value to the currently
; active page, although by changing
; this value you can write to a non-
; visible page.
;

; AX holds character on entry

        mov      BH,PAG_NUM

; Function OEh, interrupt 10h
```

```
        mov     AH,0Eh
        int     10h
        ret
APUTCH  ENDP


;
; End of Assembly Source
;-------------------------------------
```

Fig. 4-16 ends.

Fig. 4-17. The source code listing to CPROG2.ASM.

```
;-------------------------------------
; Source Listing Start
;
; File Name: CPROG2.ASM
;
; Description:
;  Demonstrates use of VIDINIT and CLRSCREEN
;  and PUTCHAR

;
; Include Macro file
;

INCLUDE SMALL.MAC

        PROG_COM
program:
        vidinit
        clrscreen
        putchar   'A'
        COM_TO_DOS

;  Load subroutines

L_VIDINIT
L_CLRSCREEN
L_PUTCHAR

; COM DOS Terminate and end source file

        END_COM

;
; End of Source Listing
;-------------------------------------
```

PUTS

PUTS puts a string to the screen. The syntax is:

PUTS *text_name*

where *text_name* = label|register

The PUTS procedure writes a string to the screen at the current cursor location in teletype fashion. The string write terminates under two circumstances:

1. 0 (NULL) In this case, the string terminates and the cursor stays right after the last character that was put to the screen
2. '$' In this case, the string terminates and the cursor goes to the next line at column 0 (NEWLINE)

PUTS (EXE Version)   The listing for the EXE version of the PUTS macro is presented in Fig. 4-18. The source code listing for the EXE version of PUTS.ASM is presented in Fig. 4-19.

Fig. 4-18. The EXE macro listing to PUTS.

```
;;----------------------------------------
;;
;; Macro: PUTS string
;;
;; Description: Prints string
;;    at the current cursor
;;    location
;;

PUTS MACRO string

;; save general purpose registers

        pushx

;; save source index register

        push    SI

;; If parameter 'string' == SI

  IFDIFI <SI>,<string>

  ;; If parameter 'string is blank then
  ;; AX holds the offset to the string

  IFB <string>
        mov     SI,AX

;; else move offset string to SI via AX

  ELSE

        lea     AX,string
        mov     SI,AX

        ENDIF

  ENDIF

;; call aputs subroutine

        EXTRN   APUTS:NEAR
```

```
        call    aputs

;; restore SI register

        pop     SI

;; restore general purpose registers

        popx

        ENDM
;;----------------------------------------
```

Fig. 4-18 ends.

Fig. 4-19. The EXE source code to PUTS.ASM.

```
;******************
; Source Code Start
;
; File Name:    PUTS.ASM
;
; char *string Prints string and
;               terminates with '\0' or '$'
;
; Returns:      Nothing
;
; On entry: SI holds the offset to the
;           string.
;
INCLUDE small.MAC
;
; Enable DOS segment-ordering at link time
;

        DOSSEG
        .MODEL SMALL
        .CODE
        PUBLIC  APUTS
APUTS PROC NEAR

; set AX to zero

        xor     AX,0

; loop label

lp1:

; move byte to AL

        mov     AL,[SI]

; is AL 0?

        cmp     AL,0

; conditional jump on yes -
; exit with no change of cursor
```

```
; location

        je      lp3

; is AL '$'?

        cmp     AL,'$'

; conditional jump on yes
; exit with CR/LF

        je      lp2

; otherwise => putchar sends byte to screen

        putchar AX

; point to next byte in string

        inc     SI

; repeat loop

        jmp     lp1

lp2:

        putchar 10
        putchar 13

lp3:

        ret
APUTS   ENDP
        END

;
; End of Assembly Source
;
```

Fig. 4-19 ends.

The PUTS.EXE demonstration program prints the "Hello World!" message to the screen. The EPROG3.EXE file size is 713 bytes and the source code listing to EPROG3.ASM is listed in Fig. 4-20.

Notice in Fig. 4-20 that all you need to do to print a string using the PUTS procedure is simply pass the name of the text buffer (in this case named 'mess') that you wish to print to the screen. That's not too hard, is it? The C version of PUTS might look like this:

```
puts (mess);
```

Take away the parenthesis/semi-colon and what have you got?

Figure 4-21 shows the source listing after the macro expansion. If you're even the least bit familiar with the look of compiler-generated assembly source listings you'll see a vague familiarity taking shape: registers saved, parameters placed into proper registers, procedure called and registers restored.

Fig. 4-20. The source code listing to EPROG3.ASM.

```
;----------------------------------------
; Source Listing Start
;
; File Name: EPROG3.ASM
;
; Description:
;  Tests: VIDINIT & PUTS
;


;
; Include Macro file
;

INCLUDE SMALL.MAC

        PROG_EXE

        PROG_DATA

mess    DB       'Hello World!',0

        PROG_CODE

        vidinit
        puts    mess

        END_EXE
        END

;
; End of Source Listing
;----------------------------------------
```

Fig. 4-21. The source listing to EPROG3.ASM after macro expansion has taken place.

```
;  PROG_EXE
        .MODEL SMALL
        .STACK 100h

;  PROG_DATA
        .DATA

mess    DB       'Hello World!',0

;  PROG_CODE
        .CODE

;  vidinit
        push    AX
        push    BX
        push    CX
        push    DX
        call    AVID
        pop     DX
        pop     CX
        pop     BX
        pop     AX
```

```
;  puts    mess
          push     AX
          push     BX
          push     CX
          push     DX
          push     SI
          lea      AX,mess
          mov      SI,AX
          call     aputs
          pop      SI
          pop      DX
          pop      CX
          pop      BX
          pop      AX

;  END_EXE
          mov      AH,4ch
          int      21h

          END
```

Fig. 4-21 ends.

PUTS (COM Version)   The L_PUTS macro subroutine loader is:

```
L_PUTS MACRO
          INCLUDE PUTS.ASM
          ENDM
```

Place the L_PUTS macro into your COM.MAC file. Note that PUTS uses PUTCHAR and that L_PUTCHAR must also be invoked. If you forget to invoke the L_PUTCHAR macro you will get a reminder that something is missing from your assembler!

The COM version PUTS macro is presented in Fig. 4-22, the COM version of the PUTS.ASM subroutine is presented in Fig. 4-23, and the COM demonstration program (CPROG3.ASM) is presented in Fig. 4-24.

Fig. 4-22. The COM macro listing to PUTS.

```
;;-------------------------------------
;;
;; Macro: PUTS string
;;
;; Description: Prints string
;;    at the current cursor
;;    location
;;

PUTS MACRO string

;; save general purpose registers

        pushx

;; save source index register
```

```
                push    SI

;; If parameter 'string' == SI

 IFDIFI <SI>,<string>

 ;; If parameter 'string is blank then
 ;; AX holds the offset to the string

  IFB <string>
                mov     SI,AX

;; else move offset string to SI via AX

   ELSE

                lea     AX,string
                mov     SI,AX

                ENDIF

 ENDIF

;; call aputs subroutine

                PUBLIC  APUTS
                call    aputs

;; restore SI register

                pop     SI

;; restore general purpose registers

                popx

                ENDM
;;----------------------------------------
```

Fig. 4-22 ends.

Fig. 4-23. The COM source code to PUTS.ASM.

```
;*******************
; Source Code Start
;
; File Name:   PUTS.ASM
;
; char *string Prints string and
;              terminates with '\0' or '$'
;
; Returns:     Nothing
;
; On entry: SI holds the offset to the
;           string.
;
INCLUDE small.MAC
;
; Enable DOS segment-ordering at link time
;
```

```
        PUBLIC  APUTS
APUTS PROC NEAR

; set AX to zero

        xor     AX,0

; loop label

lp1:

; move byte to AL

        mov     AL,[SI]

; is AL 0?

        cmp     AL,0

; conditional jump on yes -
; exit with no change of cursor
; location

        je      lp3

; is AL '$'?

        cmp     AL,'$'

; conditional jump on yes
; exit with CR/LF

        je      lp2

; otherwise => putchar sends byte to screen

        putchar AX

; point to next byte in string

        inc     SI

; repeat loop

        jmp     lp1

lp2:

        putchar 10
        putchar 13

lp3:

        ret
APUTS   ENDP

;
; End of Assembly Source
;
```

Fig. 4-23 ends.

Fig. 4-24. The source code listing to CPROG3.ASM.

```
;-------------------------------------
; Source Listing Start
;
; File Name: CPROG3.ASM
;
; Description:
;  Demonstrates use of VIDINIT and PUTS

;
; Include Macro file
;

INCLUDE SMALL.MAC

        PROG_COM

mess    DB        'Hello World!',0

program:
        vidinit
        puts    mess
        COM_TO_DOS

;  Load subroutines

L_VIDINIT
L_CLRSCREEN
L_PUTCHAR
L_PUTS

; COM DOS Terminate and end source file

        END_COM

;
; End of Source Listing
;-------------------------------------
```

It's been a while since I presented the source code to a C file and compared CHUCK to C. Now seems like a good time to present C-EPROG3.C. The source for this program is presented in Fig. 4-25. As you can see the C source listing is similar to the CHUCK listings. Let's compare executable file sizes:

```
CPROG3.COM      256 bytes (CHUCK COM)
EPROG3.EXE      713 bytes (CHUCK EXE)
C-EPROG3.EXE   4830 bytes (TURBO C)
```

These are not unexpected results. The next procedure introduced moves the cursor (MVCUR). This is done because the SWRITE function nests the MVCUR macro.

Fig. 4-25. The source code listing to C-EPROG3.C.

```
/*-----------------------------------
 * Start of source listing
 *
 * File Name: C-EPROG3.C
 *
 */

#include <stdio.h>

void main(void);

char mess[] = {"Hello World!"};

void
main()
{
puts(mess);
}

/*
 *
 * End of source listing
 *-----------------------------------
 */
```

MVCUR

MVCUR moves the text cursor to row, column. The syntax is:

mvcur *row, column*

where *row*   = memory|immediate
      column = memory|immediate

MVCUR moves the cursor in the video page indicated by PAG_NUM. It receives the row and column parameters.

MVCUR (EXE Version)   Figure 4-26 presents the listing for the EXE version of the MVCUR macro. Figure 4-27 presents the source code listing for the EXE version of MVCUR.ASM. Remember that once this source file is assembled you must add its object module to the TAB.LIB file.

Figure 4-28, the demonstration program, is the source code listing for EPROG4.ASM. This MVCUR EXE demonstration program shows how to use the MVCUR procedure.

Fig. 4-26. The EXE macro listing to MVCUR.

```
;;-----------------------------------
;;
;; Macro: MVCUR row, column
;;
;; Description: Move the cursor
```

```
;;   on the current page to row &
;;   column

MVCUR MACRO row,column

;; If parameters are not in AX,DX then move
;; parameters to registers

        pushabd

;; If AX not equal to row then...

    IFDIFI <AX>,<row>
        mov     AX,row
    ENDIF

;; If DX not euqal to column

    IFDIFI <DX>,<column>
        mov     DX,column
    ENDIF

;; Call amvcur

        EXTRN   AMVCUR:NEAR
        call    AMVCUR

;; restore saved registers

        popabd

        ENDM
;;---------------------------------------
```

Fig. 4-26 ends.

Fig. 4-27. The EXE source code to MVCUR.ASM.

```
;*******************
; Start Source File
;
; File Name     MVCUR.ASM
;
; Synopsis:     AMVCUR(row,column)
;
; int row       move cursor to this row
;
; int column    move cursor to this column
;
;
;
; Description   moves the cursor via BIOS
;               int 10h to the position
;               specified by row and column
;
;
;
; On Entry DL holds the column
; And AL holds the row
;
        DOSSEG
```

```
        .MODEL SMALL

        .DATA

        EXTRN PAG_NUM:BYTE

        .CODE

        PUBLIC AMVCUR

AMVCUR PROC NEAR

; move row => DL

        mov     DH,AL

; move video page number => BH

        mov     BH,PAG_NUM

; invoke interrupt 10h, function 2
; move the cursor

        mov     AH,2
        int     10H

; return to caller

        ret

AMVCUR ENDP

        END

; End Source Here
;****************
;
```

Fig. 4-27 ends.

Fig. 4-28. The source code listing to EPROG4.ASM.

```
;---------------------------------------
; Source Listing Start
;
; File Name: EPROG4.ASM
;
; Description:
;   Tests: VIDINIT & CLRSCREEN
;          & PUTCHAR
;

;
; Include Macro file
;

INCLUDE SMALL.MAC

; Initialize EXE file structure with STACK => 100h

        PROG_EXE
```

```
; Start of code segment

        PROG_CODE

; CHUCK video call initialization

        vidinit

; Clear the active video page

        clrscreen

; Move the cursor to row 10, column 10

        mvcur       10,10

; put the 'A' character to the screen at 10,10

        putchar     'A'

; DOS EXE terminate

        END_EXE

        END

;
; End of Source Listing
;-------------------------------------
```

Fig. 4-28 ends.

MVCUR (COM Version)   The L_MVCUR macro subroutine loader is:

```
L_MVCUR MACRO
        INCLUDE MVCUR.ASM
        ENDM
```

Add L_MVCUR to your COM.MAC file.

Figure 4-29 presents the COM version macro listing for MVCUR, Fig. 4-30 presents the COM version source code for MVCUR.ASM, and Fig. 4-31 presents the source code listing for the COM demonstration program CPROG4.ASM.

Figure 4-31 presents the source listing for the COM version demonstration program. Note that the macro L_MVCUR is invoked. Create L_MVCUR and add this macro to your COM.MAC file. Remember, L_MVCUR simply loads (using INCLUDE) MVCUR.ASM.

Fig. 4-29. The COM macro listing to MVCUR.

```
;;-------------------------------------
;;
;; Macro: MVCUR row, column
;;
;; Description: Move the cursor
```

```
;;   on the current page to row &
;;   column

MVCUR MACRO row,column

;; If parameters are not in AX,DX then move
;; parameters to registers

        pushabd

;; If AX not equal to row then...

   IFDIFI <AX>,<row>
        mov     AX,row
   ENDIF

;; If DX not equal to column then...

   IFDIFI <DX>,<column>
        mov     DX,column
   ENDIF

;; call amvcur

        PUBLIC  AMVCUR
        call    AMVCUR

;; restore saved registers

        popabd

        ENDM
;;-------------------------------------
```

Fig. 4-29 ends.

Fig. 4-30. The COM source code to MVCUR.ASM.

```
;*******************
; Start Source File
;
; File Name     MVCUR.ASM
;
; Synopsis:     AMVCUR(row,column)
;
; int row       move cursor to this row
;
; int column    move cursor to this column
;
;
;
; Description   moves the cursor via BIOS
;               int 10h to the position
;               specified by row and column
;
;
; On Entry DL holds the column
; And AL holds the row
;
```

```
                PUBLIC AMVCUR

AMVCUR PROC NEAR

; move row => DL

        mov     DH,AL

; move video page number => BH

        mov     BH,PAG_NUM

; invoke interrupt 10h, function 2
; move the cursor

        mov     AH,2
        int     10H

; return to caller

        ret

AMVCUR ENDP


; End Source Here
;****************
```

Fig. 4-30 ends.

Fig. 4-31. The source code listing to CPROG4.ASM.

```
;--------------------------------------
; Source Listing Start
;
; File Name: CPROG4.ASM
;
; Description:
;   Demonstrates use of VIDINIT and CLRSCREEN
;   and PUTCHAR and MVCUR


; Include Macro file
;

INCLUDE SMALL.MAC

; Initialize for COM program

        PROG_COM

; DATA in code segment in CHUCK COM programs
;
; ALL COM data goes between PROG_COM and the
; program: label

cval    dw      'A'

; Start of active program code
```

program:

```
; Initialize CHUCK video

        vidinit

; Clear the active display screen

        clrscreen

; Move the cursor to row 10, column 10

        mvcur       10,10

; Put the character in cval to the screen

        putchar     cval

; COM DOS terminate

        COM_TO_DOS

;  Load subroutines

L_VIDINIT
L_CLRSCREEN
L_PUTCHAR
L_MVCUR

; COM DOS Terminate and end source file

        END_COM

;
; End of Source Listing
;---------------------------------------
```

Fig. 4-31 ends.

SWRITE

SWRITE puts a text buffer to the screen at row, column. The syntax is:

SWRITE *row,column,text_buffer*

where *row*   = memory|immediate
      column   = memory|immediate
      text_buffer = label|register

SWRITE is a very clear example of how nesting macros can build new procedures very quickly. SWRITE is a combination of the MVCUR macro followed by PUTS. SWRITE is called like this:

```
swrite   4,0,text_buffer
```

The example (on page 110) could be written using MVCUR and PUTS like this:

```
mvcur    4,0
puts     text_buffer
```

The convenience of using one macro instead of two will be seen in both writing CHUCK source code and also building window procedures.

SWRITE (EXE Version)   Figure 4-32 presents the EXE version of the SWRITE macro. Note that SWRITE is composed of MVCUR and PUTS. There is no subroutine called from within the macro.

Figure 4-33 presents the source code listing to EPROG5.ASM, the demonstration program for SWRITE. The SWRITE procedure is a very convenient way to place text on a screen.

Fig. 4-32. The EXE macro listing to SWRITE.

```
;;----------------------------------------
;;
;; Macro: SWRITE
;;
;; Descritpion: Write to the
;;   screen at row and col
;;
;;

SWRITE MACRO row,column,string
       MVCUR row,column
       PUTS string
       ENDM
;;----------------------------------------
```

Fig. 4-33. The source code listing to EPROG5.ASM.

```
;----------------------------------------
; Source Listing Start
;
; File Name: EPROG5.ASM
;
; Description:
;   Tests: VIDINIT & CLRSCREEN
;          & SCWRITE

;
; Include Macro file
;

INCLUDE SMALL.MAC

; Initialize EXE file structure with STACK => 100h

       PROG_EXE

; Start of data segment
```

```
        PROG_DATA

text_buffer DB 'Hello World!',0

; Start of code segment

        PROG_CODE

; CHUCK video call initialization

        vidinit

; Clear the active video page

        clrscreen

; Write text message at row 10, column 10

        swrite      10,10,text_buffer

; DOS EXE terminate

        END_EXE

        END


;
; End of Source Listing
;-------------------------------------
```

Fig. 4-33 ends.

SWRITE (COM Version)   The listing for the COM SWRITE macro is identical to the EXE version of the macro. Figure 4-34 repeats the short listing. As with the EXE version there is no subroutine called; consequently, there will not be any assembly subroutine code.

As the SWRITE macro uses the MVCUR and PUTS macros, L_MVCUR, L_PUTS and L_PUTCHAR must be invoked in order for SWRITE to function. Figure 4-35 presents the source code listing to the demonstration program, CPROG5.ASM.

Fig. 4-34. The COM macro listing to SWRITE.

```
;;-------------------------------------
;;
;; Macro: SWRITE
;;
;; Descritpion: Write to the
;;   screen at row and col
;;
;;

SWRITE MACRO row,column,string
        MVCUR row,column
        PUTS string
        ENDM
;;-------------------------------------
```

Fig. 4-35. The source code listing to CPROG5.ASM.

```
;-------------------------------------
; Source Listing Start
;
; File Name: CPROG5.ASM
;
; Description:
;  Demonstrates use of VIDINIT and CLRSCREEN
;  and SWRITE


; Include Macro file
;
INCLUDE SMALL.MAC

; Initialize for COM program

        PROG_COM

; DATA in code segment in CHUCK COM programs
;
; ALL COM data goes between PROG_COM and the
; program: label

text_buffer DB 'Hello World!',0

; Start of active program code

program:

; Initialize CHUCK video

        vidinit

; Clear the active display screen

        clrscreen

; Display text_buffer at row 10, column 10

        swrite      10,10,text_buffer

; COM DOS terminate

        COM_TO_DOS

;  Load subroutines

L_VIDINIT
L_CLRSCREEN
L_PUTS
L_PUTCHAR
L_MVCUR

; COM DOS Terminate and end source file

        END_COM

;
; End of Source Listing
;-------------------------------------
```

Earlier I used the word "organized" to describe the assembly code produced by the CHUCK COM method of programming. In support of that statement I've disassembled the CPROG5.COM. Take a look at how the disassembler presents the file and trace the CHUCK CPROG5.ASM along with the listing presented in Fig. 4-36.

Note that the CHUCK CPROG5.ASM consisted of four procedures. Now compare those four procedures next to the disassembled code in Fig. 4-36. It is quite clear that coding in CHUCK offers the advantage of ease over pure assembly. Yes, I could have written tighter pure assembly code, but remember that CHUCK is, in a sense, a super-set of assembly and there will be code overhead:

CPROG5.COM   292 bytes
EPROG5.EXE   779 bytes

There is no need to mention the size of the C generated EXE file.

Fig. 4-36. The disassembled listing of CPROG5.COM.

```
PAGE   60,132

.286c

code_seg_a    segment
        assume   cs:code_seg_a, ds:code_seg_a

        org    100h

cprog5      proc    far

start:
        push    cs
        pop     ds
        jmp     short loc_1
        db      90h
        db      16 dup (0)
data_2      db      48h
        db      'ello World!'
        db      0
loc_1:
        push    ax
        push    bx
        push    cx
        push    dx
        call    sub_1
        pop     dx
        pop     cx
        pop     bx
        pop     ax
        push    ax
        push    bx
        push    cx
        push    dx
        call    sub_2
        pop     dx
        pop     cx
        pop     bx
```

Fig. 4-36 continued.

```
            pop     ax
            push    ax
            push    bx
            push    dx
            mov     ax,0Ah
            mov     dx,0Ah
            call    sub_5
            pop     dx
            pop     bx
            pop     ax
            push    ax
            push    bx
            push    cx
            push    dx
            push    si
            lea     ax,data_2
            mov     si,ax
            call    sub_3
            pop     si
            pop     dx
            pop     cx
            pop     bx
            pop     ax
            int     20h

cprog5      endp

;--------------------------
sub_1       proc    near
            push    cs
            pop     ds
            jmp     short loc_2
            db      90h
data_3      db      0
data_4      dw      0
data_5      dw      0
loc_2:
            mov     ah,0Fh
            int     10h

            mov     cs:data_3,bh
            cmp     al,7
            je      loc_6
            mov     cs:data_4,3DAh
            cmp     cs:data_3,0
            jne     loc_3
            mov     cs:data_5,0B800h
            jmp     short loc_ret_7
            db      90h
loc_3:
            cmp     cs:data_3,1
            jne     loc_4
            mov     cs:data_5,0B900h
            jmp     short loc_ret_7
            db      90h
loc_4:
            cmp     cs:data_3,2
            jne     loc_5
            mov     cs:data_5,0BA00h
            jmp     short loc_ret_7
```

Fig. 4-36 Continued.

```
        db      90h
loc_5:
        mov     cs:data_5,0BB00h
        jmp     short loc_ret_7
        db      90h
loc_6:
        mov     cs:data_4,3BAh
        mov     cs:data_5,0B000h

loc_ret_7:
        ret
sub_1       endp

;----------------------------
sub_2       proc    near
        mov     al,0
        mov     ch,0
        mov     cl,0
        mov     dh,18h
        mov     dl,4Fh
        mov     bh,7
        mov     ah,6
        int     10h

        mov     ah,0Fh
        int     10h

        xor     dx,dx
        mov     ah,2
        int     10h

        ret
sub_2       endp

;----------------------------
sub_3       proc    near
        xor     ax,0
loc_8:
        mov     al,[si]
        cmp     al,0
        je      loc_ret_10
        cmp     al,24h
        je      loc_9
        push    ax
        push    bx
        call    sub_4
        pop     bx
        pop     ax
        inc     si
        jmp     short loc_8
loc_9:
        push    ax
        push    bx
        mov     ax,0Ah
        call    sub_4
        pop     bx
        pop     ax
        push    ax
        push    bx
        mov     ax,00h
```

```
        call    sub_4
        pop     bx
        pop     ax

loc_ret_10:
        ret
sub_3       endp


;---------------------------
sub_4       proc    near
        mov     bh,cs:data_3
        mov     ah,0Eh
        int     10h

        ret
sub_4       endp


;---------------------------
sub_5       proc    near
        mov     dh,al
        mov     bh,cs:data_3
        mov     ah,2
        int     10h

        ret
sub_5       endp


code_seg_a   ends

        end     start
```

Fig. 4-36 ends.

PRINTF

PRINTF prints various text strings in a contiguous fashion. The syntax is:

printf   *text_buffer,text_buffer...*

PRINTF receives from 1 to 8 labels of text buffers that terminate with a 0 (NULL). OK. OK. CHUCK's PRINTF is not nearly as powerful as C's PRINTF. The CHUCK programmer is required to prepare the text buffers he wishes to print in contiguous fashion. As CHUCK does have a Integer to ASCII conversion (which is presented later in this book) preparing the buffers for PRINTF is not as gruesome as you might expect. The PRINTF demonstration programs are rather simple in this section of the text, but when the code conversion routines are presented, there is a more comprehensive use of CHUCK's PRINTF.

PRINTF (EXE Version)   Because PRINTF uses the PUTS macro, there will not be any subroutine listing. The listing for the EXE version of the PRINTF macro is presented in Fig. 4-37.

Figure 4-38 presents the source listing of the PRINTF demonstration program EPROG6.ASM.

Fig. 4-37. The EXE macro listing to PRINTF.

```
;;----------------------------------------
;;
;; Macro: PRINTF p1,p2,p3,p4,p5,p6,p7,p8
;;
;; Description: Print pre-formatted strings
;;   on a row
;;

PRINTF MACRO p1,p2,p3,p4,p5,p6,p7,p8

;; If the parameter is blank then end macro expansion...
;; Else print the text_buffer

    IFB <p1>
        EXITM
    ELSE
        puts    p1
    ENDIF

;; If the parameter is blank then end macro expansion...
;; Else print the text_buffer

    IFB <p2>
        EXITM
    ELSE
        puts    p2
    ENDIF

;; If the parameter is blank then end macro expansion...
;; Else print the text_buffer

    IFB <p3>
        EXITM
    ELSE
        puts    p3
    ENDIF

;; If the parameter is blank then end macro expansion...
;; Else print the text_buffer

    IFB <p4>
        EXITM
    ELSE
        puts    p4
    ENDIF

;; If the parameter is blank then end macro expansion...
;; Else print the text_buffer

    IFB <p5>
        EXITM
    ELSE
        puts    p5
    ENDIF

;; If the parameter is blank then end macro expansion...
;; Else print the text_buffer

    IFB <p6>
        EXITM
```

```
        ELSE
             puts    p6
        ENDIF

;; If the parameter is blank then end macro expansion...
;; Else print the text_buffer

   IFB <p7>
        EXITM
   ELSE
        puts    p7
   ENDIF

;; If the parameter is blank then end macro expansion...
;; Else print the text_buffer

   IFB <p8>
        EXITM
   ELSE
        puts    p8
   ENDIF
        ENDM
;;-------------------------------------
```

Fig. 4-37 ends.

Fig. 4-38. The source code listing to EPROG6.ASM.

```
;-------------------------------------
; Source Listing Start
;
; File Name: EPROG6.ASM
;
; Description:
;  Tests: VIDINIT & CLRSCREEN
;            & PRINTF
;
;
; Include Macro file
;

INCLUDE SMALL.MAC

; Initialize EXE file structure with STACK => 100h

        PROG_EXE

; Start of data segment

        PROG_DATA

text1_buff DB 'Hello ',0
text2_buff DB 'World!',0

; Start of code segment

        PROG_CODE

; CHUCK video call initialization
```

```
        vidinit

; Clear the active video page

        clrscreen

; Write text buffers using PRINTF

        printf      text1_buff,text2_buff

; DOS EXE terminate

        END_EXE

        END

;
; End of Source Listing
;-------------------------------------
```

Fig. 4-38 ends.

PRINTF (COM Version)   Because PRINTF uses the PUTS macro, L_PUTS and L_PUTCHAR must be invoked in order for your program to function properly. The COM version listing to the PRINTF macro is presented in Fig. 4-39.

The source code listing to CPROG6.ASM, the demonstration program for PRINTF, is presented in Fig. 4-40. Note that:

CPROG6.COM   299 bytes
EPROG6.EXE   771 bytes

Fig. 4-39. The COM macro listing to PRINTF.

```
;;-------------------------------------
;;
;; Macro: PRINTF p1,p2,p3,p4,p5,p6,p7,p8
;;
;; Description: Print pre-formatted strings
;;    on a row
;;

PRINTF MACRO p1,p2,p3,p4,p5,p6,p7,p8

;; If the parameter is blank then end macro expansion...
;; Else print the text_buffer

   IFB <p1>
        EXITM
   ELSE
        puts      p1
   ENDIF

;; If the parameter is blank then end macro expansion...
;; Else print the text_buffer

   IFB <p2>
```

```
        EXITM
    ELSE
        puts    p2
    ENDIF

;; If the parameter is blank then end macro expansion...
;; Else print the text_buffer

    IFB <p3>
        EXITM
    ELSE
        puts    p3
    ENDIF

;; If the parameter is blank then end macro expansion...
;; Else print the text_buffer

    IFB <p4>
        EXITM
    ELSE
        puts    p4
    ENDIF

;; If the parameter is blank then end macro expansion...
;; Else print the text_buffer

    IFB <p5>
        EXITM
    ELSE
        puts    p5
    ENDIF

;; If the parameter is blank then end macro expansion...
;; Else print the text_buffer

    IFB <p6>
        EXITM
    ELSE
        puts    p6
    ENDIF

;; If the parameter is blank then end macro expansion...
;; Else print the text_buffer

    IFB <p7>
        EXITM
    ELSE
        puts    p7
    ENDIF

;; If the parameter is blank then end macro expansion...
;; Else print the text_buffer

    IFB <p8>
        EXITM
    ELSE
        puts    p8
    ENDIF
        ENDM
;;-----------------------------------------
```

Fig. 4-39 ends.

Fig. 4-40. The source code listing to CPROG6.ASM.

```
;----------------------------------------
; Source Listing Start
;
; File Name: CPROG6.ASM
;
; Description:
;  Demonstrates use of VIDINIT and CLRSCREEN
;  and PRINTF
;

;
; Include Macro file
;

INCLUDE SMALL.MAC

; Initialize for COM program

        PROG_COM

; DATA in code segment in CHUCK COM programs
;
; ALL COM data goes between PROG_COM and the
; program: label

text1_buff DB 'Hello ',0
text2_buff DB 'World!',0

; Start of active program code

program:

; Initialize CHUCK video

        vidinit

; Clear the active display screen

        clrscreen

; Write text buffers using PRINTF

        printf      text1_buff,text2_buff


; COM DOS terminate

        COM_TO_DOS

;  Load subroutines

L_VIDINIT
L_CLRSCREEN
L_PUTS
L_PUTCHAR
L_MVCUR

; COM DOS Terminate and end source file

        END_COM
```

```
;
; End of Source Listing
;------------------------------------
```

Fig. 4-40 ends.

MAKEATTR

MAKEATTR makes a character attribute byte. The syntax is:

makeattr   *foreground, background, intensity, blink*

where *foreground*   = immediate
      background   = immediate
      intensity   = immediate
      blink   = immediate

MAKEATTR makes a character attribute byte where the four parameters passed are:

- *Parameter 1* foreground color
- *Parameter 2* background color
- *Parameter 3* intensity on/off toggle
- *Parameter 4* foreground blink on/off toggle

PC character can be printed to the color monitor with a variety of attributes. There are eight foreground and background colors to select from. The eight colors are defined in the DEFINES.MAC file. They are:

BLACK

BLUE

GREEN

CYAN

RED

MAGENTA

BROWN

WHITE

The foreground color may have intensity on or intensity off. Finally, the foreground color of the text may be blinking or not. Here is an example of a MAKEATTR call:

makeattr   RED,WHITE,OFF_INTEN,OFF_BLINK

The preceding MAKEATTR procedure would create an attribute byte with a RED foreground color, a WHITE background color, and its intensity and blink characteristics would be off. The eight-bit attribute value would be returned in the AL register.

The PC text mode stores the attribute byte directly after the ASCII character byte in screen memory. The character byte combined with the attribute byte will be called a *TOKEN*. A TOKEN has a 16-bit value. More on the TOKEN when the MAKETOKEN procedure is presented.

MAKEATTR (EXE Version)   Figure 4-41 presents the listing for the MAKEATTR macro. Note that the MAKEATTR demonstration programs will appear as the example programs for the SCWRITE function which directly follows MAKEATTR.

The assembly subroutine, which is called from within the MAKEATTR macro, is found in Fig. 4-42.

Fig. 4-41. The EXE macro listing to MAKEATTR.

```
;;-------------------------------------------
;; Macro: MAKEATTR fore,back,intense,blink
;;
;; Description: Create an attribute

MAKEATTR MACRO fore,back,intense,blink
        pushbcd

    IFDIFI <AX>,<fore>
        mov    AX,fore
    ENDIF

    IFDIFI <DX>,<back>
        mov    DX,back
    ENDIF

    IFDIFI <BX>,<intense>
        mov    BX,intense
    ENDIF

    IFDIFI <CX>,<blink>
        mov    CX,blink
    ENDIF

        EXTRN    MKATTR:NEAR
        call     MKATTR

        popbcd
        ENDM
;;-------------------------------------------
```

Fig. 4-42. The EXE source code to MKATTR.ASM.

```
;********************
; Source Code Start
;
; File Name:    MKATTR.ASM
;
; Synopsis:     mkAttr(fore,back,intensity,blink)
;
; int fore      foreground color
```

Fig. 4-42 continued.

```
;
; int back       background color
;
; int intensity  foreground intensity on-off
;
; int blink      blink on-off
;
; int attr       the properly aligned bits
;                for a character attribute
;
; Description: mkAttr takes the four qualities
;                of the attribute byte and
;                brings them together into the
;                attribute byte's proper bit
;                arrangement
;
; Returns:       attr

        DOSSEG

        .MODEL SMALL


        .CODE
        PUBLIC MKATTR

MKATTR PROC NEAR
;
; Save regs
;
        jmp     mk1
fore_c DB       0
back_c DB       0
inten_t DB      0
blink_t DB      0
mk1:

; save attributes to memory

        mov     fore_c,AL

        mov     back_c,DL

        mov     inten_t,BL

        mov     blink_t,CL

; 0 => AX

        xor     AX,AX

; background color => AL

        mov     AL,back_c


;
; move background 4 bits left (back*16)
;

        mov     CL,4
```

```
        shl     AL,CL

;
; OR foreground
;

        or      AL,fore_c

;
; OR intensity
;

        or      AL,inten_t

;
; OR blink
;

        or      AL,blink_t
        ret
MKATTR  ENDP

;
; End assembly source file
;

        END

; End Source Here
;****************
```

Fig. 4-42 ends.

MAKEATTR (COM Version)   The macro loader for the MAKEATTR procedure is:

```
L_MAKEATTR MACRO
        INCLUDE MKATTR.ASM
        ENDM
```

Add the L_MAKEATTR file to your COM.MAC program. The listing for the
COM version of the MAKEATTR macro is presented in Fig. 4-43. The subroutine that is called from within the COM MAKEATTR macro is presented in Fig.
4-44.

Fig. 4-43. The COM macro listing to MAKEATTR.

```
;;-------------------------------------
;; Macro: MAKEATTR fore,back,intense,blink
;;
;; Description: Create an attribute

MAKEATTR MACRO fore,back,intense,blink

        pushbcd

    IFDIFI <AX>,<fore>
        mov     AX,fore
    ENDIF
```

```
        IFDIFI <DX>,<back>
            mov     DX,back
        ENDIF

        IFDIFI <BX>,<intense>
            mov     BX,intense
        ENDIF

        IFDIFI <CX>,<blink>
            mov     CX,blink
        ENDIF

            PUBLIC  MKATTR
            call    MKATTR

            popbcd
            ENDM
;;-------------------------------------
```

Fig. 4-43 ends.

Fig. 4-44. The COM source code to MKATTR.ASM.

```
;********************
; Source Code Start
;
; File Name:    MKATTR.ASM
;
; Synopsis:     mkAttr(fore,back,intensity,blink)
;
; int fore      foreground color
;
; int back      background color
;
; int intensity  foreground intensity on-off
;
; int blink     blink on-off
;
; int attr      the properly aligned bits
;               for a character attribute
;
; Description: mkAttr takes the four qualities
;               of the attribute byte and
;               brings them together into the
;               attribute byte's proper bit
;               arrangement
;
; Returns:      attr

MKATTR PROC NEAR

; Jump over data held in code segment

        jmp     mk1

; attributes

fore_c  DB      0
back_c  DB      0
inten_t DB      0
```

```
        blink_t DB      0

        mk1:

        ; store attributes in memory

                mov     fore_c,AL

                mov     back_c,DL

                mov     inten_t,BL

                mov     blink_t,CL

        ; 0 => AX

                xor     AX,AX

        ; background color to AL

                mov     AL,back_c

        ;
        ; move background 4 bits left (back*16)
        ;

                mov     CL,4
                shl     AL,CL

        ;
        ; OR foreground
        ;

                or      AL,fore_c

        ;
        ; OR intensity
        ;

                or      AL,inten_t

        ;
        ; OR blink
        ;

                or      AL,blink_t
                ret
        MKATTR  ENDP

        ;-------------------------------------
```

Fig. 4-44 ends.

SCWRITE

SCWRITE prints a string of *n* bytes and attributes to a specific screen location. The syntax is:

SCWRITE *row,column,length,string,attribute*

where *row*   = immediate|memory
       column   = immediate|memory
       length   = immediate|memory
       string   = label of text_buffer
       attribute = immediate|memory

SCWRITE uses BIOS function 13h, interrupt 10h, to write a string to the screen. You can control where the string write starts, the number of bytes written and the character attribute used for the string. On entry:

- AH holds the function number 13h
- AL in write mode is 0 by default; string is character only and no cursor update
- BH holds video page from PAG_NUM
- BL holds attribute created by MAKEATTR
- CX holds the length of the string
- DH holds row to begin write
- DL holds column to begin write
- ES:BP points to the string

SCWRITE is a very long macro and should be invoked as few times as possible. There is no subroutine call made from SCWRITE.

SCWRITE (EXE Version)   The listing for the EXE version of the SCWRITE is presented in Fig. 4-45. As there is no subroutine called from within the SCWRITE macro the EXE example program will immediately follow.

Fig. 4-45. The EXE macro listing to SCWRITE.

```
;;--------------------------------------
;;
;; Macro: SCWRITE
;;
;; Descritpion: Write to the
;;   screen at row and col with attribute
;;
;;

SCWRITE MACRO row,column,length,string,attribute
        EXTRN PAG_NUM:BYTE

;; save regs

        pushaa
        push    BP

;; set ES to DS

        push    DS
        pop     ES
```

```
;; get offset of string

        lea     AX,string

;; transfer offset to BP

        push    AX
        pop     BP

;; get attribute into AL

        mov     AX,DS:[attribute]

;; xfer AL to BL

        mov     BL,AL

;; place video page to BH

        mov     BH,DS:[PAG_NUM]

;; AL gets row

        mov     AX,row

;; DH gets row

        mov     DH,AL

;; AL gets column

        mov     AX,column

;; DL gets column

        mov     DL,AL

;; CX gets length

        mov     CX,length

;; AL gets 0 (write mode)

        mov     AL,0

;; Function 13h, interrupt 10h

        mov     AH,13h
        int     10h

;; restore regs

        pop     BP
        popaa

        ENDM
;;------------------------------------
```

Fig. 4-45 ends.

The source code listing to EPROG7.ASM is presented in Fig. 4-46. This demonstration program prints the famous 'Hello World!' message with a BLACK foreground, WHITE background, with intensity off and foreground blink on.

Fig. 4-46. The source code listing to EPROG7.ASM.

```
;----------------------------------------
; Source Listing Start
;
; File Name: EPROG7.ASM
;
; Description:
;   Tests: VIDINIT & CLRSCREEN
;           & SCWRITE
;
;
; Include Macro file
;

INCLUDE SMALL.MAC

; Initialize EXE file structure with STACK => 100h

        PROG_EXE

; Start of data segment

        PROG_DATA

text_buff DB 'Hello World!',0
attribute DW 0

; Start of code segment

        PROG_CODE

; CHUCK video call initialization

        vidinit

; Clear the active video page

        clrscreen

; set attribute byte to

        makeattr   BLACK,WHITE,OFF_INTEN,ON_BLINK

; set attribute variable to value returned
; makeattr (RET_VAL defined in DEFINES.MAC)

        setv       [attribute],RET_VAL

; Write text buffer using scwrite

        scwrite    2,0,12,text_buff,[attribute]

; DOS EXE terminate
```

```
        END_EXE

        END

;
; End of Source Listing
;----------------------------------------
```

Fig. 4-46 ends.

SCWRITE (COM Version)   As SCWRITE does not call a subroutine from within the macro there is no need to create a loader macro. Figure 4-47 presents the listing to the SCWRITE macro.

The COM version demonstration program, CPROG7.ASM is presented in Fig. 4-48.

Fig. 4-47. The COM macro listing to SCWRITE.

```
;;----------------------------------------
;;
;; Macro: SCWRITE
;;
;; Descritpion: Write to the
;;   screen at row and col with attribute
;;
;;

SCWRITE MACRO row,column,length,string,attribute

;; save regs

        pushaa
        push    BP

;; set ES to DS

        push    DS
        pop     ES

;; get offset of string

        lea     AX,string

;; transfer offset to BP

        push    AX
        pop     BP

;; get attribute into AL

        mov     AX,CS:[attribute]

;; xfer AL to BL

        mov     BL,AL

;; place video page to BH
```

```
              mov        BH,CS:[PAG_NUM]

;; AL gets row

              mov        AX,row

;; DH gets row

              mov        DH,AL

;; AL gets column

              mov        AX,column

;; DL gets column

              mov        DL,AL

;; CX gets length

              mov        CX,length

;; AL gets 0 (write mode)

              mov        AL,0

;; Function 13h, interrupt 10h

              mov        AH,13h
              int        10h

;; restore regs

              pop        BP
              popaa

              ENDM
;;------------------------------------
```

Fig. 4-47 ends.

Fig. 4-48. The source code listing to CPROG7.ASM.

```
;------------------------------------
; Source Listing Start
;
; File Name: CPROG7.ASM
;
; Description:
;   Tests: VIDINIT & CLRSCREEN
;          & SCWRITE
;
; Include Macro file
;

INCLUDE SMALL.MAC

; Initialize for COM program

              PROG_COM
```

```
; DATA in code segment in CHUCK COM programs
;
; ALL COM data goes between PROG_COM and the
; program: label

text_buff DB 'Hello World!',0
attribute DW 0

; Start of active program code

program:

; CHUCK video call initialization

        vidinit

; Clear the active video page

        clrscreen

; set attribute byte to

        makeattr   BLACK,WHITE,OFF_INTEN,ON_BLINK

; set attribute variable to value returned
; makeattr (RET_VAL defined in DEFINES.MAC)

        setv        [attribute],RET_VAL

; Write text buffer using scwrite

        scwrite     2,0,12,text_buff,[attribute]

; COM DOS terminate

        COM_TO_DOS

L_VIDINIT
L_CLRSCREEN
;L_PUTS
;L_PUTCHAR
L_MVCUR
L_MKATTR

; COM DOS Terminate and end source file

        END_COM

;
; End of Source Listing
;------------------------------------
```

Fig. 4-48 ends.

The file sizes for EPROG7.EXE and CPROG7.COM are:

CPROG7.COM   339 bytes
EPROG7.EXE   809 bytes

As you can see the CHUCK COM version demonstration programs are always smaller than the CHUCK EXE versions programs and the Turbo C EXE programs are larger than both. You're almost to the end of Part I. Part II begins with a brief discussion on the elements of program flow and how it relates to a programming language.

Before you go on to Part II, I want to challenge you to modify a previously presented macro and make it better. When you examined the CLRSCREEN (Fig. 4-6) macro you might have thought, say, why didn't Len code this macro so I could use any screen attribute for the screen clear, as opposed to the WHITE foreground and BLACK background.

A very good question indeed. Your task? Re-write the CLRSCREEN macro so that if you do not pass a parameter (IFB - hint) then the value 7 (normal video) will pass into the BH register, otherwise the passed attribute will move to BH. The CLRSCREEN macro must be changed along with the CLRSCRN.ASM source listing.

Stop here. Take a moment to glance back at Fig. 4-6 and write the new version of the CLRSCREEN macro and CLRSCRN.ASM. Check you code with the source presented in Fig. 4-49 and 4-50.

Fig. 4-49. The EXE macro listing to the new CLRSCREEN.

```
;;--------------------------------------
;;
;; Macro: CLRSCREEN attr
;;
;; Descritpion:
;;   Clears the screen using an attribute
;;   or normal attribute if no paramteter
;;   passed
;;

CLRSCREEN MACRO attr

;; save general registers

        pushx

;; If parameter attr is blank then ...

    IFB <attr>
        mov     BH,7

;; else -> move attr to BH

    ELSE
      IFDIFI <AX>,<attr>
        mov     AX,attr
      ENDIF
        mov     BH,AL
    ENDIF

;; declare SCLR as EXTRN

        EXTRN   SCLR:NEAR

;; Call SCLR

        call    sclr
```

```
;; restore general registers

        popx

        ENDM
;;----------------------------------------
```

Fig. 4-49 ends.

Fig. 4-50. The EXE source code listing to CLRSCRN.ASM.

```
;*******************
; Source Code Start
;
; File Name:    CLRSCRN.ASM
;
; Description: Clears the screen with
;              a white foreground and
;              black background if no
;              attribute received.
;              Otherwise the attribute
;              is used.  The cursor
;              is moved to row
;              0 and column 0.
;
; Returns:      Nothing
;

        DOSSEG

        .MODEL SMALL

        .CODE
        PUBLIC  SCLR

SCLR PROC NEAR

; AL holds the number of lines to scroll
; 0 => blank the video window

        mov     AL,0

; CH holds the row of the upper left corner

        mov     CH,0

; CL holds the column of the upper left corner

        mov     CL,0

; DH holds the row of the lower right corner

        mov     DH,24

; DL holds the column of the lower right corner

        mov     DL,79

; BH holds the new screen attribute
; set in CLRSCREEN macro
```

```
; Scroll Window Up via BIOS
; Function 6, interrupt 10h

        mov     AH,6
        int     10H

; Get the current display mode
; Function 15, interrupt 10h

        mov     AH,0fh
        int     10H

; Move the cursor to row 0, column 0
; Function 2, interrupt 10h

; DL & DH hold column and row of new cursor position

        xor     DX,DX  ; 0 => DL & DH
        mov     AH,2
        int     10H
        ret
SCLR ENDP
        END


;
; End of source
;**************
;
```

Fig. 4-50 ends.

CLRSCREEN (New and Improved)

Here is the new and improved CLRSCREEN! The syntax is:

CLRSCREEN *attribute*

where *attribute* = memory|register

CLRSCREEN clears the screen with a designated attribute. If no attribute is passed then the default attribute of WHITE foreground, BLACK background, intensity off and blink off is used.

CLRSCREEN (EXE Version)   The listing to the newly updated CLRSCREEN macro is presented in Fig. 4-49. Figure 4-50 presents the EXE version source code listing to the subroutine which is called from within the CLRSCREEN macro.

The EPROG8.ASM demonstration for the new CLRSCREEN macro is presented in Fig. 4-51.

CLRSCREEN (COM Version)   The COM version of CLRSCREEN is presented in Fig. 4-52. The COM version source code listing for the subroutine which is called from within the CLRSCREEN macro is presented in Fig. 4-53.

The source code listing to CPROG8.ASM, the demonstration program, is presented in Fig. 4-54. Did you figure out how to re-write CLRSCREEN? I hope it was easy for you.

Fig. 4-51. The source code listing to EPROG8.ASM.

```
;-------------------------------------
; Source Listing Start
;
; File Name: EPROG8.ASM
;
; Description:
;   Tests: VIDINIT & CLRSCREEN procedures
;


;
; Include Macro file
;

INCLUDE SMALL.MAC

; Set up EXE small model

        PROG_EXE

; Start code segment

        PROG_CODE

; Initialize CHUCK video

        vidinit

; Make attribute using MAKEATTR
; Attribute byte returned in AL.
; RET_VAL has been defined in DEFINES.MAC  as AX.

        makeattr    BLACK,WHITE,OFF_INTEN,OFF_BLINK

; Clear the screen usingattribute returned in RET_VAL

        clrscreen   RET_VAL

; EXE DOS terminate

        END_EXE

; END of source listing

        END


;
; End of Source Listing
;-------------------------------------
;
```

Fig. 4-52. The COM macro listing to the new CLRSCREEN.

```
;;-------------------------------------
;;
;; Macro: CLRSCREEN attr
;;
;; Descritpion:
;;   Clears the screen using an attribute
```

```
;;   or normal attribute if no paramteter
;;   passed
;;

CLRSCREEN MACRO attr

;; save general registers

        pushx

;; If parameter attr is blank then ...

   IFB <attr>
        mov     BH,7

;; else -> move attr to BH

   ELSE
      IFDIFI <AX>,<attr>
        mov     AX,attr
      ENDIF
        mov     BH,AL
   ENDIF

;; declare SCLR as EXTRN

        PUBLIC  SCLR

;; Call SCLR

        call    sclr

;; restore general registers

        popx

        ENDM
;;--------------------------------------
```

Fig. 4-52 ends.

Fig. 4-53. The COM source code listing to CLRSCRN.ASM.

```
;*******************
; Source Code Start
;
; File Name:   CLRSCRN.ASM
;
; Description: Clears the screen with
;              a white foreground and
;              black background if no
;              attribute received.
;              Otherwise the attribute
;              is used.  The cursor
;              is moved to row
;              0 and column 0.
;
; Returns:     Nothing
;
```

```
SCLR PROC NEAR

; AL holds the number of lines to scroll
; 0 => blank the video window

        mov     AL,0

; CH holds the row of the upper left corner

        mov     CH,0

; CL holds the column of the upper left corner

        mov     CL,0

; DH holds the row of the lower right corner

        mov     DH,24

; DL holds the column of the lower right corner

        mov     DL,79

; BH holds the new screen attribute
; BH set in CLRSCREEN macro

; Scroll Window Up via BIOS
; Function 6, interrupt 10h

        mov     AH,6
        int     10H

; Get the current display mode
; Function 15, interrupt 10h

        mov     AH,0fh
        int     10H

; Move the cursor to row 0, column 0
; Function 2, interrupt 10h

; DL & DH hold column and row of new cursor position

        xor     DX,DX   ; 0 => DL & DH
        mov     AH,2
        int     10H
        ret
SCLR ENDP

;
; End of source
;**************
;
```

Fig. 4-53 ends.

Fig. 4-54. The source code listing to CPROG8.ASM.

```
;------------------------------------
; Source Listing Start
;
; File Name: CPROG8.ASM
;
; Description:
;   Demonstrates use of VIDINIT and CLRSCREEN
;


;
; Include Macro file
;

INCLUDE SMALL.MAC

        PROG_COM
program:

; Initialize CHUCK video

        vidinit

; Make attribute using MAKEATTR
; Attribute byte returned in AL.
; RET_VAL has been defined in DEFINES.MAC  as AX.

        makeattr    BLACK,WHITE,OFF_INTEN,OFF_BLINK

; Clear the screen usingattribute returned in RET_VAL

        clrscreen   RET_VAL

        COM_TO_DOS

;   Load subroutines

L_VIDINIT
L_CLRSCREEN
L_MAKEATTR

; COM DOS Terminate and end source file

        END_COM


;
; End of Source Listing
;------------------------------------
```

FINAL WORDS

Part I of this book covered many topics. You learned how to use the new assembly directives to create simple EXE and COM programs. Macros were defined as text expansions. Macro-defined procedures ranging from setting up the stack and segment order for EXE files to printing text buffers to the screen were presented.

I hope Part I has given you a feel for the powerful implications of using macros in assembly programming.

Hold on to your hats, though. Part II starts by presenting a brief discussion on notions of program flow and a formal introduction (at last) to CHUCK.

PART II
Adding Structure to Assembly Programs

Part II is an introduction to the control flow statements, which form the heart of the CHUCK programming language. These control flow statements add an easy means of creating looping program structure, conditional branching structure, and value filtering structure with the streamline economy of assembly.

Following the presentation of CHUCK's control flow statements the section on using CHUCK in a mixed-language programming environment is presented.

When you've finished Part II, writing nested FOR/NEXT loops in CHUCK should prove as easy as it is in your current favorite programming language. Note though, that CHUCK's programming code overhead will in all likelihood prove considerably less than most other languages.

5

Introducing the CHUCK Programming Language

Clear, organized and structured thinking will produce clear, organized and structured source code. With proper programming technique, notorious spaghetti-like languages such as BASIC and Assembly can produce organized and readable source code. Unstructured programming languages like BASIC and assembly, though, place a heavy burden on the programmer to make source code organized and readable.

On the other hand, programming languages such as C or PASCAL, have internal program flow constructs which facilitate organized and structured programming technique. For example, let's say that you need to clear a rectangle on the screen using the ASCII space (20 hex) character. The rectangle's upper left-hand corner begins at row 5, column 5, and the lower right-hand corner is located at row 15, column 25. One method of clearing the rectangle on the screen is to write spaces horizontally and when the right-hand column has been written, go to the next line and write another row. Continue this process until row 15 has been written. The pseudo code for this method might look like:

```
        set row variable to 5
start_row_loop
        set column variable to 5
        move cursor to row and column variable value
start_column_loop
        print space to screen ( 20 hex ) (update cursor)
        add 1 column variable
        is column 26?
            yes -> go to end_column_loop
        go to start_column_loop
end_column_loop
        add1 to row variable
```

```
        is row 16?
            yes -> go to end_row_loop
        go to start_row_loop
    end_row_loop
```

For those of you who have some experience in assembly try writing the code to clear a rectangular area of the screen. Here's the C code to do the job:

```
for(row = 5; row < 16; row ++)
    {
    mvCur(row,5);
    for(column = 5; column < 26; column ++)
        putchar(' ');
    }
```

Notice how C's for (...;...;...) program flow statement facilitates the implementation of the pseudo code. The assembly programmers can now compare their assembly code to the C code. In summary, adding program flow statements to a computer language improves the utility of the language by great leaps.

CHUCK's control flow statements are very easy to decipher. In a very real sense virtually all CHUCK program control flow keywords are an acronym. Anyone who views a CHUCK program will easily be able to say, "Oh, here's an endless loop which will terminate when the ALT F7 key is pressed." Being able to instantly code and recognize program flow is a powerful advantage of high-level languages. And CHUCK adds program flow constructs with the economy of assembly.

Why is it that CHUCK programs produce code significantly smaller than higher-level languages? Answer: CHUCK is not a compiled language. CHUCK does not need a compiler which uses cleverness upon cleverness upon cleverness to take the text of a language and produce object code for the linker.

CHUCK is assembled not compiled and defined by a macro script. One powerful feature of the macro script language generation technique is that every control flow construct is under your personal scrutiny and control. Once the building block technique underlying the power of CHUCK's program flow constructs is grasped, you'll be adding new program flow statements to CHUCK as their needs arise.

In other words, CHUCK as presented in this book can be thought of as Version 1.0. I'm sure this language will be modified in countless ways. As CHUCK's number one fan, I gladly volunteer to keep a record of user program flow modifications and new procedures. As you modify CHUCK version 1.0 I'd love to hear of any and all of your innovations.

CHUCK'S FOUNDATION

The basic element that allows CHUCK macros to create structure is that macros can communicate memory locations with each other. This is accomplished by giving each CHUCK program flow structure a name. In other words, C source

```
if (val = = 3)
    {
    statement1
    statement2
    }
```

reads: If val is equal to 3 then execute statement1and statement2. Otherwise if val is not equal to 3 then jump to the second bracket (}) and bypass statement1 and statement2.

Now let's examine an equivalent CHUCK program flow sequence:

```
BIFE f_name,val,3
        statement1
        statement2
EIF   f_name
```

The CHUCK BIFE example reads: The Begin IF Equal named f_name compares val with 3. If valis equal to 3 then statement1 and statement2 are executed. Otherwise, if val is not equal to three then the program bypasses statement1 and statement2 and jumps to the End IF named f_name.

That's not too hard, is it?

The C program flow structure created executable code which behaves in an identical way to the CHUCK BIFE program flow structure. Let's compare some more. CHUCK's BIFE (Begin IF Equal) is an acronym. C's if(val = = 3) is not. For some, the acronym will prove easier to remember.

For non-C programmers let's try the following test:

What does this mean?
    if(val != 3)

What does this mean?
    BIFNE name,val,3

If you figured out that BIFNE means "Begin IF Not Equal" then you already know how easy it is to decipher many CHUCK program flow statements. If you guessed that C's != means not equal, then good guess.

What I'm saying is that I think CHUCK is not too difficult to learn. Give CHUCK a chance. The ease of using CHUCK style procedures will probably come faster than using CHUCK's program control flow constructs. I believe learning CHUCK is worth the effort, though. You rarely get something for nothing.

One final thought on CHUCK's requirement that each program control flow statement must be named. I suspect that at first the construct naming convention might seem a tad awkward, but knowing when program flow structures begin and end can really be an aid finding language syntax errors. There are times when I've had a C language sequence end with

```
                    }
                put++;
                }
            counter- -;
            puts(buffer1);
            }
            newline( );
        }
    count += 5;
    }
```

and when I compiled I'd get a dreaded 'too many errors to continue compiling' message. There would be one too many or one too few closing brackets. If each program flow statement had been named, the syntax error would have been easier to find. So I judge that the requirement of naming each program flow statement is an improvement over the brackets method.

CHUCK IN PERSPECTIVE

CHUCK is a general purpose programming language closely associated with assembly language. CHUCK is a lower-level language and has been designed to fit between assembly and C in the hierarchy of languages. Although CHUCK is a low-level language it provides many structure statements, giving it some attributes of higher-level languages, such as C and PASCAL.

CHUCK does not provide any high-level facilities such as disk I/O or writing to the screen. These higher-level mechanisms must be explicitly provided by the CHUCK library built specifically for the machine on which CHUCK has been implemented.

CHUCK provides straightforward single thread program flow constructs similar in flavor to those provided by C. One advantage of the simplicity of constructs is that there are few acronym-based keywords which often can be learned in a short period of time.

As CHUCK is defined by a macro script which is interpreted by your assembler, pure assembly may be interspersed at will in CHUCK code. Of course this is a tremendous advantage for those of you who are conversant in assembly. Also, the mixed programming language requirements of CHUCK are identical to those of assembly. CHUCK data types are also identical to those of assembly.

CHUCK GROUND WORK

Let's begin by writing a program in assembly that loops to read a key from the keyboard and prints the key to the screen. When the Enter key is pressed the loop terminates.

Figure 5-1 presents the EXE version of the keyboard-looping program and Fig. 5-2 presents the COM version. The file sizes of the CHUCK/assembly key-

Fig. 5-1. The source code listing to EPROG9.ASM.

```
;----------------------------------------
; Source Listing Start
;
; File Name: EPROG9.ASM
;
; Description:
;  Keyboard looping demonstration
;


;
; Include Macro file
;

INCLUDE SMALL.MAC

; Set up EXE small model

        PROG_EXE
        PROG_CODE

        vidinit

; CHUCK ends and assembly begins

;----------------------------------------

begin_loop:
        mov     AH,0        ; read keyboard function
        int     16h         ; invoke BIOS keyboard
        cmp     AL,13       ; AL is carriage return?
        je      end_loop    ; yes -> jump to exit
        mov     AH,0Eh      ; print char function
        mov     BH,0        ; on video page 0
        int     10h         ; invoke BIOS video
        jmp     begin_loop  ; get next character
end_loop:

;----------------------------------------

; CHUCK returns

        END_EXE
        END

;
; End of Source Listing
;----------------------------------------
```

Fig. 5-2. The source code listing to CPROG9.ASM.

```
;----------------------------------------
; Source Listing Start
;
; File Name: CPROG9.ASM
;
; Description:
;  Keyboard looping demonstration
```

```
;
;
; Include Macro file
;

INCLUDE SMALL.MAC

        PROG_COM
program:
        vidinit

; CHUCK ends and assembly begins

;----------------------------------------

begin_loop:
        mov     AH,0        ; read keyboard function
        int     16h         ; invoke BIOS keyboard
        cmp     AL,13       ; AL is carriage return?
        je      end_loop    ; yes -> jump to exit
        mov     AH,0Eh      ; print char function
        mov     BH,0        ; on video page 0
        int     10h         ; invoke BIOS video
        jmp     begin_loop  ; get next character
end_loop:

;----------------------------------------

; CHUCK returns

L_VIDINIT

        END_COM

;
; End of Source Listing
;----------------------------------------
```

Fig. 5-2 ends.

board-looping demonstration programs are:

    EPROG9.EXE   643 bytes
    CPROG9.COM   157 bytes

Let's begin to modify the keyboard demonstration program. To demonstrate the impact of each change, the new source is shown, along with the sizes of the files. The steps are:

1. Add a GETCH procedure for keyboard read and replace BIOS int 10h, func 0Eh, with PUTCHAR procedure

2. Replace the 'is key carriage return' with CHUCK's BIFE/EIF (Begin IF Equal/End IF) structure

3. Replace 'get next char' via jump with BELOOP / EELOOP (Begin Endless LOOP / End Endless LOOP) structure

Before formally presenting CHUCK language macros, it will prove beneficial to discuss the GETCH macro at this time. Some of the CHUCK demonstration programs require that the user input a response which is then analyzed. The GETCH macro facilitates this procedure.

Create a file called KEYBOARD.MAC and place the GETCH macro in that file. Remember to modify your SMALL.MAC file to include KEYBOARD.MAC.

GETCH Procedure

GETCH gets the character code from the keyboard. The syntax is:

getch   *key*

where *key* = WORD in memory

The GETCH procedure uses BIOS function 0, interrupt 16h to wait for a keystroke. When the key is pressed the scan code value is returned in the AH register and the character code is returned in the AL register. If no WORD sized parameter is passed to GETCH then the character code is returned in the AL register.

Figure 5-3 presents the macro listing for the EXE version of the GETCH macro.

Fig. 5-3. The EXE macro listing to GETCH.

```
;;----------------------------------------
;; Macro: GETCH key_val
;;
;; Descritpion: Use BIOS to
;;   wait and get a character
;;

GETCH MACRO key_val

;; if key_val is legal parameter them...

IFNB <key_val>

;; save AX

        push    AX

;; 0 -> AX -> funct 0, Get key

        xor     AX,AX
        int     16h

;; AH -> scan code
;; AL -> character code

;; scan code not needed

        xor     AH,AH

;; store char val in memory
```

```
        mov      [key_val],AX

;; restore AX

        pop      AX

;; char key code returned in AL

ELSE

;; 0 -> AX -> funct 0, Get key

        xor      AX,AX
        int      16h

;; AH -> scan code
;; AL -> character code
;; scan code not needed

        xor      AH,AH

ENDIF

        ENDM
```

Fig. 5-3 ends.

EPROG9.ASM (Fig. 5-1) has been re-coded so that two procedures replace the assembly code. Figure 5-4 presents the source code listing to EPROG10.ASM.

A 'cmp' instruction with the attendant conditional jump (je) are still present in the program. Before discussing the BIFE macro, the COM version of GETCH needs to be presented.

Fig. 5-4. The source code listing to EPROG10.ASM.

```
;-------------------------------------
; Source Listing Start
;
; File Name: EPROG10.ASM
;
; Description:
;   Keyboard looping demonstration
;
;
;
; Include Macro file
;

INCLUDE SMALL.MAC

; Set up EXE small model

        PROG_EXE
        PROG_DATA

key_val DW       0
```

```
        PROG_CODE

        vidinit

; CHUCK ends and assembly begins

;----------------------------------------

begin_loop:
        getch   [key_val]    ; get key press char val
        cmp     [key_val],13 ; AL is carriage return?
        je      end_loop     ; yes -> jump to exit
        putchar [key_val]    ; print char function
        jmp     begin_loop ; get next character
end_loop:

;----------------------------------------

; CHUCK returns

        END_EXE
        END

;
; End of Source Listing
;----------------------------------------
```

Fig. 5-4 ends.

GETCH (COM Version)   Figure 5-5 presents the COM version of the GETCH macro.

Fig. 5-5. The COM macro listing to GETCH.

```
;;----------------------------------------
;;
;; Macro: GETCH key_val
;;
;; Descritpion: Use BIOS to
;;   wait and get a character
;;

GETCH MACRO key_val

;; if key_val is legal parameter them...

IFNB <key_val>

;; save AX

        push    AX

;; 0 -> AX -> funct 0, Get key

        xor     AX,AX
        int     16h

;; AH -> scan code
;; AL -> character code

;; scan code not needed
```

```
        xor     AH,AH

;; store char val in memory

        mov     [key_val],AX

;; restore AX

        pop     AX

;; char key code returned in AL

ELSE

;; 0 -> AX -> funct 0, Get key

        xor     AX,AX
        int     16h

;; AH -> scan code
;; AL -> character code
;; scan code not needed

        xor     AH,AH

ENDIF

        ENDM
```

Fig. 5-5 ends.

As with EPROG10.ASM, CPROG10.ASM now has the GETCH and PUTCHAR procedures in the source. Figure 5-6 presents the assembly listing to CPROG10.ASM. Here is a comparison of executable files.

EPROG9.EXE	643 bytes	(no procedures)
EPROG10.EXE	669 bytes	(GETCH & PUTCHAR)
CPROG9.EXE	157 bytes	(no procedures)
CPROG10.EXE	186 bytes	(GETCH & PUTCHAR)

It is easy to see that the addition of PUTCHAR and GETCH did add a few bytes to the programs. The EXE program increased by 26 bytes and the COM program increased by 29 bytes. I think that is a very reasonable price to pay for high-level-like procedures. But this is not the end. It's finally time to present the first control flow macro, BIFE.

Fig. 5-6. The source code listing to CPROG10.ASM.

```
;------------------------------------
; Source Listing Start
;
; File Name: CPROG10.ASM
;
; Description:
;   Keyboard looping demonstration
;
```

```
;
; Include Macro file
;

INCLUDE SMALL.MAC

        PROG_COM

key_val DW      0

program:
        vidinit

; CHUCK ends and assembly begins

;------------------------------------

begin_loop:
        getch    [key_val]      ; get key press char val
        cmp      [key_val],13 ; AL is carriage return?
        je       end_loop       ; yes -> jump to exit
        putchar [key_val]       ; print char function
        jmp      begin_loop ; get next character
end_loop:

;------------------------------------

;------------------------------------

; CHUCK returns

L_VIDINIT
L_PUTCHAR
        END_COM

;
; End of Source Listing
;------------------------------------
```

Fig. 5-6 ends.

CHUCK
BEGINNING PROGRAM FLOW CONSTRUCTS

The following sections describe the program flow constructs as used in CHUCK programming.

BIFE (Begin IF Equal)
EIF (End IF)

The syntax is:

```
BIFE   name,val1,val2
       statement
```

      statement
      EIF   *name*

where *name* = ASCII name for BIFE construct
       val1   = memory
       val2   = memory|immediate

BIFE is always associated with EIF (End IF). If val1 and val2 are equal then the statements between BIFE and EIF are executed. The BIFE and EIF macros for EXE files and COM files are the same. Figure 5-7 presents the listing for the BIFE macro and Fig. 5-8 presents the listing for the EIF macro.

Fig. 5-7. The macro listing to BIFE.

```
;;-------------------------------------
;; Macro BIFE name,val1,val2
;;
;; Description: If val1==val2
;;   then execute code between
;;   BIFE.. and EIF (End IF)
;;
BIFE MACRO name,val1,val2

;; save regs

        push    AX
        push    DX

;; if AX not equal to val1 then

    IFDIFI <AX>,<val1>
        mov     AX,val1
    ENDIF

;; if DX not equal to val2 then

    IFDIFI <DX>,<val2>
        mov     DX,val2
    ENDIF

;; compare AX with DX

        cmp     AX,DX

;; jump and bypass code if not equal

        jne     &name&

;; restore regs

        pop     DX
        pop     AX

        ENDM

;;-------------------------------------
;;
```

Fig. 5-8. The macro listing to EIF.

```
;;----------------------------------------
;; Macro: EIF name
;;
;; Description: End of BIF..
;;

EIF MACRO name
        LOCAL SkipLabel

;; if code executed then bypass register restore

        jmp SkipLabel

name:
        pop     DX
        pop     AX

SkipLabel:

        ENDM

;;----------------------------------------
```

The keyboard-read demonstration program enters another incarnation in Fig. 5-9 and Fig. 5-10. Figure 5-9 presents the source code listing to EPROG11.ASM and Fig. 5-10 presents the source code listing to CPROG11.ASM.

Let's compare file sizes again:

EPROG9.EXE	643 bytes	(no procedures)
EPROG10.EXE	669 bytes	(GETCH & PUTCHAR)
EPROG11.EXE	683 bytes	(GETCH & PUTCHAR)
CPROG9.EXE	157 bytes	(no procedures)
CPROG10.EXE	186 bytes	(GETCH & PUTCHAR)
CPROG11.EXE	201 bytes	(GETCH & PUTCHAR)

As you can see each CHUCK control flow construct adds a few bytes to the executable program. Macros for handling an endless loop, and breaking from an endless loop will finally make the keyboard-read program a full-fledged CHUCK program. Once fully CHUCK-ized, the C version of the CPROG12.EXE program will be presented.

Fig. 5-9. The source code listing to EPROG11.ASM.

```
;----------------------------------------
; Source Listing Start
;
; File Name: EPROG11.ASM
;
; Description:
```

```
;  Keyboard looping demonstration
;


;
; Include Macro file
;

INCLUDE SMALL.MAC

; Set up EXE small model

        PROG_EXE
        PROG_DATA

key_val DW      0

        PROG_CODE

        vidinit

; CHUCK ends and assembly begins

;--------------------------------------

begin_loop:
        getch   [key_val]    ; get key press char val
        BIFE    key_is_cr,[key_val],13
           jmp end_loop
        EIF     key_is_cr
        putchar [key_val]    ; print char function
        jmp     begin_loop ; get next character
end_loop:

;--------------------------------------

; CHUCK returns

        END_EXE
        END


;
; End of Source Listing
;--------------------------------------
```

Fig. 5-9 ends.

Fig. 5-10. The source code listing to CPROG11.ASM.

```
;--------------------------------------
; Source Listing Start
;
; File Name: CPROG11.ASM
;
; Description:
;   Keyboard looping demonstration
;


;
; Include Macro file
;
```

```
INCLUDE SMALL.MAC

        PROG_COM

key_val DW      0

program:
        vidinit

; CHUCK ends and assembly begins

;-------------------------------------

begin_loop:
begin_loop:
        getch   [key_val]    ; get key press char val
        BIFE    key_is_cr,[key_val],13
            jmp end_loop
        EIF     key_is_cr
        putchar [key_val]    ; print char function
        jmp     begin_loop ; get next character
end_loop:

;-------------------------------------

;-------------------------------------

; CHUCK returns

L_VIDINIT
L_PUTCHAR
        END_COM

;
; End of Source Listing
;-------------------------------------
```

Fig. 5-10 ends.

BELOOP (Begin Endless LOOP)
EBREAK (Endless loop BREAK)
ECONTINUE (Endless loop CONTINUE)
EELOOP (End Endless LOOP)

The syntax is:

```
BELOOP   name
      statement1
            ECONTINUE name
      statement2
            EBREAK name
      statement3
EELOOP name
```

where *name* = ASCII-valid text name

An endless loop will loop until an EBREAK statement is encountered. In the example on the previous page if statement1 permits ECONTINUE, statement3 will be bypassed but the loop will continue executing. If statement2 permits EBREAK, statement3 will also be bypassed and the endless loop will terminate.

Figure 5-11 presents the macro listing to BELOOP, Fig. 5-12 EBREAK, Fig. 5-13 ECONTINUE, and Fig. 5-14 EELOOP. Remember to add each of these macros to your CHUCK.MAC file.

Fig. 5-11. The macro listing to BELOOP.

```
;;----------------------------------------
;;
;; Macro: BELOOP label
;;
;; Description: Set beginning of
;;    Endless loop

BELOOP MACRO label

;; start of endless loop

label:

        ENDM

;;----------------------------------------
```

Fig. 5-12. The macro listing to EBREAK.

```
;;----------------------------------------
;;
;; Macro: EBREAK label
;;
;; Description:  Break out of
;;    Endless loop

EBREAK  MACRO label

;; jump beyond return jump in EELOOP

        jmp     ªª&label&

        ENDM

;;----------------------------------------
```

Fig. 5-13. The macro listing to ECONTINUE.

```
;;----------------------------------------
;;
;; Macro: ECONTINUE label
;;
;; Description: Endless Continue
;;    Endless loop (as in C continue)
```

```
ECONTINUE MACRO label

;; bypas code and continue next iteration

        jmp     a&label&

        ENDM

;;----------------------------------------
```

Fig. 5-13 ends.

Fig. 5-14. The macro listing to EELOOP.

```
;;----------------------------------------
;;
;; Macro: EELOOP label
;;
;; Description: End Endless loop and
;;    return to label

EELOOP MACRO label

;; ECONTINUE jumps here

a&label&:

;; jump to start for another iteration of loop

        jmp     label

;; EBREAK jumps here

aa&label&:

        ENDM

;;----------------------------------------
```

Figure 5-15 presents the source code listing to EPROG12.EXE, the first full-fledged CHUCK program containing structure: EPROG12.EXE. Figure 5-16 presents the source code listing to CPROG12.ASM.

Let's compare file sizes again.

EPROG9.EXE	643 bytes	(no procedures)
EPROG10.EXE	669 bytes	(GETCH & PUTCHAR)
EPROG11.EXE	683 bytes	(GETCH & PUTCHAR)
EPROG12.EXE	683 bytes	(GETCH & PUTCHAR)
CPROG9.COM	157 bytes	(no procedures)
CPROG10.COM	186 bytes	(GETCH & PUTCHAR)
CPROG11.COM	201 bytes	(GETCH & PUTCHAR)
CPROG12.COM	201 bytes	(GETCH & PUTCHAR)

Note that the BELOOP, EBREAK and EELOOP statements did not add code above the pure assembly code.

Fig. 5-15. The source code listing to EPROG12.ASM.

```
;-------------------------------------
; Source Listing Start
;
; File Name: EPROG12.ASM
;
; Description:
;  Keyboard looping demonstration
;

;
; Include Macro file
;

INCLUDE SMALL.MAC

; Set up EXE small model

        PROG_EXE
        PROG_DATA

key_val DW       0

        PROG_CODE

        vidinit


BELOOP  kb_loop               ; Begin Endless loop
        getch   [key_val]     ; get key press char val
        BIFE    key_is_cr,[key_val],13 ; is carriage return?
          EBREAK  kb_loop     ; yes -> break from emdless loop
        EIF     key_is_cr     ; End IF named key_is_cr
        putchar [key_val]     ; print char function
EELOOP  kb_loop

        END_EXE
        END

;
; End of Source Listing
;-------------------------------------
```

Fig. 5-16. The source code listing to CPROG12.ASM.

```
;-------------------------------------
; Source Listing Start
;
; File Name: CPROG12.ASM
;
; Description:
;  Keyboard looping demonstration
;

;
; Include Macro file
;
```

```
INCLUDE SMALL.MAC

        PROG_COM

key_val DW      0

program:
        vidinit

BELOOP  kb_loop                 ; Begin Endless loop
        getch   [key_val]       ; get key press char val
        BIFE    key_is_cr,[key_val],13 ; is carriage return?
            EBREAK  kb_loop     ; yes -> break from emdless loop
        EIF     key_is_cr       ; End IF named key_is_cr
        putchar [key_val]       ; print char function
EELOOP  kb_loop

L_VIDINIT
L_PUTCHAR
        END_COM


;
; End of Source Listing
;--------------------------------------
```

Fig. 5-16 ends.

Figure 5-17 presents the disassembled listing to CPROG12.COM. Experienced assembly programmers can then see how CHUCK assembles and decide if using the structure of CHUCK is worth the coding overhead. Figure 5-18 presents the source code to C-E12.C.

We have arrived at the end of Chapter 5. If you look at the disassembled listing to CPROG12.COM presented in Fig. 5-17 you'll get a good feel for how CHUCK assembles. I've added comments to the disassembly to highlight the CHUCK procedures and program flow constructs. EPROG12.EXE, CPROG12.EXE, and C-E12.EXE all function in an identical fashion. Let's compare the final executable sizes.

CPROG12.COM	201 bytes	(CHUCK)
EPROG12.EXE	683 bytes	(CHUCK)
C-E12.EXE	8768 bytes	(Turbo C)

No more disassemblies of C generated EXE files. I promise!

Fig. 5-17. The disassembled version of CPROG12.COM.

```
PAGE   60,132

.286c

data_6e         equ     3E88h
data_7e         equ     0CD0Fh

code_seg_a      segment
```

Fig. 5-17 continued.

```
                assume  cs:code_seg_a, ds:code_seg_a
                org     100h

cprog12         proc    far
start:
                push    cs
                pop     ds
                jmp     short loc_1
                db      90h
                db      16 dup (0)
data_2          dw      0
loc_1:

;
; vidinit
;
                push    ax
                push    bx
                push    cx
                push    dx
                call    sub_1
                pop     dx
                pop     cx
                pop     bx
                pop     ax

;
; BELOOP kb_loop
;
loc_2:

;
; getch [key_val]
;
                push    ax
                xor     ax,ax
                int     16h
                xor     ah,ah
                mov     cs:data_2,ax
                pop     ax

;
; BIFE key_is_cr,[key_val],13
;
                push    ax
                push    dx
                mov     ax,cs:data_2
                mov     dx,0Dh
                cmp     ax,dx
                jne     loc_3
                pop     dx
                pop     ax

;
; EBREAK kb_loop
;
                jmp     short loc_5
                db      90h, 0EBh, 3, 90h

;
```

Fig. 5-17 continued.

```
; EIF key_is_cr
;
loc_3:
                pop     dx
                pop     ax
loc_4:

;
; putchar [key_val]
;
                push    ax
                push    bx
                mov     ax,cs:data_2
                call    sub_2
                pop     bx
                pop     ax


;
; EELOOP kb_loop
;
                jmp     short loc_2

cprog12         endp


;
; vidinit subroutine
;
sub_1           proc    near
loc_5:
                push    cs
                pop     ds
                jmp     short loc_6
                db      90h
data_3          db      0
data_4          dw      0
data_5          dw      0
loc_6:
                mov     ah,0Fh
                int     10h

                mov     cs:data_3,bh
                cmp     al,7
                je      loc_10
                mov     cs:data_4,3DAh
                cmp     cs:data_3,0
                jne     loc_7
                mov     cs:data_5,0B800h
                jmp     short loc_11
                db      90h
loc_7:
                cmp     cs:data_3,1
                jne     loc_8
                mov     cs:data_5,0B900h
                jmp     short loc_11
                db      90h
loc_8:
                cmp     cs:data_3,2
                jne     loc_9
                mov     cs:data_5,0BA00h
                jmp     short loc_11
```

```
                    db        90h
loc_9:
                    mov       cs:data_5,0BB00h
                    jmp       short loc_11
                    db        90h
loc_10:
                    mov       cs:data_4,3BAh
                    mov       cs:data_5,0B000h
loc_11:
                    ret
sub_1               endp

;
; putchar subroutine
;
sub_2               proc      near
                    mov       bh,cs:data_3
                    mov       ah,0Eh
                    int       10h
                    ret
sub_2               endp


code_seg_a          ends

                    end       start
```

Fig. 5-17 ends.

Fig. 5-18. The source code listing to C-E12.C.

```
/*
 * C-E12.C
 */

#include <stdio.h>
#include <stdlib.h>

void main(void);

void
main()
{

int key;

vidInit();

for(;;)
        {
        key = getch();
        if(key==13)
                break;
        putchar(key);
        }
}
```

6

CHUCK Subroutines, SWITCH/CASE, Looping

Inherent in structured programming is the ability to declare and call subroutines. CHUCK's version of a subroutine is called a *procedure*. BPROCEDURE (Begin PROCEDURE) and EPROCEDURE (End PROCEDURE) are the CHUCK keywords to declare the beginning and end of a procedure. Declaring a procedure in CHUCK is as easy as:

```
BPROCEDURE my_procedure
        statement1
        statement2
EPROCEDURE my_procedure
```

The equivalent source in C would be:

```
void
my_procedure( )
        {
        statement1
        statement2
        }
```

The CHUCK keywords BBLOCK (Begin BLOCK of data in code segment) and EBLOCK (End BLOCK of data in code segment) are used to declare data within a procedure. Initializing a variable within a procedure is as easy as:

```
BPROCEDURE my_procedure
BBLOCK mp_data
```

```
counter DW 0
EBLOCK mp_data
        statement1
        statement2
EPROCEDURE my_procedure
```

The equivalent source in C would be

```
void
my_procedure( )
        {
        int  counter;
        statement1
        statement2
        }
```

RETURN causes a subroutine to terminate immediately. If a parameter (memory|immediate) is passed with RETURN then that value is returned in RET_VAL (the AX register). If no parameter is passed to return then the AX register remains untouched.

Figure 6-1 is the BPROCEDURE macro listing, Fig. 6-2 the EPROCEDURE macro listing, Fig. 6-3 the BBLOCK macro listing, Fig. 6-4 the EBLOCK macro listing, and Fig. 6-5 the RETURN macro listing. Figure 6-6 is the EXE version of the BPROCEDURE|EPROCEDURE demonstration program EPROG13 .ASM.

The COM version, CPROG13.ASM (Fig. 6-7), uses BBLOCK and EBLOCK to declare data in the code segment within a procedure.

Fig. 6-1. The macro listing to BPROCEDURE.

```
;;-------------------------------------
;; Macro: BPROCEDURE name
;;
;; Description: Start of procedure
;;

BPROCEDURE MACRO name

name    PROC    NEAR

        ENDM

;;-------------------------------------
```

Fig. 6-2. The macro listing to EPROCEDURE.

```
;;-------------------------------------
;; Macro: EPROCEDURE name
;;
;; Description: End of procedure
;;
```

```
EPROCEDURE MACRO name

        ret

name    ENDP

        ENDM

;;----------------------------------------
```

Fig. 6-2 ends.

Fig. 6-3. The macro listing to BBLOCK.

```
;;----------------------------------------
;; Macro: BBLOCK name
;;
;; Description: Start of data block
;;              embedded in code
;;              segment
;;

BBLOCK MACRO name

        jmp     name

        ENDM

;;----------------------------------------
```

Fig. 6-4. The macro listing to EBLOCK.

```
;;----------------------------------------
;; Macro: EBLOCK name
;;
;; Description: End of data block
;;              embedded in code
;;              segment
;;

EBLOCK MACRO name

name:

        ENDM

;;----------------------------------------
```

Fig. 6-5. The macro listing to RETURN.

```
;;----------------------------------------
;; Macro RETURN val
;;
;; Description: Return from ASMplus procedure
;;  and return WORD value is AX if requested
```

```
;;
RETURN MACRO val

;; if no parameter then just return

    IFB <val>
        ret

;; if parameter not AX then move to AX and return

    ELSEIFDIFI <AX>,<val>
        mov     AX,val
        ret

;; if parameter is AX then just return

    ELSE
        ret
    ENDIF

        ENDM

;;------------------------------------
```

Fig. 6-5 ends.

Fig. 6-6. The source code listing to EPROG13.ASM.

```
;------------------------------------
; Source Listing Start
;
; File Name: EPROG13.ASM
;
; Description:
;  Demonstrates subroutines in CHUCK


;
; Include Macro file
;

INCLUDE SMALL.MAC

; Initialize EXE file structure with STACK => 100h

        PROG_EXE

; Start of data segment

        PROG_DATA

text_buffer DB 'Hello World!',0

; Start of code segment

        PROG_CODE

        vidinit      ; CHUCK video initialization

        clrscreen    ; clear the screen
```

```
        call p_mess    ; print message

        END_EXE        ; DOS EXE terminate

;-------------------------------------
;
; Begin subroutines for EXE files here
;
;-------------------------------------

BPROCEDURE p_mess      ; begin procedure

        puts    text_buffer

EPROCEDURE p_mess      ; end procedure

;-------------------------------------
;
; End of subroutine section
;
;-------------------------------------

        END

;
; End of Source Listing
;-------------------------------------
```

Fig. 6-6 ends.

Fig. 6-7. The source code listing to CPROG13.ASM.

```
;-------------------------------------
; Source Listing Start
;
; File Name: CPROG13.ASM
;
; Description:
;   Demonstrates use of subroutines
;   and BBLOCK and EBLOCK


;
; Include Macro file
;

INCLUDE SMALL.MAC

; Initialize for COM program

        PROG_COM


program:

        vidinit        ; CHUCK video initialization

        clrscreen      ; clear the screen

        call p_mess    ; print message
```

```
        COM_TO_DOS    ; COM DOS terminate

;--------------------------------------
;
; Begin subroutines for COM files here
;
;--------------------------------------

BPROCEDURE p_mess      ; begin procedure

BBLOCK  p_mess1        ; begin data block in code

text_buffer DB 'Hello World!',0  ; data in code

EBLOCK  p_mess1        ; end data block in code

        puts     text_buffer

EPROCEDURE p_mess      ; end of procedure

;--------------------------------------
;
; End of subroutine section
;
;--------------------------------------

;  Load subroutines

L_VIDINIT
L_CLRSCREEN
L_PUTS
L_PUTCHAR

; COM DOS Terminate and end source file

        END_COM

;
; End of Source Listing
;--------------------------------------
```

Fig. 6-7 ends.

BPROCEDURE (Begin PROCEDURE)
EPROCEDURE (End PROCEDURE)
BBLOCK (Begin Data BLOCK)
EBLOCK (End Data BLOCK)
RETURN (RETURN from procedure)

BPROCEDURE begins a procedure. EPROCEDURE ends a procedure. BBLOCK begins a BLOCK, a data block in a code segment. EBLOCK ends a BLOCK in a code segment. RETURN returns from a procedure prematurely and either does or does not return a 16-bit value in AX. The syntax for the EXE CHUCK procedure is:

```
BPROCEDURE name
        statement1
```

```
        statement2
        return value
        statement3
EPROCEDURE name
```

where *name* = proper ASCII text name
     value = memory|immediate

The syntax for the COM CHUCK procedure is:

```
BPROCEDURE name
BBLOCK          data_name
value           DW  10
EBLOCK          data_name
        statement1
        statement2
            return value
        statement3
EPROCEDURE name
```

where *name* = proper ASCII text name
      value = memory|immediate

BPROCEDURE declares the start of a subroutine and EPROCEDURE declares the end of a subroutine. Note that EPROCEDURE contains an RET instruction eliminating an occasional common error for assembly programmers—forgetting of a RET instruction at the end of a subroutine.

In the syntax examples if *statement2* leads to *return value* then the procedure will return immediately placing the contents of value in the AX register. If a parameter has not been passed to RETURN then the AX register has not been modified.

Remember to add all five macros to your CHUCK.MAC file.

Note that in CPROG13.ASM the data was declared in the 'p_mess' procedure. The data also could have been declared immediately below the PROG_COM CHUCK word. The file sizes for CPROG13.COM and EPROG-13.EXE are:

```
CPROG13.COM   274 bytes
EPROG13.EXE   757 bytes
```

SWITCH (As in C SWITCH)
CASE (As in C CASE)
DEFAULT (As in C DEFAULT)
ESWITCH (End SWITCH)

SWITCH sets a value to be tested. CASE calls a procedure if the SWITCH value equals the CASE value. If no CASEed procedures are called the DEFAULT procedure is called. ESWITCH indicates the end of a SWITCH. The syntax is:

```
SWITCH    sw1,[key_val]
  CASE    sw1,procedure1,'a'
  CASE    sw1,procedure2,'b'
  CASE    sw1,procedure3,'c'
  CASE    sw1,procedure4,'x'
  DEFAULT sw1,procedure5
ESWITCH   sw1
```

where *sw1*   = legal ASCII text name
       key_val   = memory|immediate
       procedure(n) = Procedure created using BPROCEDURE . . . etc.

CHUCK's SWITCH and CASE can function in an identical fashion to the C version of SWITCH and CASE. There is one striking difference, though. With the C SWITCH and CASE you can place program statements after CASE. The program statements after the CASE is terminated with a BREAK statement. The CHUCK SWITCH/CASE scheme requires that you must call a procedure if the CASE matches the SWITCHed value. You are not permitted to use program statements in the CHUCK SWITCH/CASE scheme of things.

Here is the C version of the CHUCK syntax example:

```
switch(key_val)
    {
    case 'a':
        procedure1( );
        break;
    case 'b':
        procedure2( );
        break;
    case 'c':
        procedure3( );
        break;
    case 'x':
        procedure4( );
        break;
    default:
        procedure5( );
        break;
    }
```

Note that the CHUCK SWITCH/CASE scheme, although more restricted than the C scheme, can be coded in fewer lines.

For those programmers not familiar with C, I'll describe the SWITCH/CASE example with prose. Please note that = = means 'is equal to' and -> means 'then'.

SWITCH -> the value 'key_val' is being tested
    If 'key_val' = = 'a' -> call procedure1 -> GOTO ESWITCH
      otherwise
    If 'key_val' = = 'b' -> call procedure2 -> GOTO ESWITCH
      otherwise
    If 'key_val' = = 'c' -> call procedure3 -> GOTO ESWITCH
      otherwise
    If 'key_val' = = 'x' -> call procedure4 -> GOTO ESWITCH
      otherwise
            call procedure5 -> GOTO ESWITCH
ESWITCH

Figure 6-8 presents the SWITCH macro listing, Fig. 6-9 presents the CASE macro listing, Fig. 6-10 the DEFAULT macro listing and Fig. 6-11 the ESWITCH macro listing. Remember to add all four macros to your CHUCK-.MAC file.

Fig. 6-8. The macro listing to SWITCH.

```
;;----------------------------------------
;; Macro: SWITCH label,value
;;
;; Description: SWITCH similar to
;;   'C' SWITCH.  Compare many cases
;;   to SWITCH value
SWITCH MACRO label,value
        PUBLIC  &label&a

        jmp     SHORT &label&a

;; declare memory in CS to hold value

&label&aaa DW   0

&label&a:

;; save AX

        push    AX

;; store value in memory

        mov     AX,value
        mov     &label&aaa,AX

;; restore AX

        pop     AX

        ENDM

;;----------------------------------------
```

Fig. 6-9. The macro listing to CASE.

```
;;----------------------------------------
;; Macro: CASE label,function,val
;;
;; Description: If SWITCHed value is equal
;;   to CASE val the call function and
;;   jump to enc of switch

CASE MACRO label,function,value
        LOCAL   notfound

;; compare CASE value to value saved in memory

        cmp     &label&aaa,value

;; if not equal then jump to notfound

        jne     notfound

;; otherwise call procedure

        PUBLIC  function
        call    function

;; jump to ESWITCH bypassing other cases

        PUBLIC  &label&aa
        jmp     &label&aa

;; go on to next case

notfound:

        ENDM

;;----------------------------------------
```

Fig. 6-10. The macro listing to DEFAULT.

```
;;----------------------------------------
;; Macro: DEFAULT label,function
;;
;; Description: If SWITCHed value cases
;;   are all passed then the DEFAULT
;;   function will be called

DEFAULT MACRO label,function,value

        PUBLIC  function

;; call last procedure

        call    function

        ENDM

;;----------------------------------------
```

Fig. 6-11. The macro listing to ESWITCH.

```
;;------------------------------------
;; Macro: ESWITCH label
;;
;; Description: End of the SWITCH statement

ESWITCH MACRO label

        PUBLIC  &label&aa

;;  End of SWITCH label

&label&aa:

        ENDM

;;------------------------------------
```

Figure 6-12 presents the source code listing to EPROG14.ASM, Fig. 6-13 the source code listing to CPROG14.ASM, and Fig. 6-14 the source code to C-E14.C. All three programs are functionally identical.

The file size comparisons come next:

EPROG14.EXE	1019 bytes
CPROG14.COM	539 bytes
C-E14.EXE	8882 bytes

No surprises here.

Fig. 6-12. The source code listing to EPROG14.ASM.

```
;------------------------------------
; Source Listing Start
;
; File Name: EPROG14.ASM
;
; Description:
;  Demonstrates SWITCH / CASE

;
; Include Macro file
;

INCLUDE SMALL.MAC

; Initialize EXE file structure with STACK => 100h

        PROG_EXE

        PROG_DATA

mess1   DB      'Key a has been selected','$'
mess2   DB      'Key b has been selected','$'
mess3   DB      'Key c has been selected','$'
```

Fig. 6-12 continued.

```
mess5   DB      'Another key has been selected','$'

key_val DW      0       ; getch puts char value here
k_exit  DW      0       ; endless loop exit flag

; Start of code segment

        PROG_CODE

        vidinit         ; CHUCK video initialization
        clrscreen       ; clear the screen

; begin endless loop

BELOOP  be1

        getch   [key_val]               ; get key char value

        SWITCH  sw1,[key_val]           ; begin key comparisons
          CASE  sw1,p_mess1,'a'         ; if 'a' the call p_mess1
          CASE  sw1,p_mess2,'b'         ; if 'b' the call p_mess1
          CASE  sw1,p_mess3,'c'         ; if 'c' the call p_mess1
          CASE  sw1,p_mess4,'x'         ; if 'x' the call p_mess1
        DEFAULT sw1,p_mess5             ; call p_mess1
        ESWITCH sw1                     ; end of switch

        BIFE    be_exit,[k_exit],1 ; if k_exit is 1
                EBREAK be1              ; then break from loop
        EIF     be_exit                 ; otherwise continue
EELOOP  be1


        END_EXE         ; DOS EXE terminate

;----------------------------------------
;
; Begin subroutines for EXE files here
;
;----------------------------------------

BPROCEDURE p_mess1      ; begin procedure

        puts    mess1

EPROCEDURE p_mess1      ; end procedure

;----------------------;

BPROCEDURE p_mess2      ; begin procedure

        puts    mess2

EPROCEDURE p_mess2      ; end procedure

;----------------------;

BPROCEDURE p_mess3      ; begin procedure

        puts    mess3

EPROCEDURE p_mess3      ; end procedure
```

```
;--------------------;

BPROCEDURE p_mess4       ; begin procedure

        setv    [k_exit],1

EPROCEDURE p_mess4       ; end procedure

;--------------------;

BPROCEDURE p_mess5       ; begin procedure

        puts    mess5

EPROCEDURE p_mess5       ; end procedure

;------------------------------------
;
; End of subroutine section
;
;------------------------------------

        END

;
; End of Source Listing
;------------------------------------
```

Fig. 6-12 ends.

Fig. 6-13. The source code listing to CPROG14.ASM.

```
;--------------------.--------------------
; Source Listing Start
;
; File Name: CPROG14.ASM
;
; Description:
;  Demonstrates use of SWITCH / CASE

;
; Include Macro file
;

INCLUDE SMALL.MAC

; Initialize for COM program

        PROG_COM

mess1   DB      'Key a has been selected','$'
mess2   DB      'Key b has been selected','$'
mess3   DB      'Key c has been selected','$'

mess5   DB      'Another key has been selected','$'

key_val DW      0    ; getch puts char value here
k_exit  DW      0    ; endless loop exit flag
```

Fig. 6-13 continued.

program:

```
        vidinit         ; CHUCK video initialization

        clrscreen       ; clear the screen

; begin endless loop

BELOOP  be1

        getch   [key_val]               ; get key char value

        SWITCH  sw1,[key_val]           ; begin key comparisons
          CASE  sw1,p_mess1,'a'         ; if 'a' the call p_mess1
          CASE  sw1,p_mess2,'b'         ; if 'b' the call p_mess1
          CASE  sw1,p_mess3,'c'         ; if 'c' the call p_mess1
          CASE  sw1,p_mess4,'x'         ; if 'x' the call p_mess1
        DEFAULT sw1,p_mess5             ; call p_mess1
        ESWITCH sw1                     ; end of switch

        BIFE    be_exit,[k_exit],1 ; if k_exit is 1
                EBREAK be1              ; then break from loop
        EIF     be_exit                ; otherwise continue
EELOOP  be1

        COM_TO_DOS    ; COM DOS terminate

;------------------------------------
;
; Begin subroutines for COM files here
;
;------------------------------------

BPROCEDURE p_mess1      ; begin procedure

        puts    mess1

EPROCEDURE p_mess1      ; end procedure

;---------------------;

BPROCEDURE p_mess2      ; begin procedure

        puts    mess2

EPROCEDURE p_mess2      ; end procedure

;---------------------;

BPROCEDURE p_mess3      ; begin procedure

        puts    mess3

EPROCEDURE p_mess3      ; end procedure

;---------------------;

BPROCEDURE p_mess4      ; begin procedure
```

```
          setv     [k_exit],1

EPROCEDURE p_mess4      ; end procedure

;---------------------;

BPROCEDURE p_mess5      ; begin procedure

          puts     mess5

EPROCEDURE p_mess5      ; end procedure

;--------------------------------------
;
; End of subroutine section
;
;--------------------------------------

;  Load subroutines

L_VIDINIT
L_CLRSCREEN
L_PUTS
L_PUTCHAR

; COM DOS Terminate and end source file

          END_COM

;
; End of Source Listing
;--------------------------------------
```

Fig. 6-13 ends.

Fig. 6-14. The source code listing to C-E14.C.

```
/*
 * C-E14.C
 */

#include <stdio.h>
#include <tproto.h>

void main(void);

char mess1[] = {"Key a has been selected"};
char mess2[] = {"Key b has been selected"};
char mess3[] = {"Key c has been selected"};

char mess5[] = {"Another key has been selected"};

void
main()
{
int key_val;
int exit_val = 0;

for(;;)
```

```
            {
        key_val = getch();
        switch(key_val)
                {
                case    'a':
                        puts(mess1);
                        break;

                case    'b':
                        puts(mess2);
                        break;

                case    'c':
                        puts(mess3);
                        break;

                case    'x':
                        exit_val = 1;
                        break;

                default:
                        puts(mess5);
                        break;
                }


        if(exit_val)
                break;
        }
    }
```

Fig. 6-14 ends.

As you can imagine I've spent a great deal of time playing with CHUCK lately. One pleasure of mine is to see how CHUCK's macros expand into assembly code. With each revision of the macros I've been groaning and groaning less when I look at the disassembled listings. Figure 6-15 presents the disassembled source to CPROG14.ASM. When you examine the listing, note that I've added some comments to help you relate the CHUCK source to the assembly source.

The CHUCK source expands into plenty of assembly code. When you think of taking time to play with CHUCK recall Fig. 6-15 and say to yourself: "Do I want to program in assembly or CHUCK or C or PASCAL?" If you say "C" or "PASCAL" then look at the executable program's file sizes. If you say "assembly" then you've seen the movie "Die Hard" too many times.

Could I have written CPROG14.ASM in pure assembly and have come in with tighter code than the CHUCK version? Of course. CHUCK is a slightly higher-level language than assembly, and you'll always pay a price for some convenience.

Fig. 6-15. The disassembled listing of CPROG14.COM.

```
    .286c

    data_1e         equ     65h
    data_2e         equ     79h
```

Fig. 6-15 continued.

```
data_14e        equ         3E88h
data_15e        equ         0CD0Fh

code_seg_a      segment
                assume      cs:code_seg_a, ds:code_seg_a

                org         100h

cprog14         proc        far

start:
                push        cs
                pop         ds
                jmp         short loc_6
;
; data held in code segment
;
                db          90h
                db          16 dup (0)
data_4          db          4Bh
                db          'ey a has been selected$'
data_5          db          4Bh
                db          'ey b has be'
loc_1:
                db          65h, 6Eh, 20h, 73h, 65h, 6Ch
loc_2:
                db          65h, 63h, 74h, 65h, 64h, 24h
data_6          db          4Bh
                db          'ey c has be'
loc_3:
                db          'en selected$'
data_7          db          41h
                db          'nother key '
loc_4:
                push        7361h
                and         ss:data_1e[bp+si],ah
loc_5:
                db          'en selected$'
data_8          dw          0           ; key_val DW 0
data_9          dw          0           ; k_exit  DW 0


;
; program:
;

loc_6:

;
; vidinit
;
                push        ax
                push        bx
                push        cx
                push        dx
                call        sub_6
                pop         dx
                pop         cx
                pop         bx
                pop         ax
```

Fig. 6-15 continued.

```
;
; clrscreen
;
                push    ax
                push    bx
                push    cx
                push    dx
                mov     bh,7
loc_8:
                call    sub_7
                pop     dx
                pop     cx
                pop     bx
                pop     ax

;
; BELOOP be1
;

loc_9:

;
; getch
;
                push    ax
                xor     ax,ax
                int     16h

                xor     ah,ah
                mov     cs:data_8,ax
                pop     ax

;
; SWITCH sw1,[key_val]
                jmp     short loc_10
data_10         dw      0
loc_10:
                push    ax
loc_11:
                mov     ax,cs:data_8
                mov     cs:data_10,ax
                pop     ax

;
; CASE sw1,p_mess1,'a'
;
                cmp     cs:data_10,61h
                jne     loc_12
                call    sub_1
                jmp     short loc_19
                db      90h
loc_12:
loc_13:
;
; CASE sw1,p_mess2,'b'
;
                cmp     cs:data_10,62h
```

Fig. 6-15 continued.

```
                jne       loc_15
                call      sub_2
loc_14:
                jmp       short loc_19
                db        90h
loc_15:
;
; CASE sw1,p_mess3,'c'
;

                cmp       cs:data_10,63h
                jne       loc_16
                call      sub_3
                jmp       short loc_19
                db        90h
loc_16:
;
; CASE sw1,p_mess1,'x'
;

                cmp       cs:data_10,78h
                jne       loc_18
                call      sub_4
                jmp       short loc_19
                db        90h
loc_18:
;
; DEFAULT sw1,p_MESS5
;

                call      sub_5
loc_19:
;
; BIFE be_exit,[k_exit],1
;


                push      ax
                push      dx
                mov       ax,cs:data_9
                mov       dx,1
                cmp       ax,dx
                jne       loc_20
                pop       dx
                pop       ax
                jmp       short loc_22
                db        90h, 0EBh, 3, 90h
loc_20:
                pop       dx
                pop       ax
loc_21:
;
; EELOOP be1
;

                jmp       short loc_9
loc_22:
;
; COM_TO_DOS
;
```

Fig. 6-15 continued.

```
                int     20h

cprog14         endp

;----------------------------------------
sub_1           proc    near
                push    ax
                push    bx
                push    cx
                push    dx
                push    si
                lea     ax,data_4
                mov     si,ax
                call    sub_8
                pop     si
                pop     dx
                pop     cx
                pop     bx
                pop     ax
                ret
sub_1           endp


;----------------------------------------
sub_2           proc    near
                push    ax
                push    bx
                push    cx
                push    dx
                push    si
                lea     ax,data_5
                mov     si,ax
                call    sub_8
                pop     si
                pop     dx
                pop     cx
                pop     bx
                pop     ax
                ret
sub_2           endp

;----------------------------------------
sub_3           proc    near
                push    ax
                push    bx
                push    cx
                push    dx
                push    si
                lea     ax,data_6
                mov     si,ax
                call    sub_8
                pop     si
                pop     dx
                pop     cx
                pop     bx
                pop     ax
                ret
sub_3           endp
```

Fig. 6-15 continued.

```
;------------------------------------------
sub_4           proc    near
                mov     cs:data_9,1
                ret
sub_4           endp

;------------------------------------------
sub_5           proc    near
                push    ax
                push    bx
                push    cx
                push    dx
                push    si
                lea     ax,data_7
                mov     si,ax
                call    sub_8
                pop     si
                pop     dx
                pop     cx
                pop     bx
                pop     ax
                ret
sub_5           endp

;------------------------------------------
sub_6           proc    near
                push    cs
                pop     ds
                jmp     short loc_23
                db      90h
data_11         db      0
data_12         dw      0
data_13         dw      0
loc_23:
                mov     ah,0Fh
                int     10h

                mov     cs:data_11,bh
                cmp     al,7
                je      loc_27
                mov     cs:data_12,3DAh
                cmp     cs:data_11,0
                jne     loc_24
                mov     cs:data_13,0B800h
                jmp     short loc_28
                db      90h
loc_24:
                cmp     cs:data_11,1
                jne     loc_25
                mov     cs:data_13,0B900h
                jmp     short loc_28
                db      90h
loc_25:
                cmp     cs:data_11,2
                jne     loc_26
                mov     cs:data_13,0BA00h
                jmp     short loc_28
                db      90h
loc_26:
                mov     cs:data_13,0BB00h
```

Fig. 6-15 continued.

```
                jmp      short loc_28
                db       90h
loc_27:
                mov      cs:data_12,3BAh
                mov      cs:data_13,0B000h
loc_28:
                ret
sub_6           endp


;-------------------------------------
sub_7           proc     near
                mov      al,0
                mov      ch,0
                mov      cl,0
                mov      dh,18h
                mov      dl,4Fh
                mov      ah,6
                int      10h

                mov      ah,0Fh
                int      10h

                xor      dx,dx
                mov      ah,2
                int      10h

                ret
sub_7           endp


;-------------------------------------
sub_8           proc     near
                xor      ax,0
loc_29:
                mov      al,[si]
                cmp      al,0
                je       loc_31
                cmp      al,24h
                je       loc_30
                push     ax
                push     bx
                call     sub_9
                pop      bx
                pop      ax
                inc      si
                jmp      short loc_29
loc_30:
                push     ax
                push     bx
                mov      ax,0Ah
                call     sub_9
                pop      bx
                pop      ax
                push     ax
                push     bx
                mov      ax,0Dh
                call     sub_9
                pop      bx
                pop      ax
```

```
loc_31:
                    ret
sub_8               endp


;----------------------------------------
sub_9               proc      near
                    mov       bh,cs:data_11
                    mov       ah,0Eh
                    int       10h

                    ret
sub_9               endp

code_seg_a          ends
                    end       start
```

Fig. 6-15 ends.

BLOOP (Begin LOOP)
ELOOP (End LOOP)
BREAK (BREAK from loop)
CONTINUE (CONTINUE in loop)

BLOOP begins a loop of n iterations. ELOOP ends a loop of n iterations. BREAK breaks from a loop of n iterations. CONTINUE bypasses the code and continues the loop of n iterations. The syntax is:

```
BLOOP           L1, number
      statement1
                    CONTINUE  L1
      statement2
                    BREAK  L1
      statement3
ELOOP           L1
```

where   L1   = ASCII text name
        number = memory|immediate

BLOOP (Begin LOOP) loops n (number in the syntax example) times. In the syntax example, if BREAK and CONTINUE are not called then all statements will operate. If statement1 leads to CONTINUE then statement2 and statement3 will be bypassed and the looping will continue. If statement2 leads to BREAK then the loop will immediately terminate.

There is one restriction for BLOOP/ELOOP. The branch back is accomplished using the 'loop' instruction. This instruction has a limitation of jumping no more than 128 bytes. If your statements within the loop take up more than 128 bytes you have two options:

1. Call the body of the loop as a subroutine

or

2. Use the BELOOP/EELOOP sequence

Figure 6-16 contains the macro listing for BLOOP, Fig. 6-17 the macro listing for ELOOP, Fig. 6-18 the macro listing for BREAK and Fig. 6-19 the macro listing for CONTINUE. Remember to add these macro listings to your CHUCK-.MAC file.

Figures 6-20 and 6-21 show the final EXE and COM program listings for EPROG15.ASM and CPROG15.ASM, respectively.

The file sizes for EPROG15.EXE and CPROG15.COM are:

EPROG15.EXE   693 bytes
CPROG15.COM   208 bytes

Fig. 6-16. The macro listing to BLOOP.

```
;;-----------------------------------------
;; Macro: BLOOP label,count
;;
;; Description: Set beginning of
;;    loop with CX counter

BLOOP MACRO label,count
;; If parameters are not in AX,DX the move
;; parameters to registers

    IFDIFI <CX>,<count>
        mov     CX,count
    ENDIF

;; CX is ther count register so it must be saved

label:

        push    CX

        ENDM

;;-----------------------------------------
```

Fig. 6-17. The macro listing to ELOOP.

```
;;-----------------------------------------
;; Macro: ELOOP label
;;
;; Description: End loop and
;;    return to label

ELOOP MACRO label

;; restore CX

        pop     CX
```

```
a&label&:

        loop      label

        ENDM
```

```
;;------------------------------------
```

Fig. 6-17 ends.

Fig. 6-18. The macro listing to BREAK.

```
;;----------------------------------------
;; Macro: BREAK label
;;
;; Description: Break out of loop
;; (as in C break)

BREAK   MACRO label

;; CX is restored

        pop       CX

;; set to 0 to exit loop

        mov       CX,0

;; jump to loop instruction

        jmp       a&label&

        ENDM
```

```
;;-------------------------------------
```

Fig. 6-19. The macro listing to CONTINUE.

```
;;----------------------------------------
;; Macro: CONTINUE label
;;
;; Description: Continue loop
;; (as in C continue)

CONTINUE MACRO label

;; CX restored

        pop       CX

;; jump to label bypassing code

        jmp       a&label&

        ENDM
```

```
;;-------------------------------------
```

Fig. 6-20. The source code listing to EPROG15.ASM.

```
;----------------------------------------
; Source Listing Start
;
; File Name: EPROG15.ASM
;
; Description:
;  Demonstrates EFOR... / NEXT ...

;
; Include Macro file
;

INCLUDE SMALL.MAC

; Initialize EXE file structure with STACK => 100h

        PROG_EXE

        PROG_DATA

; Start of code segment

        PROG_CODE

        vidinit        ; CHUCK video initialization
        clrscreen      ; clear the screen

BLOOP   bl0,65         ; begin loop of 65 iterations
        putchar 'A'    ; print 'A' to screen
ELOOP   bl0

        END_EXE        ; DOS EXE terminate

        END

;
; End of Source Listing
;----------------------------------------
```

Fig. 6-21. The source code listing to CPROG15.ASM.

```
;----------------------------------------
; Source Listing Start
;
; File Name: CPROG15.ASM
;
; Description:
;  Looping demonstration
;

;
; Include Macro file
;

INCLUDE SMALL.MAC

        PROG_COM
```

```
program:
        vidinit

        clrscreen      ; clear the screen

BLOOP   bl0,65         ; begin loop of 65 iterations
        putchar 'A'    ; print 'A' to screen
ELOOP   bl0


        COM_TO_DOS

;-------------------------------------
;
; Include procedure file here
;
L_VIDINIT
L_CLRSCREEN
L_PUTCHAR
        END_COM


;
; End of Source Listing
;-------------------------------------
```

Fig. 6-21 ends.

This marks the end of Chapter 6. Chapter 7 adds conditional branching control flow macros to your CHUCK.MAC file.

7

CHUCK
Conditional Branching

In previous chapters, two types of looping were discussed. In Chapter 7, a third type of looping related to C's for(val = 10; val < = 25; val + +) is introduced. In addition to looping, a variety of condition branching control flow constructs are presented. Many of the conditional branching constructs may be combined to permit branching when values fall within discrete boundaries. Each macro presented in Chapter 7 should be added to your EXE and COM CHUCK-.MAC files.

GOTO (GO TO label)

GOTO is equivalent to assembly 'jmp' or C's 'GOTO.' The syntax is:

GOTO   *label*

where
   label = legal text name for label

GOTO is a CHUCK program statement added to satisfy the ASMplus™ marketing need to minimize assembly mnemonics in CHUCK programs. For BASIC or C programmers migrating to CHUCK, the GOTO Macro does provide another element of familiarity. The EXE version and COM version of the GOTO macro are identical. Figure 7-1 is the GOTO macro listing to GOTO.

Fig. 7-1. The macro listing to GOTO.

```
;;-----------------------------------------
;; Macro GOTO label
;;
;; Description: C like GOTO label
;;
```

```
GOTO MACRO label

        jmp     label

        ENDM

;;-------------------------------------
```

Fig. 7-1 ends.

GOTO (EXE and COM Version)   The following is an example of GOTO:

```
    .
    .
BIFE   name1, val1,75
       GOTO val1_is_75
EIF    name1
    .
    .
```

In the GOTO example the program flow could be described like this: If memory location val1 is equal to 75 then alter program flow to jump to the label val1_is_75, otherwise continue program flow in the same direction.

BIFGT (Begin IF Greater Than)

BIFGT begins IF val1 is greater than val2. The syntax is:

```
BIFGT    name,val1,val2
         statement1
EIF      name
```

where *name* = proper ASCII text label name
        val1 = memory
        val2 = memory|immediate

BIFGT functions in a similar fashion to the BIFE condition branch described earlier, except in this case statement1 executes only if val1 is greater than val2. Figure 7-2 presents the macro listing to BIFGT.

Fig. 7-2. The macro listing to BIFGT.

```
;;-------------------------------------
;; Macro BIFGT name,val1,val2 (Greater Than)
;;
;; Description: If val1 > val2
;;   then execute code between
;;   BIFGT.. and EIF (End IF)
;;

BIFGT MACRO name,val1,val2
```

```
;; save regs

        push    AX
        push    DX

;;  if val1 is not AX then...

    IFDIFI <AX>,<val1>
        mov     AX,val1
    ENDIF

;;  if val2 is not DX then...

    IFDIFI <DX>,<val2>
        mov     DX,val2
    ENDIF

;; add 1 to val2

        inc     DX

;; compare val1 with modified val2

        cmp     AX,DX

;; jump to bypass code if val1 > val2

        jl      &name&

;; otherwise restore regs and execute

        pop     DX
        pop     AX

        ENDM

;;-------------------------------------
```

Fig. 7-2 ends.

The following is the BIFGT EXE and COM example:

```
    .
    .
BIFGT     name1,val1,75
        GOTO    val1_is_greater_than_75
EIF       name1
    .
    .
```

In the BIFGT example the program flow can be described like this: If memory location val1 is greater than 75 then alter program flow to jump to the val1_is _greater_than_75, otherwise continue program flow in the same direction.

BIFLT (Begin IF Less Than)

Begin IF val1 is Less Than val2. The syntax is:

```
BIFLT   name,val1,val2
        statement1
EIF     name
```
where *name* = proper ASCII text label name
　　　 val1 = memory
　　　 val2 = memory|immediate

BIFLT functions in a similar fashion to the BIFE condition branch which had been described earlier in the text, except in this case statement1 executes only if val1 is less than val2. Figure 7-3 presents the macro listing to BIFLT.

The following is the BIFLT EXE and COM example:

```
     .
     .

BIFLT   name1,val1,75
        GOTO   val1_is_less_than_75
EIF     name1
     .
     .
```

In the BIFLT example the program flow can be described like this: If memory location val1 is less than 75 then alter program flow to jump to the label val1_is_less_than_75, otherwise continue program flow in the same direction.

Fig. 7-3. The macro listing to BIFLT.

```
;;------------------------------------------
;; Macro BIFLT name,val1,val2
;;
;; Description: If val1 < val2 (Less Than)
;;   then execute code between
;;   BIFLT.. and EIF (End IF)
;;

BIFLT MACRO name,val1,val2

;; save regs

        push    AX
        push    DX

;;  if val1 is not AX then...

    IFDIFI <AX>,<val1>
        mov     AX,val1
    ENDIF

;;  if val2 is not DX then...
```

```
        IFDIFI <DX>,<val2>
             mov    DX,val2
        ENDIF

;; sub 1 from val2

             dec    DX

;; compare val1 with modified val2

             cmp    AX,DX

;; jump to bypass code if val1 < val2

             jg     &name&

;; otherwise restore regs and execute

             pop    DX
             pop    AX

             ENDM

;;-------------------------------------
```

Fig. 7-3 ends.

BIFEGT (Begin IF Equal or Greater Than)

BIFEGT begins IF val1 is equal to or greater than val2. The syntax is:

```
BIFEGT   name,val1,val2
             statement1
EIF          name
```

where *name* = proper ASCII text label name
      val1 = memory
      val2 = memory|immediate

BIFEGT functions in a similar fashion to the BIFE condition branch described earlier, except in this case statement1 executes only if val1 is equal to or greater than val2. Figure 7-4 presents the macro listing to BIFEGT.

The following is the BIFEGT EXE and COM example:

```
        .
        .

BIFEGT   name1,val1,75
             GOTO val1_is_greater_than_75
EIF          name1

        .
        .
```

Fig. 7-4. The macro listing to BIFEGT.

```
;;-------------------------------------
;; Macro BIFEGT name,val1,val2 (EQUAL or Greater Than)
;;
;; Description: If val1 >= val2
;;   then execute code between
;;   BIFEGT.. and EIF (End IF)
;;

BIFEGT MACRO name,val1,val2

;; save regs

        push    AX
        push    DX

;;  if val1 is not AX then...

    IFDIFI <AX>,<val1>
        mov     AX,val1
    ENDIF

;;  if val2 is not DX then...

    IFDIFI <DX>,<val2>
        mov     DX,val2
    ENDIF

;; compare val1 with val2

        cmp     AX,DX

;; jump to bypass code if val1 >= val2

        jl      &name&

;; otherwise restore regs and execute

        pop     DX
        pop     AX

        ENDM

;;-------------------------------------
```

In the BIFEGT example the program flow can be described like this: If memory location val1 is equal to or greater than 75 then alter program flow to jump to the label val1_is_greater_than_75, otherwise continue program flow in the same direction.

BIFELT (Begin IF Equal or Less Than)

BIFELT begins IF val1 is equal to or less than val2. The syntax is:

.
.

```
BIFELT    name1,val1,val2
          statement1
EIF       name
```

where *name* = proper ASCII text label name
      val1 = memory
      val2 = memory|immediate

BIFELT functions in a similar fashion to the BIFE condition branch described earlier, except in this case statement1 executes only if val1 is equal to or less than val2. Figure 7-5 presents the BIFELT macro listing.

Fig. 7-5. The macro listing to BIFELT.

```
;;-----------------------------------------
;; Macro BIFELT name,val1,val2
;;
;; Description: If val1 <= val2 (EQUAL or Less Than)
;;   then execute code between
;;   BIFELT.. and EIF (End IF)
;;

BIFELT MACRO name,val1,val2

;; save regs

        push    AX
        push    DX

;;  if val1 is not AX then...

    IFDIFI <AX>,<val1>
        mov     AX,val1
    ENDIF

;;  if val2 is not DX then...

    IFDIFI <DX>,<val2>
        mov     DX,val2
    ENDIF

;; compare val1 with val2

        cmp     AX,DX

;; jump to bypass code if val1 <= val2

        jg      &name&

;; otherwise restore regs and execute

        pop     DX
        pop     AX

        ENDM

;;-----------------------------------------
```

The following is a BIFELT EXE and COM example:

```
        .
        .
BIFELT   name1,val1,75
         GOTO   val1_is_less_than_75
EIF      name1
        .
        .
```

In the BIFELT example the program flow can be described like this: If memory location val1 is equal to or less than 75 then alter program flow to jump to the label val1_is_less_than_75, otherwise continue program flow in the same direction.

BIFTRUE (Begin IF TRUE)

BIFTRUE begins IF *val1* is greater than 0. The syntax is:

```
BIFTRUE   name,val1
          statement1
EIF       name
```

where *name* = proper ASCII text label name
     val1 = memory

BIFTRUE functions in a similar fashion to the BIFE condition branch described earlier, except in this case statement1 executes only if val1 is greater than 0. Figure 7-6 presents the macro listing to BIFTRUE. The following is a BIFTRUE EXE and COM example:

```
        .
        .
BIFTRUE   name1,val1
          GOTO   val1_is_greater_than_0
EIF       name1
        .
        .
```

In the BIFTRUE example the program flow can be described like this: If memory location val1 is greater than 0 then alter the program flow to jump to the label val1_is_greater_than_0, otherwise continue program flow in the same direction.

Fig. 7-6. The macro listing to BIFTRUE.

```
;;--------------------------------------------
;; Macro BIFTRUE name,val1
;;
```

```
;; Description: If val1 > 0
;;   then execute code between
;;   BIFTRUE.. and EIF (End IF)
;;

BIFTRUE MACRO name,val1

;; save regs

        push    AX
        push    DX

;;  if val1 is not AX then...

    IFDIFI <AX>,<val1>
        mov     AX,val1
    ENDIF

;;  1 => DX

        mov     DX,1

;; compare val1 with 1

        cmp     AX,DX

;; jump to bypass code if val1 >= 1

        jl      &name&

;; otherwise restore regs and execute

        pop     DX
        pop     AX

        ENDM

;;-------------------------------------
```

Fig. 7-6 ends.

BIFFALSE (Begin IF FALSE)

BIFFALSE begins IF val1 is equal to 0. The syntax is:

```
BIFFALSE  name,val1
          statement1
EIF       name
```

where *name* = proper ASCII text label name
       val1 = memory

BIFFALSE functions in a similar fashion to the BIFE condition branch described earlier, except in this case statement1 executes only if val1 is equal to 0. Figure 7-7 presents the macro listing to BIFFALSE.

Fig. 7-7. The macro listing to BIFFALSE.

```
;;-------------------------------------------
;; Macro BIFFALSE name,val1
;;
;; Description: If val1 == 0
;;   then execute code between
;;   BIFFALSE.. and EIF (End IF)
;;

BIFFALSE MACRO name,val1

;; save regs

        push    AX
        push    DX

;;  if val1 is not AX then...

    IFDIFI <AX>,<val1>
        mov     AX,val1
    ENDIF

;;  0 => DX

        xor     DX,DX

;; compare val1 with 0

        cmp     AX,DX

;; jump to bypass code if val1 not 0

        jne     &name&

;; otherwise restore regs and execute

        pop     DX
        pop     AX

        ENDM

;;-------------------------------------------
```

The following is a BIFFALSE EXE and COM example:

```
    •
    •
BIFFALSE    name1,val1
       GOTO  val1_is_equal_to_0
EIF        name1
    •
    •
```

In the BIFFALSE example the program flow could be described like this: If memory location val1 is equal to 0 then alter program flow to jump to the label val1_is_equal_to_0, otherwise continue program flow in the same direction.

BIFxxx (Begin IFxxx)
BELSE (Begin ELSE)
EIFELSE (Begin IF ELSE)

BIFxxx begins if *xxx* is true then executes your procedure. BELSE if *xxx* is not true execute. EIFELSE ends the IF ELSE. The syntax is:

```
BIFE        name,val1,val2
       statement1
BELSE      name
       statement2
EIFELSE    name
```

where   *name* = legal ASCII text name of label
        val1 = memory
        val2 = memory|immediate

If val1 is equal to val2 then execute statement1. Otherwise if val1 is not equal to val2 then execute statement2.

BELSE & EIFELSE (EXE & COM version)   The macro listing to BELSE is presented in Fig. 7-8, and the macro listing to EIFELSE is presented in Fig. 7-9.

Fig. 7-8. The macro listing to BELSE.

```
;;--------------------------------------
;;
;; Macro BELSE name
;;
;; Description: ELSE condition
;;    if BIF... is not true

BELSE MACRO name

;; bypass ELSE condition

        jmp  &name&?

;; else condition to execute

&name&:

;; restore regs

        pop    DX
        pop    AX

        ENDM

;;--------------------------------------
```

Fig. 7-9. The macro listing to EIFELSE.

```
;;----------------------------------------
;;
;; Macro: EIFELSE name
;;
;; Description: End of BIF...BESLE
;;

EIFELSE MACRO name

;; End of IFELSE construct
&name&?:

        ENDM

;;----------------------------------------
```

The following is a BELSE and EIFELSE EXE and COM example:

```
     .
BIFGT     name1,val1,val2
     statement1
     statement2
BELSE     name1
     statement3
     statement4
EIFELSE   name1
     .
     .
```

In this example the program flow could be described like this: If memory location val1 is greater than val2 execute statement1 and statement2, otherwise execute statement3 and statement4.

BFORLTE (Begin FOR Less Than or Equal)
EFOR (End FOR)

BFORLTE begins FOR if less than or equal. EFOR ends the FOR. The syntax is:

```
BFORLTE   L1,val1,val2
     swrite   v1L1,0,text_mess
EFOR      L1
```

where *L1*   = legal ASCII name for label
     val1   = memory|immediate
     val2   = memory|immediate
     v1L1   = DW in memory created by BFORLTE

The BFORLTE example could read this way: For val1 is less than or equal to val2, execute swrite statement, and increment memory location v1L1.

The v1L1 variable is the incremental counter in the FORLTE loop. This variable is created by combining the default '*v1*' (variable 1) with '*L1*' (label name). The '*v1*' prefix is always added to the label name in the FORLTE sequence, and is always incremented. If you ever need to adjust the stop variable (val2) from within the FORLTE loop it can be accomplished by addressing v2L1 ('*v2*' + '*L1*' = "*v2L1*"). Examine the macros presented in Fig. 7-10 to see how these variables are created. The EXE and COM macro listing for BFORLTE and EFOR is presented in Fig. 7-10.

Fig. 7-10. The macro listing to BFORLTE and EFOR.

```
;;------------------------------------------
;;
;; Macro: BFORLTE label, val1, val2
;;
;; Description:
;;  Begin FOR val1 >= val2 then
;;

BFORLTE MACRO label,val1,val2
        LOCAL   loc1

;; jump over data held in code segment

        jmp     loc1

v1&label&       DW      0   ;; holds incrementing variable
v2&label&       DW      0   ;; holds stopper variable

loc1:

;; save AX reg

        push    AX

;; if AX different from val1 then ...

    IFDIFI <AX>,<val1>
        mov     AX,val1
    ENDIF

;; move incrementing variable to memory

        mov     CS:[v1&label&],AX

;; if AX different from val2 then ...

    IFDIFI <AX>,<val2>
        mov     AX,val2
    ENDIF

;; move stopper variable to memory

        mov     CS:[v2&label&],AX

;; restore AX

        pop     AX
```

```
;; increment stopper

        inc     CS:[v2&label&]

;; now variables set to initiate endless loop

BELOOP  &label&

        ENDM

;;----------------------------------------

;;----------------------------------------
;;
;; Macro: EFOR label
;;
;; Description:
;;   End FOR loop
;;

EFOR MACRO label

;; increment at end of iteration

        inc     CS:[v1&label&]

;; if incrementer variable and stopper variable
;; are equal then break from endless loop

BIFE loc&label&,CS:[v1&label&],CS:[v2&label&]

        EBREAK  &label&

EIF  loc&label&

;; if not broken then continue looping

EELOOP  &label&

        ENDM

;;----------------------------------------
```

Fig. 7-10 ends.

BFORLTE and EFOR (EXE Version)   The BFORLTE and EFOR EXE example program displays what could be the main screen of a word processor. It screams for drop-down windows. When you finish working with the routines presented in Part III you should be able to add the drop-down windows without much trouble. Figure 7-11 presents the source code listing to EPROG21.ASM.

Fig. 7-11. The source code listing to EPROG21.ASM.

```
;----------------------------------------
; Source Listing Start
;
; File Name: EPROG21.ASM
;
; Description:
```

Fig. 7-11 continued.

```
;  Demonstrates BFORLTE / EFOR


;
; Include Macro file
;

INCLUDE SMALL.MAC

; Initialize EXE file structure with STACK => 100h

        PROG_EXE

        PROG_DATA

mess1   DB        'Press any key to continue...',0
menu    DB        ' Desk  File  Edit                        '
        DB        '                              Quit ',0

; Start of code segment

        PROG_CODE

; CHUCK video initialization

        vidinit

; screen attributes:
;   BLACK => foreground
;   WHITE => background
;   INTENSITY => off
;   BLINK => off

        makeattr  BLACK,WHITE,OFF_INTEN,OFF_BLINK

; clear screen with returned attribute

        clrscreen RET_VAL

; write menu bar to the screen

        puts    menu

; print vertical bars on the screen

BFORLTE L1,2,22
        mvcur   v1L1,0
        putchar 179
        mvcur   v1L1,79
        putchar 179
EFOR    L1

; print horizontal lines

BFORLTE L2,0,79
        mvcur   1,v1L2
        putchar 196
        mvcur   2,v1L2
        putchar 196
        mvcur   23,v1L2
        putchar 196
```

```
        EFOR    L2

; print corners

                mvcur   23,0
                putchar 192

                mvcur   23,79
                putchar 217

                mvcur   2,0
                putchar 218

                mvcur   2,79
                putchar 191

; write message to press key

                swrite  3,1,mess1

; wait for key press

                getch

; clear the screen

                clrscreen

                END_EXE         ; DOS EXE terminate

                END

;
; End of Source Listing
;-------------------------------------
;
```

Fig. 7-11 ends.

BFORLTE & EFOR (COM Example)   The example for the BFORLTE and
EFOR COM version is shown in Fig. 7-12, the source code for CPROG21.ASM.

The file sizes are:

EPROG21.EXE   1339 bytes
CPROG21.COM   1866 bytes

Chapter 7 finishes the current control flow constructs in CHUCK Version
1.0. No doubt these will expand and improve over time.

Fig. 7-12. The source code listing to CPROG21.ASM.

```
;-------------------------------------
; Source Listing Start
;
; File Name: CPROG21.ASM
;
```

Fig. 7-12 continued.

```
; Description:
;  Demonstration of VDPUTCH
;


;
; Include Macro file
;

INCLUDE SMALL.MAC

        PROG_COM

mess1   DB      'Press any key to continue...',0
menu    DB      ' Desk  File  Edit                    '
        DB      '                              Quit ',0

program:

; CHUCK video initialization

        vidinit

; screen attributes:
;   BLACK => foreground
;   WHITE => background
;   INTENSITY => off
;   BLINK => off

        makeattr  BLACK,WHITE,OFF_INTEN,OFF_BLINK

; clear screen with returned attribute

        clrscreen RET_VAL

; write menu bar to the screen

        puts    menu

; print vertical bars on the screen

BFORLTE L1,2,22
        mvcur   v1L1,0
        putchar 179
        mvcur   v1L1,79
        putchar 179
EFOR    L1

; print horizontal lines

BFORLTE L2,0,79
        mvcur   1,v1L2
        putchar 196
        mvcur   2,v1L2
        putchar 196
        mvcur   23,v1L2
        putchar 196
EFOR    L2

; print corners
```

```
        mvcur   23,0
        putchar 192

        mvcur   23,79
        putchar 217

        mvcur   2,0
        putchar 218

        mvcur   2,79
        putchar 191

; write message to press key

        swrite  3,1,mess1

; wait for key press

        getch

; clear the screen

        clrscreen

        COM_TO_DOS

;---------------------------------------
;
; Include procedure file here
;

L_VIDINIT
L_MVCUR
L_CLRSCREEN
L_MAKEATTR
L_PUTS
L_PUTCHAR

        END_COM

;
; End of Source Listing
;---------------------------------------
_____
```

Fig. 7-12 ends.

8

CHUCK
Mixed-Language
Programming

In today's programming environment it is very important for all languages to be able to function in a mixed-language environment. For example, let's say you are writing an applications program in standard C. You've designed a screen display using CHUCK and you would like to integrate the CHUCK generated screen in your plain vanilla C program. Can you?

Of course! Because CHUCK is really assembly in disguise, any programming language that has hooks to assembly can use CHUCK modules and procedures. In Chapter 8, the technique of using CHUCK program modules in a C programming environment is described. Also, in one example the program module is integrated into the standard C library, the 'C'erious Tools library and the TAB CHUCK library. With this example, TURBO C and Watcom C examples are provided.

USING A CHUCK-GENERATED
OBJECT MODULE WITH C

Figure 8-1 presents the source code listing to CMOD1.ASM. Actually, CMOD1.ASM is a modification of EPROG21.ASM (the last EXE demonstration program in Chapter 7, Fig. 7-11). EPROG21.EXE displayed what looked like a drop-down window interface-type text editor. CMOD1.ASM is the assembly file that creates the object module, which will be used with TURBO or MICRO-SOFT C.

Notice that there isn't a stack set up by the CMOD1 object module because it is being called from the C program. Also, see that the program now has a procedure named _DRAW_BOX. Figure 8-2 presents the TURBO C listing for TESTMOD1.C. This file calls DRAW_BOX( ).

Fig. 8-1. The source code listing to CMOD1.ASM.

```
;---------------------------------------
; Source Listing Start
;
; File Name: CMOD1.ASM
;
; Description:
;   Using CHUCK program module from C
;
;
; Include Macro file
;

INCLUDE SMALL.MAC

        DOSSEG

        .MODEL SMALL

        PROG_DATA

mess1   DB      'Press any key to continue...',0
menu    DB      ' Desk  File  Edit                    '
        DB      '                          Quit ',0

; Start of code segment

        PROG_CODE

; Pre-underscore for function name for
;   TURBO C and Microsoft C.
;   Watcom C uses a post-uncerscore (DRAW_SCRN_)

        PUBLIC  _DRAW_SCRN ; pre-underscore

; Declare C procedure

BPROCEDURE _DRAW_SCRN

; preserve caller's stack frame and
; and set up your own stack frame

        push    BP
        mov     BP,SP

; CHUCK video initialization

        vidinit

; screen attributes:
;   BLACK => foreground
;   WHITE => background
;   INTENSITY => off
;   BLINK => off

        makeattr  BLACK,WHITE,OFF_INTEN,OFF_BLINK

; clear screen with returned attribute
```

Fig. 8-1 continued.

```
        clrscreen RET_VAL

; write menu bar to the screen

        puts    menu

; print vertical bars on the screen

BFORLTE L1,2,22
        mvcur   v1L1,0
        putchar 179
        mvcur   v1L1,79
        putchar 179
EFOR    L1

; print horizontal lines

BFORLTE L2,0,79
        mvcur   1,v1L2
        putchar 196
        mvcur   2,v1L2
        putchar 196
        mvcur   23,v1L2
        putchar 196
EFOR    L2

; print corners

        mvcur   23,0
        putchar 192

        mvcur   23,79
        putchar 217

        mvcur   2,0
        putchar 218

        mvcur   2,79
        putchar 191

; write message to press key

        swrite  3,1,mess1

; wait for key press

        getch

; clear the screen

        clrscreen

; restore caller's stack frame

        pop     BP

EPROCEDURE _DRAW_SCRN

        END
```

```
;
; End of Source Listing
;------------------------------------
;
```

Fig. 8-1 ends.

Fig. 8-2. The source code listing to TESTMOD1.C.

```
/*
 * File Name: TESTMOD1.C
 *
 * Description:
 *  Uses CHUCK procedure
 */

/* Include 'C'erious Library header files */

#include <tproto.h>

/* Function prototypes */

void main(void);         /* no command line params */
void DRAW_SCRN(void);    /* CHUCK procedure         */

void
main()
{
DRAW_SCRN();
}

/*
 * End of source file
 */
```

TURBO C and MicroSoft C, by default, use a pre-underscore for all procedures and variables contained in object modules. That is why the CHUCK procedure is named _DRAW_BOX but is called from C by the name of DRAW_BOX ( ). Watcom C, however, uses different parameter calling conventions from those of MicroSoft and TURBO C and also uses a post-underscore for procedures.

_DRAW_BOX   CHUCK's TURBO and MicroSoft C procedure name

DRAW_BOX_   CHUCK's Watcom C procedure name

Because CHUCK is not a case-sensitive language the assembler, by default, capitalizes all letters regardless of how they appear in the CHUCK source listing. C, however, is a case-sensitive language and that is why all CHUCK procedures must be capitalized.

For those of you with TURBO C, the command line to compile TESTMOD1.C and link it with the CMOD1.OBJ object module and the TAB CHUCK library is:

```
tcc testmod1.c cmod1.obj tab.lib
```

TESTMOD1.EXE is a program that has used a CHUCK-created object module along with TAB's CHUCK library. As you can see, calling a CHUCK program module that doesn't receive parameters from C is very easy to do. The steps are:

1. Create the CHUCK module with the procedure name beginning with an underscore (a post-underscore Watcom C)

2. In the C listing create a CHUCK function prototype remembering to capitalize the name

3. Call the CHUCK C function as any normal C function

PASSING ARGUMENTS FROM TURBO C TO CHUCK OBJECT MODULES

Most high-level languages permit you to pass variables for the procedure's use and permit the procedure to return a variable. For example, the CHUCK 'strlen' (find string length) procedure receives the offset of the string and returns the string length. If you program in a high-level language other than C, consult your compiler's manual to learn more about using assembly language generated object modules with your programs.

The ARG Directive

Assembly programs may now receive a parameter from C by using the wonderfully convenient ARG directive. ARG automatically generates correct stack offsets for the variables that you specify. The following is an ARG example:

```
_DRAW_ATTR PROC NEAR
        ARG     Attribute:word,Length:WORD
        push    BP
        mov     BP,SP
        mov     AX,[Attribute]
        mov     CX,[Length]
```

In the ARG example a procedure named _DRAW_ATTR is declared. C will be passing two word (int) sized parameters to the procedure. _DRAW_ATTR needs to have the attribute (1st parameter) go to the AX register and the length (2nd parameter) go to the CX register. TURBO C and MicroSoft C pass the arguments to functions on the stack. I won't describe the old methods to get information off the stack here (once again "too ugleee"). The ARG directive simplifies things dramatically.

Figure 8-3 presents the source code listing to the CMOD2.ASM file. The CMOD1.ASM file has been modified to allow the calling C program to set the screen attributes, as opposed to the default settings in CMOD1.ASM. Note here that the ARG parameter (Attribute) is passed directly to a the CHUCK procedure 'clrscreen'. What could be easier than that?

Fig. 8-3. The source code listing to CMOD2.ASM.

```
;-------------------------------------
; Source Listing Start
;
; File Name: CMOD2.ASM
;
; Description:
;  Using CHUCK program module from C
;  where CHUCK procedure receives one
;  parameter from C.
;

;
; Include Macro file
;

INCLUDE SMALL.MAC

        DOSSEG

        .MODEL SMALL

        PROG_DATA

mess1   DB      'Press any key to continue...',0
menu    DB      ' Desk  File  Edit                        '
        DB      '                              Quit ',0

; Start of code segment

        PROG_CODE

; Pre-underscore for function name for
;  TURBO C and Microsoft C.
;  Watcom C uses a post-uncerscore (DRAW_SCRN_)

        PUBLIC  _DRAW_SCRN ; pre-underscore

; Declare C procedure

BPROCEDURE _DRAW_SCRN

; Define argument list

        ARG     Attribute:WORD

; preserve caller's stack frame and
; and set up your own stack frame

        push    BP
        mov     BP,SP

; CHUCK video initialization

        vidinit

; screen attributes:
;  Received as parameter from C
;  and passed to clrscreen
```

Fig. 8-3 continued.

```
                clrscreen [Attribute]

; write menu bar to the screen

        puts    menu

; print vertical bars on the screen

BFORLTE L1,2,22
        mvcur   v1L1,0
        putchar 179
        mvcur   v1L1,79
        putchar 179
EFOR    L1

; print horizontal lines

BFORLTE L2,0,79
        mvcur   1,v1L2
        putchar 196
        mvcur   2,v1L2
        putchar 196
        mvcur   23,v1L2
        putchar 196
EFOR    L2

; print corners

        mvcur   23,0
        putchar 192

        mvcur   23,79
        putchar 217

        mvcur   2,0
        putchar 218

        mvcur   2,79
        putchar 191

; write message to press key

        swrite  3,1,mess1

; wait for key press

        getch

; clear the screen

        clrscreen

; restore caller's stack frame

        pop     BP

EPROCEDURE _DRAW_SCRN

        END
```

```
;
; End of Source Listing
;-----------------------------------
;
```

Fig. 8-3 ends.

Figure 8-4 presents the source code listing to TESTMOD2.C. This C program uses the 'C'erious library function 'mkAttr(...)' to create the attribute which is passed to DRAW_BOX. For C aficionados the mkAttr (..) function is called as a parameter in DRAW_SCRN.

DRAW_SCRN(mkAttr(WHITE,RED,OFF_INTENSITY,OFF_BLINK));

The 'C'erious 'mkAttr(...)' function is called and returns a value which is then passed to DRAW_SCRN. If you think that 'C'erious 'mkAttr(...)' function is related to CHUCK's 'makeattr...' you're correct. It is my dream to create a C and assembly development environment which will permit programmers to easily migrate between CHUCK and C with 'C'erious. That's a topic for another title, though.

Fig. 8-4. The source code listing to TESTMOD2.C.

```
/*
 * File Name: TESTMOD2.C
 *
 * Description:
 *   Uses CHUCK procedure where
 *   CHUCK procedure is passed one
 *   parameter.
 */

/* Include 'C'erious Library header files */

#include <tproto.h>

/* Function prototypes */

void main(void);        /* no command line params */
void DRAW_SCRN(int);    /* CHUCK procedure        */

void
main()
{
/*
 * DRAW_SCRN receives the attribute
 * returned from the 'C'erious mkAttr(...)
 * function. 'C'erious mkAttr functions in the
 * same way as CHUCK's makeattr.
 */

DRAW_SCRN(mkAttr(WHITE,RED,OFF_INTENSITY,OFF_BLINK));
}

/*
 * End of source file
 */
```

The TURBO C compile and link command line to create TESTMOD2.EXE is:

```
tcc testmod2.c cmod2.obj tab.lib tsrt2sp.lib
```

In this mixed-language program you're using the TURBO C library, the CHUCK TAB library and the 'C'erious library.

PASSING ARGUMENTS FROM WATCOM C TO CHUCK OBJECT MODULES

Watcom C is my absolute favorite C compiler (in the quality of the executable code it creates). Watcom C by default passes parameters (under most circumstances) using registers and not the stack. If you're a Watcom C user, consult the user's guide section on parameter passing conventions. You'll see that for INT (WORD) sized parameters they are passed in the following order:

AX DX BX CX

Sound familiar?

Figure 8-5 presents the source code listing to the WMOD2.ASM. WMOD2.OBJ will be used by the Watcom linker. Note that the AX register which holds the C passed attribute value is stuffed to memory and then used by CHUCK's 'makeattr...' procedure. Figure 8-6 presents the Watcom C source code listing to WTESTMOD.C. See the post-underscore to DRAW_SCRN_ and how AX is stuffed into 'h_attr'.

Fig. 8-5. The source code listing to WMOD2.ASM.

```
;--------------------------------------------
; Source Listing Start
;
; File Name: WMOD2.ASM
;
; Description:
;   Using CHUCK program module from C
;   where CHUCK procedure receives one
;   parameter from C. Watcom version
;   passes first word parameter in the
;   AX register.
;
;
; Include Macro file
;
INCLUDE SMALL.MAC

        DOSSEG

        .MODEL SMALL

        PROG_DATA
```

Fig. 8-5 continued.

```
h_attr  DW      ?
mess1   DB      'Press any key to continue...',0
menu    DB      ' Desk  File  Edit                        '
        DB      '                              Quit ',0

; Start of code segment

        PROG_CODE

; Pre-underscore for function name for
;  TURBO C and Microsoft C.
;  Watcom C uses a post-uncerscore (DRAW_SCRN_)

        PUBLIC  DRAW_SCRN_ ; post-underscore

; Declare C procedure

BPROCEDURE DRAW_SCRN_

; preserve caller's stack frame and
; and set up your own stack frame

        push    BP
        mov     BP,SP

; move attribute to h_attr

        setv    h_attr,AX

; CHUCK video initialization

        vidinit

; screen attributes:
;  Received as parameter from C
;  and passed to clrscreen

        clrscreen [h_attr]

; write menu bar to the screen

        puts    menu

; print vertical bars on the screen

BFORLTE L1,2,22
        mvcur   v1L1,0
        putchar 179
        mvcur   v1L1,79
        putchar 179
EFOR    L1

; print horizontal lines

BFORLTE L2,0,79
        mvcur   1,v1L2
        putchar 196
        mvcur   2,v1L2
```

```
            putchar 196
            mvcur   23,v1L2
            putchar 196
EFOR    L2

; print corners

            mvcur   23,0
            putchar 192

            mvcur   23,79
            putchar 217

            mvcur   2,0
            putchar 218

            mvcur   2,79
            putchar 191

; write message to press key

            swrite  3,1,mess1

; wait for key press

            getch

; clear the screen

            clrscreen

; restore caller's stack frame

            pop     BP

EPROCEDURE DRAW_SCRN_

            END

;
; End of Source Listing
;------------------------------------
```

Fig. 8-5 ends.

Fig. 8-6. The source code listing to WTESTMOD.C.

```
/*
 * File Name: WTESTMOD.C
 *
 * Description:
 *   Uses CHUCK procedure where
 *   CHUCK procedure is passed one
 *   parameter.
 */

/* Include 'C'erious Library header files */

#include <tproto.h>
```

```
/* Function prototypes */

void main(void);        /* no command line params */
void DRAW_SCRN(int);    /* CHUCK procedure        */

void
main()
{
/*
 * DRAW_SCRN receives the attribute
 * returned from the 'C'erious mkAttr(...)
 * function. 'C'erious mkAttr functions in the
 * same way as CHUCK's makeattr.
 */

DRAW_SCRN(mkAttr(WHITE,RED,OFF_INTENSITY,OFF_BLINK));
}

/*
 * End of source file
 */
```

Fig. 8-6 ends.

The command line used to compile and link WTESTMOD.EXE is:

wcl wtestmod.c wmod2.obj tab.lib tsrw6sp.lib

Here the C source is linked with the CHUCK-created 'wmod2.obj', the CHUCK TAB library, and the Watcom version of the 'C'erious library. Note that the TAB library is the same for integrating CHUCK with other languages.

Finally let's compare the sizes of the executable files:

TESTMOD2.EXE	3181 bytes	(TURBO C)
WTESTMOD.EXE	2804 bytes	(Watcom C)
EPROG21.EXE	1129 bytes	(CHUCK EXE)
CPROG21.COM	866 bytes	(CHUCK COM)

Using CHUCK in a mixed-language environment is no more difficult than using assembly, and might actually prove easier in certain circumstances.

FINAL WORDS

Part II added additional program flow macros to CHUCK's arsenal. Although CHUCK's macros for controlling program flow aren't as rich as those of higher-level languages, they do prove robust enough to handle virtually all program flow conditions.

Part III starts by discussing what categories of procedures should be added to CHUCK in order to increase the practicality of the language. Once the categories are developed the source for library routines follows.

PART III
Adding Procedures to CHUCK's Library

The CHUCK language is really defined by the program flow statements. But what good is a language that doesn't have any intrinsic procedures that write to the screen, operate on a disk, or send a byte to the printer? In Part III you will be adding routines to enhance your CHUCK library. It is these library routines that lend CHUCK a large measure of its power for programmers.

It is useful to divide the CHUCK library routines into broad categories in order to get a grasp on individual procedures. The categories for CHUCK Version 1.0 are:

- Writing to the Screen
- Window Management Procedures
- Cursor Procedures
- Code Conversion Procedures
- Keyboard Read Procedures
- Print Procedures
- Math Routines
- Character Procedures
- Disk I/O Procedures
- String and Memory Procedures

Part III concentrates on presenting a selection of procedures from these categories. Once these selected procedures are operational you'll discover that programming in CHUCK truly comes to life.

9

Direct Video Access

Reiterating what was briefly mentioned in the explanation of the SCWRITE procedure, the PC holds the information displayed on the screen in what is called *Video Ram. Direct Video Access* means that the program changes the screen display by writing directly to the screen RAM as opposed to letting the BIOS do the work. Writing to screen RAM directly is very fast.

Remembering that screen RAM holds the character byte and then its attribute byte, it is easy to create routines that alter just the character, just the attribute, or both at the same time.

The direct video access routines begin by writing data to the screen, and then by reading data from the screen. All the assembly direct video foundation routines might seem a bit complex to the uninitiated, but by using the CHUCK procedure interface, integrating them into your programs should prove very easy.

DIRECT VIDEO ACCESS PROCEDURES

The following direct video routines are presented in this chapter:

- VDPUTCH   puts a character to a row and column location
- VDATTR   changes a length of attributes at row and column location
- VDCHAR   puts a character and attribute to row and column location
- VDWRITE   writes a string at row and column location using a specified attribute
- SAVESCRN   saves the screen to memory
- RESTSCRN   restores a previously saved screen from memory
- VDRDCHAR   reads a video token (8-bit character and 8-bit attribute make a 16-bit token)
- VDTOKEN   writes the video token to the screen

These routines will appear on most machines to change the screens as quickly as a page flip. Each of the procedures should be placed in a file called DVIDEO.MAC. Be sure to include this macro file in your CHUCK assemblies by modifying SMALL.MAC to include DVIDEO.MAC.

VDPUTCH

VDPUTCH puts a character to the screen at the designated row and column. The syntax is:

vdputch   *row,col,*'A'

where *row* = memory|immediate
     col = memory|immediate
    'A' = memory|immediate

VDPUTCH puts a character to a specified screen location using direct video access. The xPROG16 demonstration programs use a (well-touted) nested looping scheme to print a rectangular box of 'A's on the screen. Note that the rectangular window of 'A's appears quickly.

VDPUTCH (EXE Version)   The macro listing for VDPUTCH is shown in Fig. 9-1. Figure 9-2 presents the subroutine called from within VDPUTCH, and Fig. 9-3 the EXE demonstration program.

Fig. 9-1. The EXE macro listing to VDPUTCH.

```
;;----------------------------------------
;;
;; Macro: VDPUTCH row,col,cval
;;
;; Description:
;;   Write a character at row col
;;   using direct video
;;

VDPUTCH MACRO row,col,cval

;; save regs

        pushaa

;; load regs with parameters

    IFDIFI <AX>,<row>
        mov     AX,row
    ENDIF

    IFDIFI <DX>,<col>
        mov     DX,col
    ENDIF

    IFDIFI <BX>,<cval>
        mov     BX,cval
```

```
        ENDIF

;; call subroutine

        EXTRN    AVDPUTCH:NEAR
        call     avdputch

;; restore regs

        popaa

        ENDM

;;-------------------------------------
```

Fig. 9-1 ends.

Fig. 9-2. The EXE source code listing to VDPUTCH.ASM.

```
;-------------------------------------
; vdputch.asm
;
; vdoutch(row,col,cval)
;
; int row      row of string write
; int col      column of string write
; int cval     write a character to the screen


        DOSSEG

        .MODEL SMALL

        .DATA

        EXTRN    SCRNSEG:WORD
avdprow   DB    0
avdpcol   DB    0
avdpchar  DB    0

        .CODE

        PUBLIC  avdputch

avdputch PROC NEAR

;; save parameters to memory
        push    ES
        push    DI

        mov     avdprow,AL
        mov     avdpcol,DL
        mov     avdpchar,BL

        mov     CX,SCRNSEG      ; SCRNSEG set by vidinit
        mov     ES,CX           ; reset extra seg

        push    ES              ; save EX
        xor     AX,AX           ; 0 -> AX
```

```
        mov     AL,[avdprow]   ; row -> AL
        mov     BL,160         ; 80 chars wide * 2
        mul     BL             ; row * scrn width  -> AX
        mov     CL,[avdpcol]   ; column to CL
        xor     CH,CH          ; 0 -> CH
        shl     CX,1           ; col * 2
        add     AX,CX          ; column + (row * scrn width)
        mov     DI,AX          ; point DI to scrn
        pop     ES             ; restore ES

        mov     AL,[avdpchar]  ; character to AL
        stosb                  ; AL -> screen

        pop     DI
        pop     ES
        ret

avdputch ENDP

        END

;----------------------------------------
```

Fig. 9-2 ends.

Fig. 9-3. The source code listing to EPROG16.ASM.

```
;----------------------------------------
; Source Listing Start
;
; File Name: EPROG16.ASM
;
; Include Macro file
;

INCLUDE SMALL.MAC

; Initialize EXE file structure with STACK => 100h

        PROG_EXE

        PROG_DATA

row     DW      ?
col     DW      ?

; Start of code segment

        PROG_CODE

        vidinit        ; CHUCK video initialization
        clrscreen      ; clear the screen

;
; Print rectangle of 'A's  on screen
; starting at: row 5
;              col 10
;

        setv    row,5  ; set start row at 5
```

```
        setv    col,10  ; set start column at 10
BLOOP   bl1,15          ; loop 15 rows
  BLOOP bl0,65          ; loop 65 columns
        vdputch row,col,'A'
        add1    col     ; increment column
  ELOOP bl0
  setv  col,10          ; reset column to 10
  add1  row             ; go to next row
ELOOP   bl1


        END_EXE         ; DOS EXE terminate

        END


;
; End of Source Listing
;-------------------------------------
```

Fig. 9-3 ends.

VPPUTCH (COM Version)

The COM macro listing is presented in Fig. 9-4. Figure 9-5 is the source code listing to the subroutine called from within VDPUTCH, VDPUTCH.ASM. Figure 9-6 presents the source code listing to the COM version demonstration program, CPROG16.ASM.

Fig. 9-4. The COM macro listing to VDPUTCH.

```
;;--------------------------------------
;;
;; Macro: VDPUTCH row,col,cval
;;
;; Description:
;;  Write a character at row col
;;  using direct video
;;

VDPUTCH MACRO row,col,cval

;; save regs

        pushaa

;; load regs with parameters

    IFDIFI <AX>,<row>
        mov     AX,row
    ENDIF

    IFDIFI <DX>,<col>
        mov     DX,col
    ENDIF

    IFDIFI <BX>,<cval>
        mov     BX,cval
    ENDIF

;; call subroutine
```

```
        PUBLIC  AVDPUTCH
        call    avdputch

;; restore regs

        popaa

        ENDM

;;---------------------------------------
```

Fig. 9-4 ends.

Fig. 9-5. The COM source code listing to VDPUTCH.ASM.

```
;---------------------------------------
; vdputch.asm
;
; vdputch(row,col,cval)
;
; int row      row of string write
; int col      column of string write
; int cval     write a character to the screen
;


avdputch PROC NEAR

        jmp     a?putch

avdprow    DB    0
avdpcol    DB    0
avdpchar   DB    0

a?putch:

;; save parameters to memory

        mov     avdprow,AL
        mov     avdpcol,DL
        mov     avdpchar,BL

        mov     CX,SCRNSEG     ; SCRNSEG set by vidinit
        mov     ES,CX          ; reset extra seg

        push    ES             ; save EX
        xor     AX,AX          ; 0 -> AX
        mov     AL,[avdprow]   ; row -> AL
        mov     BL,160         ; 80 chars wide * 2
        mul     BL             ; row * scrn width  -> AX
        mov     CL,[avdpcol]   ; column to CL
        xor     CH,CH          ; 0 -> CH
        shl     CX,1           ; col * 2
        add     AX,CX          ; column + (row * scrn width)
        mov     DI,AX          ; point DI to scrn
        pop     ES             ; restore ES

        mov     AL,[avdpchar]  ; character to AL
        stosb                  ; AL -> screen
```

```
        ret

avdputch ENDP

;----------------------------------------
```

Fig. 9-5 ends.

Fig. 9-6. The source code listing to CPROG16.ASM.

```
;----------------------------------------
; Source Listing Start
;
; File Name: CPROG16.ASM
;
;


;
; Include Macro file
;

INCLUDE SMALL.MAC

        PROG_COM

row     DW      ?
col     DW      ?

program:

        vidinit        ; CHUCK video initialization
        clrscreen      ; clear the screen


;
; Print rectangle of 'A's  on screen
; starting at: row 5
;              col 10
;

        setv    row,5   ; set start row at 5
        setv    col,10  ; set start column at 10
BLOOP   bl1,15          ; loop 15 rows
  BLOOP bl0,65          ; loop 65 columns
        vdputch  row,col,'A'
        add1     col    ; increment column
  ELOOP bl0
  setv  col,10          ; reset column to 10
  add1  row             ; go to next row
ELOOP   bl1

        COM_TO_DOS

;----------------------------------------
;
; Include procedure file here
;

L_VIDINIT
L_CLRSCREEN
```

```
L_VDPUTCH

        END_COM

;
; End of Source Listing
;------------------------------------
;
```

Fig. 9-6 ends.

Figure 9-7 presents the disassembled listing to CPROG16.COM. Instead of my commenting the file, why don't you try to trace the flow of CPROG16. I think it will prove instructive as to how the nested looping is accomplished.

Fig. 9-7. The disassembled listing to CPROG16.COM.

```
PAGE   60,132

.286c

data_10e        equ      6A2h
data_11e        equ      1688h
data_12e        equ      1E88h
data_13e        equ      3E88h
data_14e        equ      0CD0Fh

code_seg_a      segment
                assume   cs:code_seg_a, ds:code_seg_a

                org      100h

cprog16         proc     far

start:
                push     cs
                pop      ds
                jmp      short loc_1
                db       90h
                db       16 dup (0)
data_2          dw       0
data_3          dw       0
loc_1:

;
; hint --------------------------------
;
                push     ax
                push     bx
                push     cx
                push     dx
                call     sub_1
                pop      dx
                pop      cx
                pop      bx
                pop      ax
;
; hint --------------------------------
```

Fig. 9-7 continued.

```
;
                        push    ax
                        push    bx
                        push    cx
                        push    dx
                        mov     bh,7
                        call    sub_2
                        pop     dx
                        pop     cx
                        pop     bx
                        pop     ax
;
; hint ------------------------------
;
                        mov     cs:data_2,5
                        mov     cs:data_3,0Ah
                        mov     cx,0Fh

locloop_2:
                        push    cx
                        mov     cx,41h


;
; hint ------------------------------
;

locloop_3:
                        push    cx
                        push    ax
                        push    bx
                        push    cx
                        push    dx
                        push    si
                        push    di
                        push    es
                        mov     ax,cs:data_2
                        mov     dx,cs:data_3
                        mov     bx,41h
                        call    sub_3
                        pop     es
                        pop     di
                        pop     si
                        pop     dx
                        pop     cx
                        pop     bx
                        pop     ax
                        inc     cs:data_3
                        pop     cx
                        loop    locloop_3


;
; hint ------------------------------
;
                        mov     cs:data_3,0Ah
                        inc     cs:data_2
                        pop     cx
                        loop    locloop_2
```

Fig. 9-7 continued.

```
;
; hint -------------------------------
;

                int     20h

cprog16         endp

;
;------------------------------------
;

sub_1           proc    near
                push    cs
                pop     ds
                jmp     short loc_4
                db      90h
data_4          db      0
data_5          dw      0
data_6          dw      0
loc_4:
                mov     ah,0Fh
                int     10h

                mov     cs:data_4,bh
                cmp     al,7
                je      loc_8
                mov     cs:data_5,3DAh
                cmp     cs:data_4,0
                jne     loc_5
                mov     cs:data_6,0B800h
                jmp     short loc_9
                db      90h
loc_5:
                cmp     cs:data_4,1
                jne     loc_6
                mov     cs:data_6,0B900h
                jmp     short loc_9
                db      90h
loc_6:
                cmp     cs:data_4,2
                jne     loc_7
                mov     cs:data_6,0BA00h
                jmp     short loc_9
                db      90h
loc_7:
                mov     cs:data_6,0BB00h
                jmp     short loc_9
                db      90h
loc_8:
                mov     cs:data_5,3BAh
                mov     cs:data_6,0B000h
loc_9:
                ret
sub_1           endp
;
;------------------------------------
;

sub_2           proc    near
```

```
                           mov      al,0
                           mov      ch,0
                           mov      cl,0
                           mov      dh,18h
                           mov      dl,4Fh
                           mov      ah,6
                           int      10h

                           mov      ah,0Fh
                           int      10h

                           xor      dx,dx
                           mov      ah,2
                           int      10h

                           ret
sub_2                      endp


;
;------------------------------------
;

sub_3                      proc     near
                           jmp      short loc_10
                           db       90h
data_7                     db       0
data_8                     db       0
data_9                     db       0
loc_10:
                           mov      cs:data_7,al
                           mov      cs:data_8,dl
                           mov      cs:data_9,bl
                           mov      cx,cs:data_6
                           mov      es,cx
                           push     es
                           xor      ax,ax
                           mov      al,cs:data_7
                           mov      bl,0A0h
                           mul      bl
                           mov      cl,cs:data_8
                           xor      ch,ch
                           shl      cx,1
                           add      ax,cx
                           mov      di,ax
                           pop      es
                           mov      al,cs:data_9
                           stosb
                           ret
sub_3                      endp

code_seg_a                 ends
                           end      start
```

Fig. 9-7 ends.

VDATTR

VDATTR changes the length of screen attributes at a designated row and column. The syntax is:

vdattr　　row,col,length,attr

where *row*　=　memory|immediate
　　　　col　=　memory|immediate
　　　length　=　memory|immediate
　　　　attr　=　memory|immediate

VDATTR changes the attribute a length number of characters starting at row and col. VDATTR is very useful for writing highlight bar routines.

　　　Figure 9-8 presents the macro listing for VDATTR, Fig. 9-9 the source code listing for the EXE version of VDATTR.ASM, Fig. 9-10 the demonstration program EPROG17.ASM, Fig. 9-11 the COM version of the VDATTR macro, Fig. 9-12 the source code listing to the COM version of VDATTR.ASM, and Fig. 9-13 the source code listing to CPROG17.ASM.

VDATTR (EXE Version)　　The EXE version is demonstrated in Figs. 9-8 and 9-9. The VDATTR EXE example is shown in Fig. 9-10.

VDATTR (COM Version)　　The COM version is demonstrated in Figs. 9-11 and 9-12. The VDATTR COM example is shown in Fig. 9-13.

Fig. 9-8. The EXE macro listing to VDATTR.

```
;;--------------------------------------
;;
;; Macro: VDATTR row,col,len,attr
;;
;; Description:
;;   Change attribute of row without
;;   altering characters (highlighting)
;;

VDATTR MACRO row,col,len,attr

;; save regs

        pushaa

;; load regs with parameters

    IFDIFI <AX>,<row>
        mov     AX,row
    ENDIF

    IFDIFI <DX>,<col>
        mov     DX,col
    ENDIF

    IFDIFI <BX>,<len>
```

```
                    mov        BX,len
              ENDIF

              IFDIFI <CX>,<attr>
                    mov        CX,attr
              ENDIF

;; call subroutine

                    EXTRN      AVDATTR:NEAR
                    call       avdattr

;; restore regs

                    popaa

                    ENDM

;;----------------------------------------
```

Fig. 9-8 ends.

Fig. 9-9. The EXE source code listing to VDATTR.ASM.

```
;
; vdAttr.asm
;
; vdAttr row,col,len,attr
;
; int row      row of string write
; int col      column of string write
; int len      number of bytes to write
; int attr     attribute of screen write
;


              DOSSEG
              .MODEL SMALL

              .DATA
              EXTRN      SCRNSEG:WORD
avdprow  DB        23
avdpcol  DB        0
avdplen  DW        40
avdpattr DB        7
              .CODE
              PUBLIC  avdattr
avdattr PROC NEAR
              mov        avdprow,AL
              mov        avdpcol,DL
              mov        avdplen,BX
              mov        avdpattr,CL

              mov        CX,SCRNSEG
              mov        ES,CX          ; reset extra seg

              push       ES             ; save EX
              xor        AX,AX          ; 0 -> AX
              mov        AL,[avdprow]   ; row -> AL
              mov        BL,160         ; 80 chars wide * 2
```

```
        mul     BL              ; row * scrn width  -> AX
        mov     CL,[avdpcol]    ; column to CL
        xor     CH,CH           ; 0 -> CH
        shl     CX,1            ; col * 2
        add     AX,CX           ; column + (row * scrn width)
        mov     DI,AX           ; point DI to scrn
        pop     ES              ; restore ES


        cld                     ; direction increment
        mov     CX,[avdplen]    ; string length parameter
vdr1:
        inc     DI              ; bypass character byte
        mov     AL,[avdpattr]   ; attribute to AL
        stosb                   ; AL -> screen
        loop    vdr1
        ret
avdattr ENDP
        END
```

Fig. 9-9 ends.

Fig. 9-10. The source code listing to EPROG17.ASM.

```
;----------------------------------------
; Source Listing Start
;
; File Name: EPROG17.ASM
;
; Description:
;  Demonstrates VDATTR
;
;
; Include Macro file
;

INCLUDE SMALL.MAC

; Initialize EXE file structure with STACK => 100h

        PROG_EXE

        PROG_DATA

row     DW      ?
col     DW      ?
attr1   DW      ?

; Start of code segment

        PROG_CODE

        vidinit         ; CHUCK video initialization
        clrscreen       ; clear the screen

;
; Print rectangle of 'A's  on screen
; starting at: row 5
;             col 10
; and highlight the first row
```

```
          makeattr   BLACK,WHITE,OFF_INTEN,OFF_BLINK
          setv       attr1,RET_VAL

          setv       row,5    ; set start row at 5
          setv       col,10   ; set start column at 10
BLOOP     bl1,15              ; loop 15 rows
  BLOOP   bl0,65              ; loop 65 columns
          vdputch    row,col,'.'
          add1       col      ; increment column
  ELOOP   bl0
  setv    col,10              ; reset column to 10
  add1    row                 ; go to next row
ELOOP     bl1

          vdattr     5,10,65,attr1  ; highlight top row of '.'

          END_EXE             ; DOS EXE terminate

          END

;
; End of Source Listing
;------------------------------------
```

Fig. 9-10 ends.

Fig. 9-11. The COM macro listing to VDATTR.

```
;;----------------------------------------
;;
;; Macro: VDATTR row,col,len,attr
;;
;; Description:
;;  Change attribute of row without
;;  altering characters (highlighting)
;;

VDATTR MACRO row,col,len,attr

;; save regs

        pushaa

;; load regs with parameters

    IFDIFI <AX>,<row>
        mov     AX,row
    ENDIF

    IFDIFI <DX>,<col>
        mov     DX,col
    ENDIF

    IFDIFI <BX>,<len>
        mov     BX,len
    ENDIF
```

```
        IFDIFI <CX>,<attr>
            mov     CX,attr
        ENDIF

;; call subroutine

            PUBLIC  AVDATTR
            call    avdattr

;; restore regs

            popaa

            ENDM

;;-------------------------------------
;;
```

Fig. 9-11 ends.

Fig. 9-12. The COM source code listing to VDATTR.ASM.

```
;-------------------------------------
;
;
; vdattr.asm
;
; vdAttr row,col,len,attr
;
; int row      row of string write
; int col      column of string write
; int len      number of bytes to write
; int attr     attribute of screen write
;

avdattr PROC NEAR

            jmp     a?attr

avdatrow    DB      23
avdatcol    DB      0
avdplen     DW      40
avdpattr    DB      7

a?attr:
            mov     avdatrow,AL
            mov     avdatcol,DL
            mov     avdplen,BX
            mov     avdpattr,CL

            mov     CX,SCRNSEG
            mov     ES,CX           ; reset extra seg

            push    ES              ; save EX
            xor     AX,AX           ; 0 -> AX
            mov     AL,[avdatrow]   ; row -> AL
            mov     BL,160          ; 80 chars wide * 2
            mul     BL              ; row * scrn width  -> AX
            mov     CL,[avdatcol]   ; column to CL
            xor     CH,CH           ; 0 -> CH
            shl     CX,1            ; col * 2
            add     AX,CX           ; column + (row * scrn width
```

```
        mov     DI,AX          ; point DI to scrn
        pop     ES             ; restore ES


        cld                    ; direction increment
        mov     CX,[avdplen]   ; string length parameter
vdr1:
        inc     DI             ; bypass character byte
        mov     AL,[avdpattr]  ; attribute to AL
        stosb                  ; AL -> screen
        loop    vdr1
        ret
avdattr ENDP

;----------------------------------------
```

Fig. 9-12 ends.

Fig. 9-13. The source code listing to CPROG17.ASM.

```
;----------------------------------------
; Source Listing Start
;
; File Name: CPROG17.ASM
;


;
; Include Macro file
;

INCLUDE SMALL.MAC

        PROG_COM

row     DW      ?
col     DW      ?
attr1   DW      ?

program:

        vidinit         ; CHUCK video initialization
        clrscreen       ; clear the screen


;
; Print rectangle of 'A's  on screen
; starting at: row 5
;              col 10
; and highlight the first row
;

        makeattr  BLACK,WHITE,OFF_INTEN,OFF_BLINK
        setv      attr1,RET_VAL

        setv      row,5  ; set start row at 5
        setv      col,10 ; set start column at 10
BLOOP   bl1,15           ; loop 15 rows
  BLOOP bl0,65           ; loop 65 columns
        vdputch   row,col,'.'
        add1      col    ; increment column
```

```
     ELOOP bl0
        setv  col,10          ; reset column to 10
        add1  row             ; go to next row
     ELOOP bl1

              vdattr    5,10,65,attr1  ; highlight tio row of '.'

              COM_TO_DOS

;---------------------------------------
;
; Include procedure file here
;

     L_VIDINIT
     L_CLRSCREEN
     L_VDPUTCH
     L_VDATTR
     L_MAKEATTR

              END_COM

;
; End of Source Listing
;---------------------------------------
;
```

Fig. 9-13 ends.

VDCHAR

VDCHAR writes a character and attribute to row and column. The syntax is:

vdchar   *row,col,char,attribute*

where *row*   =   memory|immediate
      col   =   memory|immediate
      char   =   memory|immediate
      attribute =   memory|immediate

VDCHAR writes a character and its attribute to a row and column screen location.

Figure 9-14 presents the EXE version of the VDCHAR macro, Fig. 9-15 the source code listing to the EXE version of VDCHAR, Fig. 9-16 the EXE demonstration program EPROG18.ASM, Fig. 9-17 the COM version of the VDCHAR macro, Fig. 9-18 the COM version of the source code to VDCHAR.ASM and Fig. 9-19 the COM demonstration program CPROG18.ASM.

VDCHAR (EXE Version)   The VDCHAR EXE version is demonstrated in Figs. 9-14 and 9-15. The VDCHAR EXE example is shown in Fig. 9-16. After running EPROG18 you should see inverse 'A's at the screen's corners.

VDCHAR (COM Version)   The VDCHAR COM version is shown in Figs. 9-17 and 9-18. The VDCHAR COM example is shown in Fig. 9-19.

Fig. 9-14. The EXE macro listing to VDCHAR.

```
;;----------------------------------------
;;
;; Macro: VDCHAR row,col,cval,attr
;;
;; Description:
;;   Write a char and attr to the screen
;;   using direct video
;;

VDCHAR MACRO row,col,cval,aval

;; save regs

        pushaa

;; load regs with parameters

    IFDIFI <AX>,<row>
        mov     AX,row
    ENDIF

    IFDIFI <DX>,<col>
        mov     DX,col
    ENDIF

    IFDIFI <BX>,<cval>
        mov     BX,cval
    ENDIF

    IFDIFI <CX>,<aval>
        mov     CX,aval
    ENDIF

;; call subroutine

        EXTRN   AVDCHAR:NEAR
        call    avdchar

;; restore regs

        popaa

        ENDM

;;----------------------------------------
```

Fig. 9-15. The EXE source code listing to VDCHAR.ASM.

```
;----------------------------------------
;
; vdchar.asm
;
; vdchar row,col,cval,attr
;
; int row      row of string write
; int col      column of string write
```

```
; int len      number of bytes to write
; int char     attribute of screen write
;


        DOSSEG
        .MODEL SMALL

        .DATA
        EXTRN    SCRNSEG:WORD
avdprow   DB    0
avdpcol   DB    0
avdpchar  DB    0
avdpattr  DB    0

        .CODE

        PUBLIC  avdchar

avdchar PROC NEAR
;
; relocate parameters to memory
;

        mov     avdprow,AL
        mov     avdpcol,DL
        mov     avdpchar,BL
        mov     avdpattr,CL

        mov     CX,SCRNSEG
        mov     ES,CX           ; reset extra seg

        push    ES              ; save EX
        xor     AX,AX           ; 0 -> AX
        mov     AL,[avdprow]    ; row -> AL
        mov     BL,160          ; 80 chars wide * 2
        mul     BL              ; row * scrn width  -> AX
        mov     CL,[avdpcol]    ; column to CL
        xor     CH,CH           ; 0 -> CH
        shl     CX,1            ; col * 2
        add     AX,CX           ; column + (row * scrn width)
        mov     DI,AX           ; point DI to scrn
        pop     ES              ; restore ES

        mov     AL,[avdpchar]   ; character to AL
        stosb                   ; AL -> screen
        mov     AL,[avdpattr]   ; character to AL
        stosb                   ; AL -> screen
        ret

avdchar ENDP

        END


;-----------------------------------
```

Fig. 9-15 ends.

Fig. 9-16. The source code listing to EPROG18.ASM.

```
;----------------------------------------
; Source Listing Start
;
; File Name: EPROG18.ASM
;
; Description:
;  Demonstrates VDCHAR


;
; Include Macro file
;

INCLUDE SMALL.MAC

; Initialize EXE file structure with STACK => 100h

        PROG_EXE

        PROG_DATA

attr1   DW      0

; Start of code segment

        PROG_CODE

        vidinit        ; CHUCK video initialization
        clrscreen      ; clear the screen

;

        makeattr  BLACK,WHITE,OFF_INTEN,OFF_BLINK
        setv      attr1,RET_VAL

;
; Print character to screen using attribute attr1
;

        vdchar    0,79,'A',attr1
        vdchar    24,79,'A',attr1
        vdchar    24,0,'A',attr1
        vdchar    0,0,'A',attr1

        END_EXE              ; DOS EXE terminate

        END

;
; End of Source Listing
;----------------------------------------
```

Fig. 9-17. The COM macro listing to VDCHAR.

```
;;----------------------------------------
;;
;; Macro: VDCHAR row,col,cval,attr
;;
;; Description:
```

```
;;   Write a char and attr to the screen
;;   using direct video
;;

VDCHAR MACRO row,col,cval,aval

;; save regs

        pushaa

;; load regs with parameters

   IFDIFI <AX>,<row>
        mov     AX,row
   ENDIF

   IFDIFI <DX>,<col>
        mov     DX,col
   ENDIF

   IFDIFI <BX>,<cval>
        mov     BX,cval
   ENDIF

   IFDIFI <CX>,<aval>
        mov     CX,aval
   ENDIF

;; call subroutine

        PUBLIC  AVDCHAR
        call    avdchar

;; restore regs

        popaa

        ENDM

;;--------------------------------------
```

Fig. 9-17 ends.

Fig. 9-18. The COM source code listing to VDCHAR.ASM.

```
;--------------------------------------
;
; vdchar.asm
;
; vdchar row,col,cval,attr
;
; int row     row of string write
; int col     column of string write
; int len     number of bytes to write
; int char    attribute of screen write
;

avdchar PROC NEAR

        jmp     a?vdchar

avdcharrow    DB 0
```

```
avdcharcol   DB 0
avdcharchar  DB 0
avdcharattr  DB 0

a?vdchar:

;
; relocate parameters to memory
;

        mov     avdcharrow,AL
        mov     avdcharcol,DL
        mov     avdcharchar,BL
        mov     avdcharattr,CL

        mov     CX,SCRNSEG
        mov     ES,CX           ; reset extra seg

        push    ES              ; save EX
        xor     AX,AX           ; 0 -> AX
        mov     AL,[avdcharrow]  ; row -> AL
        mov     BL,160          ; 80 chars wide * 2
        mul     BL              ; row * scrn width  -> AX
        mov     CL,[avdcharcol]   ; column to CL
        xor     CH,CH           ; 0 -> CH
        shl     CX,1            ; col * 2
        add     AX,CX           ; column + (row * scrn width)
        mov     DI,AX           ; point DI to scrn
        pop     ES              ; restore ES

        mov     AL,[avdcharchar] ; character to AL
        stosb                   ; AL -> screen
        mov     AL,[avdcharattr] ; character to AL
        stosb                   ; AL -> screen
        ret

avdchar ENDP

;---------------------------------------
```

Fig. 9-18 ends.

Fig. 9-19. The source code listing to CPROG18.ASM.

```
;---------------------------------------
; Source Listing Start
;
; File Name: CPROG18.ASM
;
;


; Include Macro file
;

INCLUDE SMALL.MAC

        PROG_COM
```

```
    attr1   DW      0

program:

        vidinit         ; CHUCK video initialization
        clrscreen       ; clear the screen

;

        makeattr  BLACK,WHITE,OFF_INTEN,OFF_BLINK
        setv      attr1,RET_VAL


;
; Print character to screen using attribute attr1
;

        vdchar    0,79,'A',attr1
        vdchar    24,79,'A',attr1
        vdchar    24,0,'A',attr1
        vdchar    0,0,'A',attr1


        COM_TO_DOS

;-------------------------------------
;
; Include procedure file here
;

L_VIDINIT
L_CLRSCREEN
L_MAKEATTR
L_VDCHAR


        END_COM

;
; End of Source Listing
;-------------------------------------
```

Fig. 9-19 ends.

VDWRITE

VDWRITE writes a string of length bytes with a specified attribute. The syntax is:

```
vdwrite     row,col,string_length,buff_name,attribute
```

where *row*   = memory|immediate
      col   = memory|immediate
      string_length = memory|immediate
      buff_name   = label of text buffer
      attribute   = immediate|memory

VDWRITE functions in an identical fashion to the BIOS-based SCWRITE call. VDWRITE is fast and is useful for highlighting specific text entries on the screen. As the VDWRITE macro does not call a subroutine, the EXE and COM versions are identical. Also, note that the VDCHAR procedure is used and in the COM version the L_VDCHAR macro must be invoked in order to link properly. A VDWRITE EXE example is shown in Fig. 9-21. A VDWRITE COM example is shown in Fig. 9-22.

The file sizes for EPROG19.EXE and CPROG19.COM are:

EPROG19.EXE   944 bytes
CPROG19.COM   470 bytes

Fig. 9-20. The EXE and COM macro listing to VDWRITE.

```
;;-----------------------------------------
;;
;; Macro: VDWRITE row,col,length,buffer,attribute
;;
;; Description:
;;   Direct video version of SCWRITE.
;;

VDWRITE MACRO row1,col1,len1,buff1,attr1
        LOCAL loc_1,row,col,len,buff,attr,cval

;; jump over data held in code

        jmp     loc_1

row     DW      0
col     DW      0
len     DW      0
buff    DW      0
attr    DW      0
cval    DW      0

loc_1:

;; save regs

        pushx

;; move parameters to memory

    IFDIFI <AX>,<row1>
        mov     AX,row1
        mov     row,AX
    ELSE
        mov     row,AX
    ENDIF

    IFDIFI <AX>,<col1>
        mov     AX,col1
        mov     col,AX
    ELSE
        mov     col,AX
    ENDIF

    IFDIFI <AX>,<len1>
        mov     AX,len1
        mov     len,AX
```

```
  ELSE
        mov     len,AX
  ENDIF

        lea     AX,buff1
        mov     buff,AX

  IFDIFI <AX>,<attr1>
        mov     AX,attr1
        mov     attr,AX
  ELSE
        mov     attr,AX
  ENDIF
```

;; use CHUCK looping to count bytes

```
BLOOP   vdw?1,CS:[len]
        xor     AX,AX                  ; 0 => AX
        mov     BX,CS:[buff]           ; string ptr => BX
        mov     AL,BYTE PTR[BX]        ; 8 bit char => AL
        mov     CS:[cval],AX           ; 16 bit char => cval
        vdchar CS:[row],CS:[col],CS:[cval],CS:[attr]
        inc     CS:[col]               ; next column
        inc     CS:[buff]              ; point to next char
ELOOP   vdw?1
```

;; restore regs

```
        popx

        ENDM
```

;;--------------------------------------

Fig. 9-20 ends.

Fig. 9-21. The source code listing to EPROG19.ASM.

```
;--------------------------------------
; Source Listing Start
;
; File Name: EPROG19.ASM
;
; Description:
;  Demonstrates VDWRITE

;
; Include Macro file
;

INCLUDE SMALL.MAC

; Initialize EXE file structure with STACK => 100h

        PROG_EXE

        PROG_DATA

attr1   DW      0
mess1   DB      'Hello World!',0
```

```
; Start of code segment

        PROG_CODE

        vidinit      ; CHUCK video initialization
        clrscreen    ; clear the screen

;

        makeattr  BLACK,WHITE,OFF_INTEN,OFF_BLINK
        setv      attr1,RET_VAL

        vdwrite   10,10,12,mess1,attr1

        END_EXE            ; DOS EXE terminate

        END


  End of Source Listing
  --------------------------------------
```

Fig. 9-21 ends.

Fig. 9-22. The source code listing to CPROG19.ASM.

```
;----------------------------------------
; Source Listing Start
;
; File Name: CPROG19.ASM
;

;
; Include Macro file
;

INCLUDE SMALL.MAC

        PROG_COM

attr1   DW        0
mess1   DB        'Hello World!',0

program:

        vidinit      ; CHUCK video initialization
        clrscreen    ; clear the screen

;

        makeattr  BLACK,WHITE,OFF_INTEN,OFF_BLINK
        setv      attr1,RET_VAL

        vdwrite   10,10,12,mess1,attr1

        COM_TO_DOS

;----------------------------------------
;
; Include procedure file here
;
```

```
L_VIDINIT
L_CLRSCREEN
L_MAKEATTR
L_VDCHAR

        END_COM


;
; End of Source Listing
;------------------------------------
;
```

Fig. 9-22 ends.

SAVESCRN
RESTSCRN

SAVESCRN saves the screen to memory. RESTSCRN restores a previously saved screen from memory. The syntax is:

```
savescreen
restscreen
```

Saving the screen image using SAVESCRN is extremely easy. All the internal memory image buffers are automatically allocated. Examine the assembly source for the EXE version and the COM version. There is a difference in memory allocation. (More on the differences later.) Note also that in the COM version L_SAVESCRN must be invoked as the last macro loader in the source file.

SAVESCRN and RESTSCRN (EXE Version)   The EXE macro listings of SAVESCRN and RESTSCRN are shown in Fig. 9-23. Figure 9-24 shows the source code listing to SAVESCRN.ASM. This file contains all the assembly routines required by SAVESCRN and RESTSCRN. Figure 9-25 presents EPROG20.ASM which demonstrates how SAVESCRN and RESTSCRN are used.

Fig. 9-23. The EXE macro listing to SAVESCRN and RESTSCRN.

```
;;----------------------------------------
;;
;; Macro: SAVESCRN
;;
;; Descritpion: Save the currently
;;   displayed screen to memory
;;

SAVESCRN MACRO

;; save regs

        pushaa

;; call subroutine
```

```
        EXTRN    SSCRN:NEAR
        call     sscrn

;; restore regs

        popaa

        ENDM

;;--------------------------------------

;;--------------------------------------
;;
;; Macro: RESTSCRN
;;
;; Descritpion: Restores a previously
;;   saved screen from memory to the screen
;;

RESTSCRN MACRO

;; save regs

        pushaa

;; call subroutine

        EXTRN    RSCRN:NEAR
        call     rscrn

;; restore regs

        popaa

        ENDM

;;--------------------------------------
```

Fig. 9-23 ends.

Fig. 9-24. The EXE source code listing to SAVESCRN.ASM.

```
;*******************
; Source Code Start
;
; File Name:    SAVESCRN.ASM
;
; Synopsis:     sscrn
;               rscrn
;
; Description: Saves and restores screen to 2000 WORDS
;               allocated in code segment
;
; Returns:      Nothing
;

        DOSSEG
```

Fig. 9-24 continued.

```
        .MODEL SMALL

        .DATA
        EXTRN   SCRNSEG:WORD
buffseg DW      0
sscrnf  DW      0

        .CODE

        PUBLIC  sscrn,rscrn

sscrn PROC NEAR
        cmp     [sscrnf],1 ; first time called?
        je      no1sscrn ; no-> jump

; dynamically allocate memory for screen image
; using DOS memory allocate function 48h, int 21h

        push    DX
        mov     BX,100h ; AX     ; num of 16 byte para to BX
        mov     AH,48h  ; DOS allocate me function
        int     21      ; Invoke DOS
        pop     DX

; store memory segment from dos allocate

        mov     [buffseg],AX
        mov     [sscrnf],1 ; Set bypass flag
no1sscrn:
        mov     CX,SCRNSEG ; color addr
bs1:
        mov     ES,CX   ; save scrn seg
        mov     DI,0    ; offset to 0

        push    DS      ; save DS

        mov     AX,[buffseg] ; move scrn buffer seg to DS
        mov     DS,AX
        xor     SI,SI   ; set offset SI to 0

        mov     CX,4000 ; move 4000 bytes
lp1:
        mov     AX,ES:[DI] ; get scrn byte
        mov     DS:[SI],AX ; to buffer
        inc     DI      ; next byte
        inc     SI
        loop    lp1     ; loop until 4000 bytes moved
        pop     DS
        ret
sscrn ENDP

;
; Synopsis:    restScrn
;
; Description: restores screen from 2000 WORDS
;              allocated in code segment
;
; Returns:     Nothing
;
```

```
rscrn PROC NEAR
        push    DS
        mov     CX,SCRNSEG
bs11:
        mov     ES,CX
        mov     DI,0     ; offset to 0
        mov     AX,DS:buffseg ; move scrn buffer seg to DS
        mov     DS,AX
        xor     SI,SI    ; set offset SI to 0
        mov     CX,4000 ; move 4000 bytes
lp11:
        mov     AX,DS:[SI] ; buffer byte
        mov     ES:[DI],AX ; to display RAM
        inc     DI       ; next byte
        inc     SI
        loop    lp11     ; loop until 4000 bytes moved
        pop     DS
        ret
rscrn ENDP

        END


;
; End of assembly source listing
;********************************
```

Fig. 9-24 ends.

Fig. 9-25. The source code listing to EPROG20.ASM.

```
;---------------------------------------
; Source Listing Start
;
; File Name: EPROG20.ASM
;
; Description:
;  Demonstrates SAVESCRN & RESTSCRN


;
; Include Macro file
;

INCLUDE SMALL.MAC

; Initialize EXE file structure with STACK => 100h

        PROG_EXE

        PROG_DATA

attr1   DW      0
mess1   DB      'Press any key to continue...',0

; Start of code segment

        PROG_CODE

        vidinit         ; CHUCK video initialization
```

```
        savescrn        ; save the screen

        clrscreen       ; clear the screen

;
        makeattr  BLACK,WHITE,OFF_INTEN,OFF_BLINK
        setv      attr1,RET_VAL

        vdwrite   10,10,28,mess1,attr1

        getch

        restscrn

        mvcur     23,0

        END_EXE             ; DOS EXE terminate

        END

;
; End of Source Listing
;-------------------------------------
;
```

Fig. 9-25 ends.

SAVESCRN and RESTSCRN (COM Version)

The COM macro listings of the SAVESCRN and RESTSCRN are shown in Fig. 9-26. Figure 9-27 is the COM source code listing of SAVESCRN.ASM. The SAVESCRN and RESTSCRN COM example are shown in Fig. 9-28, the source code listing to CPROG20.ASM.

Let's compare the file sizes of EPROG20.EXE and CPROG20.COM.

EPROG20.EXE   1144 bytes
CPROG20.COM   4611 bytes

What! No, I didn't make a mistake. Do you know why the COM file is larger?

The answer is that the screen requires 2000 words of memory to hold the screen image. The EXE version of SAVESCRN uses the DOS memory allocate function to allocate the 2000 words of memory at runtime. The COM version of SAVESCRN allocates the memory by declaring a large buffer in the source code.

Remember, COM programs cannot dynamically allocate memory.

Fig. 9-26. The COM macro listing to SAVESCRN and RESTSCRN.

```
;;-------------------------------------
;;
;; Macro: SAVESCRN
;;
;; Descritpion: Save the currently
;;   displayed screen to memory
;;
SAVESCRN MACRO
```

```
;; save regs

        pushaa

;; call subroutine

        PUBLIC  SSCRN
        call    sscrn

;; restore regs

        popaa

        ENDM

;;----------------------------------------

;;----------------------------------------
;;
;;
;; Macro: RESTSCRN
;;
;; Descritpion: Restores a previously
;;   saved screen from memory to the screen
;;

RESTSCRN MACRO

;; save regs

        pushaa

;; call subroutine

        PUBLIC  RSCRN
        call    rscrn

;; restore regs

        popaa

        ENDM

;;----------------------------------------
```

Fig. 9-26 ends.

Fig. 9-27. The COM source code listing to SAVESCRN.ASM.

```
;*******************
; Source Code Start
;
; File Name:   SAVESCRN.ASM
;
; Synopsis:    sscrn
;              rscrn
;
; Description: Saves and restores screen to 2000 WORDS
;              allocated in code segment
```

```
;
; Returns:     Nothing
;


sscrn PROC NEAR
        mov     CX,SCRNSEG
bs1:
        mov     ES,CX   ; save scrn seg
        mov     DI,0    ; offset to 0
        lea     AX,SCRN
        mov     SI,AX
        mov     CX,4000 ; move 4000 bytes
lpss:
        mov     AX,ES:[DI] ; get scrn byte
        mov     [SI],AX ; to buffer
        inc     DI      ; next byte
        inc     SI
        loop    lpss    ; loop until 4000 bytes moved
        ret
sscrn ENDP

rscrn PROC NEAR
        mov     CX,SCRNSEG
bs11:
        mov     ES,CX
        mov     DI,0    ; offset to 0
        lea     AX,SCRN
        mov     SI,AX
        mov     CX,4000 ; move 4000 bytes
lp11:
        mov     AX,[SI] ; buffer byte
        mov     ES:[DI],AX ; to display RAM
        inc     DI      ; next byte
        inc     SI
        loop    lp11    ; loop until 4000 bytes moved
        ret
SCRN    DW      2000 DUP(0)
rscrn ENDP
```

Fig. 9-27 ends.

Fig. 9-28. The source code listing to CPROG20.ASM.

```
;----------------------------------------
; Source Listing Start
;
; File Name: CPROG20.ASM
;


;
; Include Macro file
;

INCLUDE SMALL.MAC

        PROG_COM
```

```
attr1   DW      0
mess1   DB      'Press any key to continue...',0

program:

        vidinit         ; CHUCK video initialization

        savescrn        ; save the screen

        clrscreen       ; clear the screen


        makeattr  BLACK,WHITE,OFF_INTEN,OFF_BLINK
        setv      attr1,RET_VAL

        vdwrite   10,10,28,mess1,attr1

        getch

        restscrn

        mvcur     23,0

        COM_TO_DOS

;---------------------------------------
;
; Include procedure file here
;

L_VIDINIT
L_MVCUR
L_CLRSCREEN
L_MAKEATTR
L_VDCHAR

; L_SAVESCRN must always be included last!

L_SAVESCRN

        END_COM

;
; End of Source Listing
;---------------------------------------
```

Fig. 9-28 ends.

VDRDCHAR
VDTOKEN

VDRDCHAR reads a 16-bit video token (8-bit character and 8-bit attribute combine to form a 16-bit video token) from the screen. VDTOKEN writes a 16-bit video token to the screen. The syntax is:

```
vdrdchar    row,column
vdtoken     row,column,token
```

where *row*   = memory|immediate
      column = memory|immediate
      token = memory|immediate|register

In a sense, VDRDCHAR and VDTOKEN are linked together. These routines are used to read and write various segments of screen memory using direct video access. They will prove vital in writing a series of sharp pop-up window management routines.

VDRDCHAR and VDTOKEN (EXE Version)   The EXE version macro listing for VDRDCHAR and VDTOKEN is shown in Fig. 9-29. Figure 9-30 presents the source code listing to VDRDCHAR.ASM and Fig. 9-31 the source code listing to VDTOKEN.ASM. Figure 9-32 is the source code listing to EPROG22.ASM, the VDRDCHAR and VDTOKEN EXE example.

Fig. 9-29. The EXE macro listing to VDRDCHAR and VDTOKEN.

```
;;------------------------------------------
;;
;; Macro: VDRDCHAR row,col
;;
;; Description:
;;   Read a token from the screen
;;   using direct video
;;

VDRDCHAR MACRO row,col

;; save regs

        push    ES
        push    DI
        pushbcd

;; load regs with parameters

    IFDIFI <AX>,<row>
        mov     AX,row
    ENDIF

    IFDIFI <DX>,<col>
        mov     DX,col
    ENDIF

;; call subroutine
```

```
              EXTRN    AVDRDCHAR:NEAR
              call     avdrdchar

;; restore regs

              popbcd
              pop      DI
              pop      ES

              ENDM

;;-------------------------------------

;;-------------------------------------
;;
;;
;; Macro: VDTOKEN row,col,token
;;
;; Description:
;;   Write a token to the screen
;;   using direct video (for saving and restoring
;;   screen rectangles)
;;

VDTOKEN MACRO row,col,token

;; save regs

              pushaa

;; load regs with parameters

       IFDIFI <AX>,<row>
              mov      AX,row
       ENDIF

       IFDIFI <DX>,<col>
              mov      DX,col
       ENDIF

       IFDIFI <BX>,<token>
              mov      BX,token
       ENDIF

;; call subroutine

              EXTRN    AVDTOKEN:NEAR
              call     avdtoken

;; restore regs

              popaa
              ENDM

;;-------------------------------------
```

Fig. 9-29 ends.

Fig. 9-30. The EXE source code listing to VDRDCHAR.ASM.

```
;-------------------------------------
; Source Code Start
;
; File Name:    VDRDCHAR.ASM
;
; Synopsis:     vdrdchar row,column
;
; int row       row where token will be read from
;
; int column    column where the token will be
;               read from
;
; Returns:      returns screen token in RET_VAL (AX)
;


        DOSSEG

        .MODEL SMALL


        .DATA
        EXTRN   SCRNSEG:WORD
prow    DB      0
pcol    DB      0

        .CODE
        PUBLIC  avdrdchar
avdrdchar PROC NEAR

        push    ES
        push    DI

;
; Parameters to memory
;
        mov     [prow],AL
        mov     [pcol],DL


;
; active video page screen segment to ES
;

        mov     CX,SCRNSEG
        mov     ES,CX           ; reset extra seg


;
; Calculate screen address
;
        xor     AX,AX           ; 0 -> AX
        mov     AL,[prow]       ; row -> AL
        mov     BL,160          ; 80 chars wide * 2
        mul     BL              ; row * scrn width  -> AX
        mov     CL,[pcol]       ; column to CL
        XOR     CH,CH           ; 0 -> CH
        shl     CX,1            ; col * 2
        add     AX,CX           ; column + (row * scrn width)
        mov     DI,AX           ; point DI to scrn
```

```
;
; Screen token from memory => AX
;
        mov     AX,WORD PTR ES:[DI]
        pop     DI
        pop     ES
        ret

avdrdchar ENDP

        END

;---------------------------------------
```

Fig. 9-30 ends.

Fig. 9-31. The EXE source code listing to VDTOKEN.ASM.

```
;---------------------------------------
;
; vdtoken.asm
;
; vdtoken row,col,token
;
; row      row of string write
; col      column of string write
; token    16 bit token (8 bit Char &
;          8 bit attribute)
;

        DOSSEG
        .MODEL SMALL

        .DATA

        EXTRN    SCRNSEG:WORD

avdprow   DB    0
avdpcol   DB    0
avdptoken DW    0

        .CODE

        PUBLIC  avdtoken

avdtoken PROC NEAR
;
; Parameters to memory
;
        push    ES
        push    DI

        mov     avdprow,AL
        mov     avdpcol,DL
        mov     avdptoken,BX


;
; active video page screen segment to ES
```

```
;

        mov     CX,SCRNSEG
        mov     ES,CX           ; reset extra seg

;
; Calculate screen address
;

        xor     AX,AX           ; 0 -> AX
        mov     AL,[avdprow]    ; row -> AL
        mov     BL,160          ; 80 chars wide * 2
        mul     BL              ; row * scrn width  -> AX
        mov     CL,[avdpcol]    ; column to CL
        xor     CH,CH           ; 0 -> CH
        shl     CX,1            ; col * 2
        add     AX,CX           ; column + (row * scrn width)
        mov     DI,AX           ; point DI to scrn

;
; Store screen token to memory
;

        mov     AX,[avdptoken] ; character to AL
        stosw                   ; AX -> screen

        pop     DI
        pop     ES
        ret

avdtoken ENDP

        END
```

;-------------------------------------

Fig. 9-31 ends.

Fig. 9-32. The source code listing to EPROG22.ASM.

```
;-------------------------------------
; File Name: EPROG22.ASM
;

include SMALL.MAC

        PROG_EXE

        PROG_DATA

token   DW      0
ulr     DW      5
ulc     DW      5
lrr     DW      15
lrc     DW      45
attr1   DW      0
sbuff   DW      (40*12) DUP(0)

        PROG_CODE
```

Fig. 9-32 continued.

```
          vidinit

;-----------------------------------
; save the rectangle

          push    BX
          lea     BX,sbuff

BFORLTE L0,[ulr],[lrr]
   BFORLTE L1,[ulc],[lrc]
      vdrdchar v1L0,v1L1
      mov       WORD PTR [BX],RET_VAL
      add2      BX
   EFOR    L1
EFOR    L0

          pop     BX


;-------------------------------------
; Draw the window

          makeattr   BLUE,WHITE,OFF_INTEN,OFF_BLINK
          setv    attr1,RET_VAL

          maketoken  ' ',attr1
          setv    token,RET_VAL

BFORLTE L3,[ulr],[lrr]
   BFORLTE L4,[ulc],[lrc]
      vdtoken  v1L3,v1L4,token
   EFOR    L4
EFOR    L3



;-------------------------------------
;
;
; wait for key press
;

          getch

;-------------------------------------
; write the old screen                   •

          push    BX
          lea     BX,sbuff

BFORLTE L5,[ulr],[lrr]
   BFORLTE L6,[ulc],[lrc]
          mov       AX,WORD PTR [BX]
          mov       [token],AX
          vdtoken   v1L5,v1L6,[token]
          add2      BX
   EFOR    L6
EFOR    L5

          pop     BX
;
```

```
;----------------------------------------
;
        mvcur    24,0

        END_EXE

        END

;----------------------------------------
;
```

Fig. 9-32 ends.

VDRDCHAR and VDTOKEN (COM Version)   The macro listing to the COM version of VDRDCHAR and VDTOKEN is shown in Fig. 9-33. Figure 9-34 is the COM version source code listing to VDRDCHAR.ASM, and Fig. 9-35 is the COM version source code listing to VDTOKEN.ASM. Figure 9-36 is the source code listing to CPROG22.ASM.

CPROG22.COM and EPROG22.EXE present the underground code to saving and restoring rectangular regions of the screen, better known as windows. Using the FORLTE/EFOR combined with VDRDCHAR and VDTOKEN you will be able to pop-up windows with the best.

Fig. 9-33. The COM macro listing to VDRDCHAR and VDTOKEN.

```
;;----------------------------------------
;;
;; Macro: VDRDCHAR row,col
;;
;; Description:
;;   Read a token from the screen
;;   using direct video
;;

VDRDCHAR MACRO row,col

;; save regs

        push     ES
        push     DI
        pushbcd

;; load regs with parameters

    IFDIFI <AX>,<row>
        mov      AX,row
    ENDIF

    IFDIFI <DX>,<col>
        mov      DX,col
    ENDIF

;; call subroutine

        PUBLIC   AVDRDCHAR
        call     avdrdchar
```

```
;; restore regs

        popbcd
        pop     DI
        pop     ES

        ENDM

;;----------------------------------------

;;----------------------------------------
;;
;; Macro: VDTOKEN row,col,token
;;
;; Description:
;;   Write a token to the screen
;;   using direct video (for saving and restoring
;;   screen rectangles)
;;

VDTOKEN MACRO row,col,token

;; save regs

        pushaa

;; load regs with parameters

   IFDIFI <AX>,<row>
        mov     AX,row
   ENDIF

   IFDIFI <DX>,<col>
        mov     DX,col
   ENDIF

   IFDIFI <BX>,<token>
        mov     BX,token
   ENDIF

;; call subroutine

        PUBLIC  AVDTOKEN
        call    avdtoken

;; restore regs

        popaa

        ENDM

;;----------------------------------------
```

Fig. 9-33 ends.

Fig. 9-34. The COM source code listing to VDRDCHAR.ASM.

```
;---------------------------------------
; Source Code Start
;
; File Name:    VDRDCHAR.ASM
;
; Synopsis:     vdrdchar row,column
;
; int row       row where token will be read from
;
; int column    column where the token will be
;               read from
;
; Returns:      returns screen token in RET_VAL (AX)
;


avdrdchar PROC NEAR
        push    ES
        push    DI
        jmp     avd?rd

avd?rdprow      DB      0
avd?rdpcol      DB      0

avd?rd:

;
; Parameters to memory
;
        mov     [avd?rdprow],AL
        mov     [avd?rdpcol],DL


;
; active video page screen segment to ES
;

        mov     CX,SCRNSEG
        mov     ES,CX           ; reset extra seg


;
; Calculate screen address
;

        xor     AX,AX           ; 0 -> AX
        mov     AL,[avd?rdprow]     ; row -> AL
        mov     BL,160          ; 80 chars wide * 2
        mul     BL              ; row * scrn width  -> AX
        mov     CL,[avd?rdpcol]     ; column to CL
        XOR     CH,CH           ; 0 -> CH
        shl     CX,1            ; col * 2
        add     AX,CX           ; column + (row * scrn width)
        mov     DI,AX           ; point DI to scrn


;
; Screen token from memory => AX
;

        mov     AX,WORD PTR ES:[DI]
```

```
        pop     DI
        pop     ES
        ret

avdrdchar ENDP

;------------------------------------
```

Fig. 9-34 ends.

Fig. 9-35. The COM source code listing to VDTOKEN.ASM.

```
;------------------------------------
;
; vdtoken.asm
;
; vdtoken row,col,token
;
; row     row of string write
; col     column of string write
; token   16 bit token (8 bit Char &
;         8 bit attribute)
;


avdtoken PROC NEAR
        jmp     avd?tok

avd??prow   DB  0
avd??pcol   DB  0
avd??ptoken DW  0

avd?tok:
;
; Parameters to memory
;

        mov     avd??prow,AL
        mov     avd??pcol,DL
        mov     avd??ptoken,BX


;
; active video page screen segment to ES
;

        mov     CX,SCRNSEG
        mov     ES,CX           ; reset extra seg

;
; Calculate screen address
;

        push    ES              ; save EX
        xor     AX,AX           ; 0 -> AX
        mov     AL,[avd??prow]  ; row -> AL
        mov     BL,160          ; 80 chars wide * 2
        mul     BL              ; row * scrn width  -> AX
        mov     CL,[avd??pcol]  ; column to CL
        xor     CH,CH           ; 0 -> CH
```

```
        shl     CX,1          ; col * 2
        add     AX,CX         ; column + (row * scrn width)
        mov     DI,AX         ; point DI to scrn
        pop     ES            ; restore ES

;
; Store screen token to memory
;

        mov     AX,[avd??ptoken] ; character to AL
        stosw                 ; AX -> screen
        ret

avdtoken ENDP

;-------------------------------------
```

Fig. 9-35 ends.

Fig. 9-36. The source code listing to CPROG22.ASM.

```
;---------------------------------------
; Source Listing Start
;
; File Name: CPROG22.ASM
;
; Description:
;   Demonstration of VDRDCHAR & VDTOKEN
;

;
; Include Macro file
;

INCLUDE SMALL.MAC

        PROG_COM

token   DW      0
ulr     DW      5
ulc     DW      5
lrr     DW      15
lrc     DW      45
attr1   DW      0
sbuff   DW      (40*12) DUP(0)

program:

        vidinit

;-------------------------------------
; save the rectangle

        push    BX
        lea     BX,sbuff

BFORLTE L0,[ulr],[lrr]
   BFORLTE L1,[ulc],[lrc]
      vdrdchar v1L0,v1L1
```

Fig. 9-36 continued.

```
        mov         WORD PTR [BX],RET_VAL
        add2        BX
    EFOR    L1
EFOR    L0

        pop     BX


;----------------------------------------
; Draw the window

        makeattr   BLUE,WHITE,OFF_INTEN,OFF_BLINK
        setv    attr1,RET_VAL

        maketoken  ' ',attr1
        setv    token,RET_VAL

BFORLTE L3,[ulr],[lrr]
   BFORLTE L4,[ulc],[lrc]
      vdtoken   v1L3,v1L4,token
   EFOR    L4
EFOR    L3




;----------------------------------------
;
; wait for key press
;

        getch

;----------------------------------------
; write the old screen

        push    BX
        lea     BX,sbuff

BFORLTE L5,[ulr],[lrr]
   BFORLTE L6,[ulc],[lrc]
        mov         AX,WORD PTR [BX]
        mov      [token],AX
        vdtoken   v1L5,v1L6,[token]
        add2        BX
   EFOR    L6
EFOR    L5

        pop     BX
;
;----------------------------------------
        mvcur   24,0

        COM_TO_DOS

;----------------------------------------
;
; Include procedure file here
;

L_VIDINIT
```

```
L_MVCUR
L_CLRSCREEN
L_MAKEATTR
L_VDRDCHAR
L_VDTOKEN

        END_COM

;
; End of Source Listing
;--------------------------------------
```
_____

Fig. 9-36 ends.

10

Miscellaneous and Cursor Procedures

This chapter contains sound, procedure-calling, make-a-token, and cursor procedures. All of the macros should be added to your VIDEO.MAC file. As the two miscellaneous procedures do not call subroutines they can be used in your EXE and COM version of VIDEO.MAC. MAKETOKEN is a procedure that receives an 8-bit character and 8-bit attribute and returns the 16-bit token in the AX register. CPROC calls a procedure you have written but automatically saves the BX, CX and DX registers before the 'call' and restores them after your procedure had returned.

INTRODUCTION

The following sections discuss the CHUCK procedures in detail.

MAKETOKEN

MAKETOKEN creates a 16-bit video token from an 8-bit character and an 8-bit attribute. The syntax is:

    maketoken   asc_char,attribute

where *asc_char* = memory|immediate|register
      attribute   = memory|immediate|register

MAKETOKEN is useful when using the direct video procedure VDTOKEN. VDTOKEN writes 16-bit video tokens to the screen. Note that this macro should be added to your COM version and EXE version VIDEO.MAC file.

MAKETOKEN (EXE AND COM Version)

The EXE and COM macro listing to MAKETOKEN is shown in Fig. 10-1. The following is a MAKETOKEN EXE and COM example:

```
        •
        •
makeattr    RED,WHITE,ON_INTEN,ON_BLINK
setv        [attribute],RET_VAL
maketoken   'A',[attribute]
setv        [token],RET_VAL
vdtoken     0,0,[token]
        •
        •
```

Fig. 10-1. The EXE and COM macro listing to MAKETOKEN.

```
;;------------------------------------
;; Macro: MAKETOKEN asc_char,attr
;;
;; Description:
;;  Combine the two 8 bit values into
;;  a word contained in AX

MAKETOKEN MACRO asc_char,attr

;; save DX

        push DX

;; if AX different from asc_char then...

    IFDIFI <AX>,<asc_char>
        mov     AX,asc_char
    ENDIF

;; if DX different from attr then...

    IFDIFI <DX>,<attr>
        mov     DX,attr
    ENDIF

;; mov attr to AH so
;;   AL => character
;;   AH => attribute

        mov     AH,DL

;; restore DX

        pop     DX

;; token returned in AX register

        ENDM

;;------------------------------------
;;
```

The example code creates an 8-bit attribute where the foreground is red, the background is white, the intensity is on and the foreground blink is on. This attribute is stored in the 16-bit WORD in memory, attribute. MAKETOKEN then combines the character 'A' with the attribute and places the 16-bit video token in 16-bit memory, token. The video token is then put to the screen via direct video at row 0, column 0.

CPROC

CPROC calls one of your procedures. The syntax is:

cproc   *your_ procedure*

where *your_ procedure* = legal text name for procedure

CPROC saves the BX, CX, and DX registers, calls your procedure, and then restores the registers. This procedure-call macro should always be used when calling any procedure you've written that uses the CHUCK program flow macros.

CPROC (EXE and COM Versions)   The macro listing to CPROC is shown in Fig. 10-2. The following is a CPROC EXE and COM example:

```
        .
        .
cproc   how_many
setv    [number],RET_VAL
        .
        .
```

The example shows that you have called a procedure you've written named how_many. The how_many procedure returns a value in the AX (RET_VAL) register. SETV stores RET_VAL in 16-bit memory named number.

Fig. 10-2. The EXE and COM macro listing to CPROC.

```
;;----------------------------------------
;;
;; Macro: CPROC name_proc
;;
;; Descritpion: Calls procedure while
;;   saving BX,CX,DX and leaving AX for
;;   word values returned by your procedure
;;

CPROC MACRO name_proc

;; save BX, CX, DX

        pushbcd

;; call your procedure
```

```
        call     name_proc

;; restore BX, CX, DX

        popbcd

        ENDM

;;----------------------------------------
```

Fig. 10-2 ends.

ONCURSOR
OFFCURSOR

ONCURSOR makes the cursor visible (enable). OFFCURSOR makes the cursor invisible (disable). The syntax is:

oncursor
offcursor

There are times when a video display would look cleaner if the PC's cursor were not forever blinking. ONCURSOR and OFFCURSOR provide two very simple procedures to accomplish this task.

ONCUR and OFFCUR (EXE Version)   Figure 10-3 presents the EXE version of the ONCURSOR and OFFCURSOR macros. Figure 10-4 presents the EXE version of the source code to the subroutines ONCUR and OFFCUR in ONCUR.ASM. The following is an ONCURSOR and OFFCURSOR EXE example:

```
        .
    offcursor
        .
; you program here
        .
    oncursor
        .
```

ONCURSOR and OFFCURSOR (COM Version)   Figure 10-5 presents the macro listing to the COM version of OFFCURSOR and ONCURSOR. Figure 10-6 presents the COM version source code listing to ONCUR.ASM. L_ONCURSOR is the name of the COM loader macro.

```
    L_ONCURSOR MACRO
            INCLUDE ONCUR.ASM
            ENDM
```

Fig. 10-3. The EXE ONCURSOR and OFFCURSOR macro listing.

```
;;----------------------------------------
;;
;; Macro: OFFCURSOR
;;
;; Description: Turn off the cursor
;;

OFFCURSOR MACRO

;; save AX, BX, CX, DX

        pushx

;; call subroutine

        EXTRN   OFFCUR:NEAR
        call    offcur

;; restore AX, BX, CX, DX

        popx

        ENDM

;;----------------------------------------

;;----------------------------------------
;;
;; Macro: ONCURSOR
;;
;; Description: Turn on the cursor
;;

ONCURSOR MACRO

;; save AX, BX, CX, DX

        pushx

;; call subroutine

        EXTRN   ONCUR:NEAR
        call    oncur

;; restore AX, BX, CX, DX

        popx

        ENDM

;;----------------------------------------
```

Fig. 10-4. The EXE source code listing to ONCUR.ASM.

```
;*******************
; Start Source File
;
; File Name      ONCUR.ASM
;
; Name           oncur
;                offcur
;
; Description    enables the cursor by
;                turning bit 5 of CH on
;                after current shape is
;                obtained.  The modified
;                current shape is then
;                used to set the cursor
;                or disables by turnin bit
;                5 off
;

        DOSSEG
;
        .MODEL SMALL
;
        .CODE

        PUBLIC ONCUR,OFFCUR

ONCUR PROC NEAR
        mov     AH,3    ; read cursor position & config
        int     10H     ; BIOS video int
        and     CH,0dfh ; enable cursor
        mov     AH,1    ; set cursor type
        int     10H     ; BIOS video int
        ret
ONCUR ENDP


;
; Set the start of OFFCUR
;
OFFCUR PROC NEAR
        mov     AH,3    ; read cursor position & config
        int     10H     ; BIOS int 10h
        or      CH,020h ; disable cursor
        mov     AH,1    ; set cursor type
        int     10H     ; int 10h
        ret
OFFCUR ENDP

        END

; End Source Here
;****************
;
```

Fig. 10-5. The COM ONCURSOR and OFFCURSOR macro listing.

```
;;----------------------------------------
;;
;; Macro: OFFCURSOR
;;
;; Description: Turn off the cursor
;;

OFFCURSOR MACRO

;; save AX, BX, CX, DX

        pushx

;; call subroutine

        PUBLIC  OFFCUR
        call    offcur

;; restore AX, BX, CX, DX

        popx

        ENDM

;;----------------------------------------


;;----------------------------------------
;;
;; Macro: ONCURSOR
;;
;; Description: Turn on the cursor
;;

ONCURSOR MACRO

;; save AX, BX, CX, DX

        pushx

;; call subroutine

        PUBLIC ONCUR
        call    oncur

;; restore AX, BX, CX, DX

        popx

        ENDM

;;----------------------------------------
;;
```

Fig. 10-6. The COM source code listing to ONCUR.ASM.

```
;*******************
; Start Source File
;
; File Name      ONCUR.ASM
;
; Name           oncur
;                offcur
;
; Description    enables the cursor by
;                turning bit 5 of CH on
;                after current shape is
;                obtained.  The modified
;                current shape is then
;                used to set the cursor
;                or disables by turnin bit
;                5 off
;

ONCUR PROC NEAR
        mov     AH,3    ; read cursor position & config
        int     10H     ; BIOS video int
        and     CH,0dfh ; enable cursor
        mov     AH,1    ; set cursor type
        int     10H     ; BIOS video int
        ret
ONCUR ENDP


;
; Set the start of OFFCUR
;
OFFCUR PROC NEAR
        mov     AH,3    ; read cursor position & config
        int     10H     ; BIOS int 10h
        or      CH,020h ; disable cursor
        mov     AH,1    ; set cursor type
        int     10H     ; int 10h
        ret
OFFCUR ENDP

; End Source Here
;*******************
```

Add the macro (on page 278) to your COM.MAC file. The following is an
ONCURSOR and OFFCURSOR COM example:

```
        .

        .

        offcursor

        .

; you program here

        .

        oncursor

        .
```

SAVECURLOC
RESTCURLOC

SAVECURLOC saves the current cursor location. RESTCURLOC restores a previously saved cursor location. The syntax is:

    savecurloc
    restcurloc

SAVECURLOC and RESTCURLOC provide convenient ways to save the current cursor location and restore the previously saved cursor location. These routines are useful when jumping from one screen or window to another and then returning in a stack-like (last on/first off) fashion.

SAVECURLOC and RESTCURLOC (EXE Version)   Figure 10-7 presents the EXE version source code listing to the SAVECURLOC and RESTCURLOC macros. Figure 10-8 presents the source code listing to SCLOC.ASM. This assembly file contains the source for both saving and restoring the cursor location.

Fig. 10-7. The EXE macro listing to SAVECURLOC and RESTCURLOC.

```
;;------------------------------------
;;
;; Macro: SAVECURLOC
;;
;; Description: Saves current cursor
;;   loaction
;;

SAVECURLOC MACRO

;; save AX, BX, CX, DX

        pushx

;; call subroutine

        EXTRN   SCLOC:NEAR
        call    scloc

;; restore regs

        popx

        ENDM

;;-------------------------------------


;;-------------------------------------
;;
;; Macro: RESTCURLOC
;;
;; Description: Restores a previously
;;   saved cursor location
```

```
;;

RESTCURLOC MACRO

;; save AX, BX, CX, DX

        pushx

;; call subroutine

        EXTRN   RCLOC:NEAR
        call    rcloc

;; restore regs

        popx

        ENDM

;;---------------------------------------
```

Fig. 10-7 ends.

Fig. 10-8. The EXE source code listing to SCLOC.ASM.

```
;*******************
; Source Code Start
;
; File Name:   SCLOC.ASM
;
; Synopsis:    sCloc
;
; Description: Uses BIOS to get the
;              current location of the
;              cursor and saves is to
;              memory
;
;
; Returns:     Nothing
;
;
;
; Enable DOS segment-ordering at link time
;

        DOSSEG

;
; Set the memory model for simplified segmentation
; directives
;

        .MODEL SMALL

        .DATA

        EXTRN PAG_NUM:BYTE
```

```
l?_cur_row DB 0
l?_cur_col DB 0


        .CODE
        PUBLIC  SCLOC,RCLOC

SCLOC PROC NEAR
        mov     AH,3            ; BIOS cur location
        int     10h             ; BIOS int
        mov     l?_cur_row,DH   ; move row
        mov     l?_cur_col,DL   ; move column
        ret
SCLOC ENDP

;
; Synopsis:    rCloc
;
; Description: Uses previously saved
;              cursor location as
;              setting for new cursor
;              location
;
; Returns:     Nothing
;


;
; Set the start of the function
;

RCLOC PROC NEAR
        mov     DH,l?_cur_row
        mov     DL,l?_cur_col
        mov     BH,PAG_NUM
        mov     AH,2
        int     10H       ; BIOS video int
        ret
RCLOC ENDP

        END

;
; End of assembly listing
;**************************
;
```

Fig. 10-8 ends.

The SAVECURLOC and RESTCURLOC EXE example is shown in Fig. 10-9. Figure 10-9 presents the source code listing to EPROG23.ASM. This program demonstrates the use of ONCUR/OFFCUR, SAVECURLOC/RESTCURLOC, and SAVESCRN/RESTSCRN. EPROG23.ASM is a modification of EPROG21.ASM.

SAVECURLOC and RESTCURLOC (COM Version)   Figure 10-10 presents the macro listing to the COM version of SAVECURLOC and RESTCURLOC. Figure 10-11 presents the source code listing to SCLOC.ASM and Fig. 10-12

the listing to the example program CPROG23.ASM. L_SAVECURLOC is the
macro loader for SCLOC.ASM.

```
L_SAVECURLOC MACRO
        INCLUDE SCLOC.ASM
        ENDM
```

Add this macro to your COM.MAC file.

Fig. 10-9. The source code listing to EPROG23.ASM.

```
;------------------------------------
; Source Listing Start
;
; File Name: EPROG23.ASM
;
; Description:
;  Demonstrates ONCUR / OFFCUR
;               SAVECURLOC / RESTCURLOC
;
; Include Macro file
;

INCLUDE SMALL.MAC

; Initialize EXE file structure with STACK => 100h

        PROG_EXE

        PROG_DATA

mess1   DB      'Press any key to continue...',0
menu    DB      ' Desk  File  Edit                    '
        DB      '                           Quit ',0

; Start of code segment

        PROG_CODE

; CHUCK video initialization

        vidinit

; Save current screen configuration
;
; 1) save the screen image via direct video access
; 2) save cursor location
; 3) turn off the cursor

        savescrn
        savecurloc
        offcursor


; screen attributes:
;    BLACK => foreground
;    WHITE => background
;    INTENSITY => off
```

Fig. 10-9 continued.

```
;   BLINK => off

        makeattr  BLACK,WHITE,OFF_INTEN,OFF_BLINK

; clear screen with returned attribute

        clrscreen RET_VAL

; write menu bar to the screen

        puts    menu

; print vertical bars on the screen

BFORLTE L1,2,22
        mvcur   v1L1,0
        putchar 179
        mvcur   v1L1,79
        putchar 179
EFOR    L1

; print horizontal lines

BFORLTE L2,0,79
        mvcur   1,v1L2
        putchar 196
        mvcur   2,v1L2
        putchar 196
        mvcur   23,v1L2
        putchar 196
EFOR    L2

; print corners

        mvcur   23,0
        putchar 192

        mvcur   23,79
        putchar 217

        mvcur   2,0
        putchar 218

        mvcur   2,79
        putchar 191

; write message to press key

        swrite  3,1,mess1

; wait for key press

        getch


; Restore previous screen configuration
;
; 1) restore the screen image via direct video access
; 2) restore cursor location
; 3) turn on the cursor
```

```
        restscrn
        restcurloc
        oncursor


        END_EXE          ; DOS EXE terminate

        END

;
; End of Source Listing
;-----------------------------------
```

Fig. 10-9 ends.

Fig. 10-10. The COM macro listing to SAVECURLOC and RESTCURLOC.

```
;;-----------------------------------------
;;
;; Macro: SAVECURLOC
;;
;; Descritpion: Saves current cursor
;;   loaction
;;

SAVECURLOC MACRO

;; save AX, BX, CX, DX

        pushx

;; call subroutine

        PUBLIC  SCLOC
        call    scloc

;; restore regs

        popx

        ENDM

;;-----------------------------------------

;;-----------------------------------------
;;
;; Macro: RESTCURLOC
;;
;; Descritpion: Restores a previously
;;   saved cursor location
;;

RESTCURLOC MACRO

;; save AX, BX, CX, DX

        pushx

;; call subroutine
```

```
        PUBLIC  RCLOC
        call    rcloc

;; restore regs

        popx

        ENDM

;;---------------------------------------
```

Fig. 10-10 ends.

Fig. 10-11. The COM source code listing to SCLOC.ASM.

```
;******************
; Source Code Start
;
; File Name:    SCLOC.ASM
;
; Synopsis:     sCloc
;
; Description: Uses BIOS to get the
;              current location of the
;              cursor and saves is to
;              memory
;
;
;
; Returns:      Nothing
;

SCLOC PROC NEAR

        jmp     ?scloc1

l?_cur_row DB 0
l?_cur_col DB 0

?scloc1:

        mov     AH,3            ; BIOS cur location
        int     10h             ; BIOS int
        mov     CS:[l?_cur_row],DH   ; move row
        mov     CS:[l?_cur_col],DL   ; move column
        ret
SCLOC ENDP


;
; Synopsis:     rCloc
;
; Description: Uses previously saved
;              cursor location as
;              setting for new cursor
;              location
;
;
; Returns:      Nothing
;


;
; Set the start of the function
```

```
;

RCLOC PROC NEAR
        mov     DH,CS:[l?_cur_row]
        mov     DL,CS:[l?_cur_col]
        mov     BH,CS:[PAG_NUM]
        mov     AH,2
        int     10H      ; BIOS video int
        ret
RCLOC ENDP

;
; End of assembly listing
;*************************
;
```

Fig. 10-11 ends.

Fig. 10-12. The source code listing to CPROG23.ASM.

```
;-------------------------------------
; Source Listing Start
;
; File Name: CPROG23.ASM
;
;

;
; Include Macro file
;

INCLUDE SMALL.MAC

        PROG_COM

mess1   DB      'Press any key to continue...',0
menu    DB      ' Desk  File  Edit                        '
        DB      '                              Quit ',0

program:

; CHUCK video initialization

        vidinit

; Save current screen configuration
;
; 1) save the screen image via direct video access
; 2) save cursor location
; 3) turn off the cursor

        savescrn
        savecurloc
        offcursor


; screen attributes:
;   BLACK => foreground
;   WHITE => background
;   INTENSITY => off
```

Fig. 10-12 continued.

```
;    BLINK => off

        makeattr  BLACK,WHITE,OFF_INTEN,OFF_BLINK

; clear screen with returned attribute

        clrscreen RET_VAL

; write menu bar to the screen

        puts    menu

; print vertical bars on the screen

BFORLTE L1,2,22
        mvcur   v1L1,0
        putchar 179
        mvcur   v1L1,79
        putchar 179
EFOR    L1

; print horizontal lines

BFORLTE L2,0,79
        mvcur   1,v1L2
        putchar 196
        mvcur   2,v1L2
        putchar 196
        mvcur   23,v1L2
        putchar 196
EFOR    L2

; print corners

        mvcur   23,0
        putchar 192

        mvcur   23,79
        putchar 217
        mvcur   2,0
        putchar 218

        mvcur   2,79
        putchar 191

; write message to press key

        swrite  3,1,mess1

; wait for key press

        getch

; Restore previous screen configuration
;
; 1) restore the screen image via direct video access
; 2) restore cursor location
; 3) turn on the cursor

        restscrn
```

```
            restcurloc
            oncursor

            COM_TO_DOS

;-------------------------------------
;
; Include procedure file here
;

L_VIDINIT
L_MVCUR
L_CLRSCREEN
L_MAKEATTR
L_PUTCHAR
L_PUTS
L_ONCURSOR
L_SAVECURLOC

L_SAVESCRN

            END_COM

;
; End of Source Listing
;-------------------------------------
```

Fig. 10-12 ends.

ONSOUND
OFFSOUND
BEEP

ONSOUND uses the PC's timer to create a tone through the speaker. OFFSOUND turns the tone off. BEEP beeps the speaker via BIOS (that familiar annoying beep). The syntax is:

```
onsound   tone
offsound
beep
```

where *tone* = memory|immediate

The PC's sound capabilities are quite poor compared to other microcomputers which have dedicated sound processors built-in. Nonetheless, you can get a tone from the machine. The two methods presented here use different methods to "eeeek" a sound. ONSOUND uses the PC's timers and vibrates the built-in speaker. OFFSOUND terminates the sound started with ONSOUND. BEEP uses the BIOS to beep. BEEP stops automatically.

ONSOUND, OFFSOUND, BEEP (EXE Version)   Figure 10-13 presents the EXE version of the macro listing to all three sound macros. Figure 10-14 presents the source code listing to ONSOUND.ASM and Fig. 10-15 presents the source code listing to EPROG24.ASM, the ONSOUND, OFFSOUND and BEEP EXE example.

Fig. 10-13. The EXE macro listing to sound procedures.

```
;;----------------------------------------
;; Macro: BEEP
;;
;; Description: Beep the consol speaker
;;

BEEP MACRO

        putchar 7

        ENDM

;;----------------------------------------
;; Macro: ONSOUND tone
;;
;; Description: turn on the PC speaker
;;   at tone value

ONSOUND MACRO tone

        pushx

    IFDIFI <AX>,<tone>
        mov     AX,tone
    ENDIF

        EXTRN   ONSND:NEAR
        call    onsnd

        popx

        ENDM

;;----------------------------------------

;;----------------------------------------
;; Macro: OFFSOUND
;;
;; Description: Turn off the PC speaker
;;

OFFSOUND MACRO

        pushx

        EXTRN   OFFSND:NEAR
        call    offsnd

        popx

        ENDM

;;----------------------------------------
```

Fig. 10-14. The EXE source code listing to ONSOUND.ASM.

```
;
; Name: ONSOUND.ASM
;
;                 int  ret
;
; Entry: AX holds (int) tone
;
; Description   ONSND  => turn on sound
;               OFFSND => turn off sound
;

INCLUDE SMALL.MAC

        MODEL    SMALL

        .CODE

        PUBLIC ONSND,OFFSND

BPROCEDURE onsnd
        jmp      onsnd1
tone    DW       0        ; reserve word to stuff tone
onsnd1:
        mov      tone,AX ; stuff tone for later use
        mov      AL,0b6H ; tell timer prep for new sound
        out      43H,AL
        mov      AX,tone ; new tone to timer, LSB
        out      42H,AL
        mov      AL,AH   ; MSB -> LSB
        out      42H,AL  ; LSB -> timer
        in       AL,61H  ; enable speaker output via timer
        or       AL,3
        out      61H,AL
EPROCEDURE onsnd


;
; Turn off the soune
;

BPROCEDURE offsnd
        in       AL,61H  ; disable speaker output via timer
        and      AL,0fcH
        out      61H,AL
EPROCEDURE offsnd

        END
```

Fig. 10-15. The source code listing to EPROG24.ASM.

```
;-------------------------------------
; File Name: EPROG24.ASM
;
; Descripion:
;  Demonstraiton of sound procedures
;

INCLUDE SMALL.MAC
```

```
        PROG_EXE

        PROG_CODE

        vidinit

BFORLTE L1,50,500
    BFORLTE L2,200,400
    EFOR    L2
    onsound v1L1
EFOR    L1

        offsound

        END_EXE

        END

;-------------------------------------
```

Fig. 10-15 ends.

ONSOUND, OFFSOUND, BEEP (COM Version)   The macro loader for the
ONSOUND and OFFSOUND macros is:

```
L_ONSOUND MACRO
        INCLUDE ONSOUND.ASM
        ENDM
```

Add the ONSOUND macro to your COM.MAC file. Figure 10-16 presents the
com version of the sound macros. Figure 10-17 is the COM code listing to
ONSOUND.ASM. The ONSOUND, OFFSOUND, BEEP COM example is shown
in Fig. 10-18, the source code listing to CPROG24.ASM.

Fig. 10-16. The COM macro listing to sound procedures.

```
;----------------------------------------
; Macro: BEEP
;
; Description: Beep the consol speaker
;

BEEP MACRO
        putchar 7
        ENDM

;----------------------------------------

;----------------------------------------
; Macro: ONSOUND tone
;
; Description: turn on the PC speaker
;   at tone value
ONSOUND MACRO tone

        pushx
```

```
   IFDIFI <AX>,<tone>
        mov     AX,tone
   ENDIF

        PUBLIC  ONSND
        call    onsnd

        popx

        ENDM

;------------------------------------

;------------------------------------
; Macro: OFFSOUND
;
; Description: Turn off the PC speaker
;
OFFSOUND MACRO

        pushx

        PUBLIC  OFFSND
        call    offsnd

        popx

        ENDM

;------------------------------------
```

Fig. 10-16 ends.

Fig. 10-17. The COM source code listing to ONSOUND.ASM.

```
;------------------------------------
;
; Name: ONSOUND.ASM
;
;
; Entry: AX holds (int) tone
;
; Description   ONSND  => turn on sound
;               OFFSND => turn off sound
;

INCLUDE SMALL.MAC


BPROCEDURE onsnd
        jmp     onsnd1
tone    DW      0         ; reserve word to stuff tone
onsnd1:
        mov     tone,AX ; stuff tone for later use
        mov     AL,0b6H ; tell timer prep for new sound
        out     43H,AL
        mov     AX,tone ; new tone to timer, LSB
        out     42H,AL
        mov     AL,AH   ; MSB -> LSB
```

```
        out     42H,AL  ; LSB -> timer
        in      AL,61H  ; enable speaker output via timer
        or      AL,3
        out     61H,AL
EPROCEDURE onsnd


;
; Turn off the soune
;

BPROCEDURE offsnd
        in      AL,61H  ; disable speaker output via timer
        and     AL,0fcH
        out     61H,AL
EPROCEDURE offsnd

;--------------------------------------
```

Fig. 10-17 ends.

Fig. 10-18. The source code listing to CPROG24.ASM.

```
;--------------------------------------
;
; CPROG24.ASM
;
; Description:
;   Sound demonstration program
;

INCLUDE SMALL.MAC

        PROG_COM
program:
        vidinit

BFORLTE L1,50,500
   BFORLTE L2,200,400
   EFOR   L2
   onsound v1L1
EFOR    L1

        offsound

        COM_TO_DOS
L_VIDINIT
L_ONSOUND
        END_COM

;--------------------------------------
```

11

String Handling and Code Conversion

This chapter contains four basic string handling procedures and two simple code conversion routines. Five of the six routines are used in Part IV's two demonstration programs.

STRLEN returns the length of a string terminated with a NULL (0) or a '$'. STRCPY copies a string terminated with a NULL (0) or '$' from source to destination. STRNCPY copies *n* bytes of a string from source to destination and MEMSET sets *n* bytes of a string to a specified value.

ITOA converts a 16-bit integer to an ASCII string and ITOHEX converts a 16-bit integer to a HEX ASCII string.

STRING HANDLING AND CODE CONVERSION PROCEDURES

The following sections discuss the string handling and code conversion procedures in detail.

STRLEN

STRLEN returns the length of a string terminated with a NULL (0) or '$'. The syntax is:

strlen   *buffer*

where *buffer* = legal label name

STRCPY

STRCPY copies one string terminating with a NULL (0) or a '$' to another string. The syntax is:

strcpy   *destination,source*

where *destination* = legal label name
    source = legal label name

STRNCPY

STRNCPY copies one string of *n* bytes to another string. The syntax is:

strncpy   *destination,source*

where *destination* = legal label name
    source = legal label name

MEMSET

MEMSET sets *n* bytes of a string to a specified value. The syntax is:

memset   *buffer,value,number_of_bytes*

where *buffer* = legal label name
    value = memory|immediate
    number_of_bytes = memory|immediate

STRING (EXE Version)   Figure 11-1 presents the macro listing to the specified string handling procedures. Create a file named STRING.MAC and type in Fig. 11-1's macros. Figures 11-2 through 11-5 present the assembly subroutines called from within the string handling macros.

Fig. 11-1. The EXE macro listing to string procedures.

```
;-------------------------------------
;
; Macro: MEMSET buffer,value,number
;
; Description: Sets buffer of size number
;    to value
;

MEMSET MACRO buffer,value,number
        pushx
        push    DI
    IFDIFI <buffer>,<DI>
        lea     AX,buffer
        mov     DI,AX
    ENDIF
    IFDIFI <AX>,<value>
        mov     AX,value
    ENDIF
    IFDIFI <CX>,<number>
        mov     CX,number
    ENDIF
        EXTRN   AMEMSET:NEAR
        call    AMEMSET
        pop     DI
        popx
        ENDM
```

Fig. 11-1 continued.

```
;----------------------------------------
;
; Macro: STRCPY dest,srce
;
; Description: Copy source string to
;    destination string. The source string
;    is terminated with 0 or '$'
;

STRCPY MACRO dest,srce
        push    AX
        push    DX
        push    DI
        push    SI
    IFIDNI <AX>,<dest>
        mov     DI,AX
    ELSEIFIDNI <DI>,<DI>
    ELSE
        lea     DI,dest
    ENDIF
    IFIDNI <DX>,<srce>
        mov     SI,DX
    ELSEIFIDNI <SI>,<SI>
    ELSE
        lea     SI,srce
    ENDIF
        EXTRN   ASTRCPY:NEAR
        call    ASTRCPY
        pop     SI
        pop     DI
        pop     DX
        pop     AX
        ENDM

;----------------------------------------
;
; Macro: STRNCPY dest,srce,num
;
; Description: Copy source string to
;    destination string of num bytes.
;

STRNCPY MACRO dest,srce,num
        push    AX
        push    CX
        push    DX
        push    DI
        push    SI
    IFIDNI <AX>,<dest>
        mov     DI,AX
    ELSEIFIDNI <DI>,<DI>
    ELSE
        lea     DI,dest

    ENDIF
    IFIDNI <DX>,<srce>
        mov     SI,DX
    ELSEIFIDNI <SI>,<SI>
    ELSE
        lea     SI,srce
```

```
        ENDIF
        IFDIFI <CX>,<NUM>
                mov      CX,num
        ENDIF
                EXTRN    ASTRNCPY:NEAR
                call     ASTRNCPY
                pop      SI
                pop      DI
                pop      DX
                pop      CX
                pop      AX
                ENDM


;------------------------------------
;
; Macro: STRLEN buffer
;
; Description: Returns the string length
;   of the buffer not including terminating
;   0 or '$'
;

STRLEN MACRO buffer
                push     BX
        IFDIFI <BX>,<buffer>
                lea      BX,buffer
        ENDIF
                EXTRN    ASTRLEN:NEAR
                call     ASTRLEN
                pop      BX
                ENDM
```

Fig. 11-1 ends.

Fig. 11-2. The EXE source code listing to STRLEN.ASM.

```
;------------------------------------
;
; File Name: STRLEN.ASM
;
; Description: Return the length of a
;   string not including the terminating
;   NULL or '$'
;
INCLUDE SMALL.MAC


        DOSSEG

        .MODEL SMALL

        PROG_CODE

        PUBLIC ASTRLEN

ASTRLEN PROC NEAR
        xor      AX,AX        ; AX = 0
```

```
astrlen1:
        cmp     BYTE PTR [BX],0
        je      exit_strlen

        cmp     BYTE PTR [BX],'$'
        je      exit_strlen

        inc     AX
        inc     BX
        jmp     astrlen1

exit_strlen:
        ret

ASTRLEN ENDP

        END

;--------------------------------------
```

Fig. 11-2 ends.

Fig. 11-3. The EXE source code listing to STRCPY.ASM.

```
;--------------------------------------
;
;
; File Name: STRCPY.ASM
;
; Description: Copy source string to destination
;    string until terminating 0 or '$' is
;    found

INCLUDE SMALL.MAC

        DOSSEG

        .MODEL SMALL

        PROG_CODE

        PUBLIC ASTRCPY

ASTRCPY PROC NEAR
        push    AX
        push    ES
        push    DS
        pop     ES

astrcpy1:
        mov     AL,BYTE PTR [SI]
        cmp     BYTE PTR [SI],0
        je      exit_strcpy
        cmp     BYTE PTR [SI],'$'
        je      exit_strcpy
        mov     BYTE PTR [DI],AL
        inc     SI
        inc     DI
        jmp     astrcpy1
```

```
exit_strcpy:
        pop     ES
        pop     AX

        ret

ASTRCPY ENDP

        END
```

;-------------------------------------

Fig. 11-3 ends.

Fig. 11-4. The EXE source code listing to STRNCPY.ASM.

```
;-------------------------------------
;
; File Name: STRNCPY.ASM
;
; Description: Copy source string to destination
;   string using n number of bytes

INCLUDE SMALL.MAC

        DOSSEG

        .MODEL SMALL

        PROG_CODE

        PUBLIC ASTRNCPY

ASTRNCPY PROC NEAR
        push    AX
        push    ES
        push    DS  ; move DS to ES
        pop     ES
        cld
REP     movsb           ; move the string
        pop     ES
        pop     AX
        ret

ASTRNCPY ENDP

        END
```

;-------------------------------------

Fig. 11-5. The EXE source code listing to MEMSET.ASM.

```
;-------------------------------------
;
; File Name: MEMSET.ASM
;
```

```
; Description: Sets buffer of num bytes
;   to a value
;
; DI holds pointer to buffer
; CX holds number of bytes to change
; AX holds value to change bytes
;

INCLUDE SMALL.MAC


        DOSSEG

        .MODEL SMALL

        PROG_CODE

        PUBLIC AMEMSET

AMEMSET PROC NEAR

        jcxz    exit_memset ; CX = 0 -> exit

        cld                 ; increment fwd
        push    ES
        push    DS          ; DS => ES
        pop     ES

REP     stosb
        pop     ES

exit_memset:
        ret

AMEMSET ENDP

        END

;----------------------------------------
```

Fig. 11-5 ends.

STRING (COM Version)

STRING (COM Version)   Figure 11-6 presents the macro listing to the specified string handling procedures. Create a COM version file named STRING.MAC and type in Fig. 11-6's macros. Figures 11-7 through 11-10 present the assembly subroutines called from within the string handling macros.

Fig. 11-6. The COM macro listing to string procedures.

```
;----------------------------------------
;
; Macro: MEMSET buffer,value,number
;
; Description: Sets buffer of size number
;   to value
;
```

Fig. 11-6 continued.

```
MEMSET MACRO buffer,value,number
        pushx
        push    DI
   IFDIFI <buffer>,<DI>
        lea     AX,buffer
        mov     DI,AX
   ENDIF
   IFDIFI <AX>,<value>
        mov     AX,value
   ENDIF
   IFDIFI <CX>,<number>
        mov     CX,number
   ENDIF
        PUBLIC  AMEMSET
        call    AMEMSET
        pop     DI
        popx
        ENDM


;-------------------------------------
;
; Macro: STRCPY dest,srce
;
; Description: Copy source string to
;   destination string. The source string
;   is terminated with 0 or '$'
;

STRCPY MACRO dest,srce
        push    AX
        push    DX
        push    DI
        push    SI
   IFIDNI <AX>,<dest>
        mov     DI,AX
   ELSEIFIDNI <DI>,<DI>
   ELSE
        lea     DI,dest
   ENDIF
   IFIDNI <DX>,<srce>
        mov     SI,DX
   ELSEIFIDNI <SI>,<SI>
   ELSE
        lea     SI,srce
   ENDIF
        PUBLIC  ASTRCPY
        call    ASTRCPY
        pop     SI
        pop     DI
        pop     DX
        pop     AX
        ENDM


;-------------------------------------
;
; Macro: STRNCPY dest,srce,num
;
; Description: Copy source string to
;   destination string of num bytes.
;
```

```
STRNCPY MACRO dest,srce,num
        push    AX
        push    CX
        push    DX
        push    DI
        push    SI
    IFIDNI <AX>,<dest>
        mov     DI,AX
    ELSEIFIDNI <DI>,<DI>
    ELSE
        lea     DI,dest

    ENDIF
    IFIDNI <DX>,<srce>
        mov     SI,DX
    ELSEIFIDNI <SI>,<SI>
    ELSE
        lea     SI,srce
    ENDIF
    IFDIFI <CX>,<NUM>
        mov     CX,num
    ENDIF
        PUBLIC  ASTRNCPY
        call    ASTRNCPY
        pop     SI
        pop     DI
        pop     DX
        pop     CX
        pop     AX
        ENDM


;-------------------------------------
;
; Macro: STRLEN buffer
;
; Description: Returns the string length
;   of the buffer not including terminating
;   0 or '$'
;

STRLEN MACRO buffer
        push    BX
    IFDIFI <BX>,<buffer>
        lea     BX,buffer
    ENDIF
        PUBLIC  ASTRLEN
        call    ASTRLEN
        pop     BX
        ENDM
```

Fig. 11-6 ends.

Fig. 11-7. The COM source code listing to STRLEN.ASM.

```
;-------------------------------------
;
; File Name: STRLEN.ASM
;
; Description: Return the length of a
```

```
;  string not including the terminating
;  NULL or '$'
;

ASTRLEN PROC NEAR
        xor     AX,AX       ; AX = 0

astrlen1:
        cmp     BYTE PTR [BX],0
        je      exit_strlen

        cmp     BYTE PTR [BX],'$'
        je      exit_strlen

        inc     AX
        inc     BX
        jmp     astrlen1

exit_strlen:
        ret

ASTRLEN ENDP

;-------------------------------------
```

Fig. 11-7 ends.

Fig. 11-8. The COM source code listing to STRCPY.ASM.

```
;-------------------------------------
;
; File Name: STRCPY.ASM
;
; Description: Copy source string to destination
;    string until terminating 0 or '$' is
;    found

ASTRCPY PROC NEAR
        push    AX
        push    ES
        push    DS
        pop     ES

astrcpy1:
        mov     AL,BYTE PTR [SI]
        cmp     BYTE PTR [SI],0
        je      exit_strcpy
        cmp     BYTE PTR [SI],'$'
        je      exit_strcpy
        mov     BYTE PTR [DI],AL
        inc     SI
        inc     DI
        jmp     astrcpy1

exit_strcpy:
        pop     ES
        pop     AX

        ret

ASTRCPY ENDP

;-------------------------------------
```

Fig. 11-9. The COM source code listing to STRNCPY.ASM.

```
;---------------------------------------
;
; File Name: STRNCPY.ASM
;
; Description: Copy source string to destination
;   string using n number of bytes

ASTRNCPY PROC NEAR
        push    AX
        push    ES
        push    DS  ; move DS to ES
        pop     ES
        cld
REP     movsb           ; move the string
        pop     ES
        pop     AX
        ret

ASTRNCPY ENDP


;---------------------------------------
```

Fig. 11-10. The COM source code listing to MEMSET.ASM.

```
;---------------------------------------
;
; File Name: MEMSET.ASM
;
; Description: Sets buffer of num bytes
;   to a value
;
; DI holds pointer to buffer
; CX holds number of bytes to change
; AX holds value to change bytes
;

AMEMSET PROC NEAR

        jcxz    exit_memset ; CX = 0 -> exit

        cld                     ; increment fwd
        push    ES
        push    DS              ; DS => ES
        pop     ES

REP     stosb
        pop     ES

exit_memset:
        ret

AMEMSET ENDP

;---------------------------------------
```

ITOA
ITOHEX

ITOA performs an integer-to-ASCII string conversion. ITOHEX performs an integer-to-ASCII HEX string conversion. The syntax is:

```
itoa     value,buffer,justify
itohex   value,buffer,justify
```

where *value* = memory|immediate
    buffer = legal label name
    justify = immediate

The ITOA and ITOHEX code conversion routines take a 16-bit binary value and convert it to an ASCII string. The ITOA routine is a signed conversion and the ITOHEX is unsigned. Note that if the *justify* parameter is blank the digits are placed in the buffer. If *justify* is equal to 0 then the digits are right justified in five places and non-digit spaces are padded with ' ' characters. If *justify* is equal to 1 then the digits are right justified in five places and non-digit spaces are padded with '0' characters.

Create a file called STDLIB.MAC and add the code conversion macros to that file. Remember to add STDLIB.MAC to your SMALL.MAC file.

ITOA and ITOHEX (EXE Version)   Figure 11-11 presents the macro listing for the EXE versions of ITOA and ITOHEX. Figure 11-12 and Fig. 11-13 present the assembly subroutines called from within the ITOA and ITOHEX macros.

Fig. 11-11. The EXE macro listing to ITOA and ITOHEX.

```
;-------------------------------------
;
; Macro: ITOA val, buffer, justify
;
; Description - signed integer to ascii
;
ITOA MACRO val,string,just
        pushbcd
    IFDIFI <AX>,<val>
        mov       AX,val
    ENDIF
    IFDIFI <BX>,<string>
        lea       BX,string
    ENDIF
        EXTRN     AITOA:NEAR
        call      AITOA
    IFB <just>
        popbcd
    ELSE
        mov       AX,just
        finum     BX,AX
        popbcd
    ENDIF
```

Fig. 11-11 continued.

```
        ENDM


;------------------------------------
;
; Macro: FINUM buffer,lead
;
; Description: Place an ascii buffer
;  holding an integer right justified
;  into a field of width of 6 spaces with
;  leading chars of (0) spaces or (1) zeros.
;
FINUM MACRO buffer,lead
        push    SI
        push    DI
        pushbcd
    IFDIFI <BX>,<buffer>
        lea     BX,buffer
    ENDIF
    IFDIFI <AX>,<lead>
        mov     AX,lead
    ENDIF
        EXTRN   AFINUM:NEAR
        call    AFINUM
        popbcd
        pop     DI
        pop     SI
        ENDM

;------------------------------------
;
; Macro: ITOHEX val, buffer, justify
;
; Description - signed integer to ascii
;
ITOHEX MACRO val,string,just
        pushbcd
    IFDIFI <AX>,<val>
        mov     AX,val
    ENDIF
    IFDIFI <BX>,<string>
        lea     BX,string
    ENDIF
        EXTRN   AITOHEX:NEAR
        call    AITOHEX
    IFB <just>
        popbcd
    ELSE
        mov     AX,just
        finumhex BX,AX
        popbcd
    ENDIF
        ENDM

;------------------------------------
;
; Macro: FINUMHEX buffer,lead
;
```

```
; Description: Place an ascii buffer
;   holding an integer right justified
;   into a field of width of 6 spaces with
;   leading chars of (0) spaces or (1) zeros.
;

FINUMHEX MACRO buffer,lead
        push    SI
        push    DI
        pushbcd
    IFDIFI <BX>,<buffer>
        lea     BX,buffer
    ENDIF
    IFDIFI <AX>,<lead>
        mov     AX,lead
    ENDIF
        EXTRN   AFINUMHEX:NEAR
        call    AFINUMHEX
        popbcd
        pop     DI
        pop     SI
        ENDM
```

Fig. 11-11 ends.

Fig. 11-12. The EXE source code listing to ITOA.ASM.

```
;-------------------------------------
;
; File Name: ITOA.ASM
;
; Integer to ascii -> no greater than unsigned 8FFFF
;
; On entry: AX holds 16 bit number
;           BX holds offset to buffer at least 8 bytes
;           DX holds 0: no block format
;                    1: block format
;
INCLUDE SMALL.MAC

        DOSSEG

        .MODEL SMALL

        PROG_DATA

aitoaptr DW     0
aitoaax  DW     0
aitoaneg DB     0
aitoabuf DB     10 DUP(0)
finumtog DW     0
finumptr DW     0
finumb   DB     8 DUP(0)
finumlen DW     0

        PROG_CODE

        PUBLIC AITOA,AFINUM

BPROCEDURE aitoa
```

Fig. 11-12 continued.

```
                xor     DX,DX        ; 0 => DX
                mov     aitoaneg,0 ; clear flag
                mov     aitoaptr,BX ; save pointer to buffer
                mov     aitoaax,AX ; save 16 bit value
                lea     BX,aitoabuf ; set pointer to local buffer
;
                cmp     AX,0        ; is AX negative
                jge     isposi1    ; jump on positive
                neg     AX          ; AX is hegative so turn positive
                mov     aitoaneg,1 ; set negative flag
isposi1:

                add     BX,6        ; adjust pointer in aitoabuf
                mov     CX,10       ; divisor
                cmp     AX,0        ; special case of 0
                je      itoa_0      ; place '0' in buffer
aitoa1:
                cmp     AX,0        ; At last digit?
                je      aitoa2      ; yes do pickup and exit
                div     CX          ; divide by 10
                add     DX,'0'      ; make binary ascii
                mov     BYTE PTR [BX],DL ; move ascii digit to buffer
                dec     BX          ; back up pointer
                xor     DX,DX       ; clear DX
                jmp     aitoa1      ; get next digit
aitoa2:
                cmp     aitoaneg,0
                je      isposi2
                mov     BYTE PTR [BX],'-'
                jmp     exit_aitoa
isposi2:
                inc     BX
                jmp     exit_aitoa
itoa_0:
                mov     BYTE PTR [BX],'0'
exit_aitoa:
                mov     AX,aitoaptr
                mov     DI,AX
                mov     SI,BX
                strcpy  DI,SI
                mov     AX,aitoaptr
                ret
EPROCEDURE aitoa

; Name: FINUM
;
;
; Description: (F)ormat (I)nteger (NUM)ber
;   Take an integer number and right justify
;   into buffer with leading 0s or spaces
;

AFINUM  PROC    NEAR
                mov     finumptr,BX ; save ptr to ascii int
                mov     finumtog,AX ; save fill toggle
                strlen  BX          ; get length of ascii int to AX
                mov     finumlen,AX ; and save
                cmp     finumtog,1  ; toggle set to ' ' fill
                je      finum2      ; yes -> jump
                memset  finumb,'0',6 ; otherwise '0' fill
```

```
        mov     finumb,' '    ; for minus
        jmp     finum3

finum2:
        memset  finumb,' ',6  ; ' ' fill

finum3:
        mov     BX,finumptr   ; left justify minus
        cmp     BYTE PTR [BX],'-' ; Negative number?
        jne     finum4        ; NO -> jump
        mov     finumb,'-'    ; place '-' at left column
        inc     finumptr      ; bypass '-' in string &
        sub1    finumlen      ; decrease ascii num len

finum4:
        lea     CX,finumb     ; set DI ptr to finumb
        mov     DI,CX
        add     DI,6          ; DI points to end of finumb
        sub     DI,finumlen   ; right just ascii int in finumb
        mov     BX,finumptr   ; move ptr to ascii int to SI
        mov     SI,BX
        strcpy  DI,SI         ; copy ascii int to finumb
        lea     CX,finumb     ; return pointer to finumb in
        mov     SI,CX
        mov     CX,aitoaptr
        mov     DI,CX
        strncpy DI,SI,6
        mov     AX,aitoaptr   ; AX reg

        ret
AFINUM  ENDP

        END
```

;-------------------------------------

Fig. 11-12 ends.

Fig. 11-13. The EXE source code listing to ITOHEX.ASM.

```
;-------------------------------------
;
; File Name: ITOHEX.ASM
;
; Integer to HEX ascii
;
; On entry: AX holds 16 bit number
;           BX holds offset to buffer at least 8 bytes
;           DX holds 0: no block format
;                   1: block format
;

INCLUDE SMALL.MAC

        DOSSEG

        .MODEL SMALL

        PROG_DATA
```

Fig. 11-13 continued.

```
aitohexptr DW    0
aitohexax  DW    0
aitohexb   DB    10 DUP(0)
ihextab    DB    '0123456789ABCDEF',0
finumhextog DW   0
finumhexptr DW   0
finumhexb        DB 10 DUP(0)
finumhexlen DW   0

        PROG_CODE

        PUBLIC AITOHEX,AFINUMHEX

BPROCEDURE aitohex
        memset  aitohexb,0,10
        xor     DX,DX
        mov     aitohexptr,BX
        mov     aitohexax,AX
        lea     BX,aitohexb

        add     BX,4        ; adjust pointer in buffer
        mov     CX,16       ; divisor
        cmp     AX,0        ; special case of 0
        je      itohex_0     ; place '0' in buffer

aitohex1:
        cmp     AX,0        ; At last digit?
        je      aitohex2     ; yes do pickup and exit
        div     CX          ; divide by 10
        push    AX
        push    BX
        xor     AX,AX
        lea     BX,ihextab
        mov     AL,DL
        xlat                ; ascii hex to AL
        pop     BX
        mov     BYTE PTR [BX],AL ; move ascii digit to buffer
        pop     AX
        dec     BX          ; back up pointer
        xor     DX,DX       ; clear DX
        jmp     aitohex1     ; get next digit

aitohex2:
        inc     BX
        jmp     exit_aitohex

itohex_0:
        mov     BYTE PTR [BX],'0'

exit_aitohex:
        mov     AX,aitohexptr
        mov     DI,AX
        mov     SI,BX
        strcpy  DI,SI
        mov     AX,aitohexptr
        ret
EPROCEDURE aitohex

;
; Name: FINUMHEX
```

```
;
; Description: (F)ormat (I)nteger (NUM)ber int (HEX)idecimal
;   Take an integer number and right justify
;   into buffer with leading 0s or spaces

AFINUMHEX        PROC    NEAR
        memset  finumhexb,0,10
        mov     finumhexptr,BX    ; save ptr to ascii int
        mov     finumhextog,AX    ; save fill toggle
        strlen  BX                ; get length of ascii int to AX
        mov     finumhexlen,AX    ; and save
        cmp     finumhextog,1     ; toggle set to ' ' fill
        je      finumhex2         ; yes -> jump
        memset  finumhexb,'0',4   ; otherwise '0' fill
;       mov     finumhexb,' '     ; for minus
        jmp     finumhex3

finumhex2:
        memset  finumhexb,' ',4   ; ' ' fill

finumhex3:
        lea     CX,finumhexb      ; set DI ptr to finumhexb
        mov     DI,CX
        add     DI,3              ; DI points to end of finumhexb
        sub     DI,finumhexlen    ; right just ascii int in finumhexb
        mov     BX,finumhexptr    ; move ptr to ascii int to SI
        mov     SI,BX
        inc     DI
        strcpy  DI,SI             ; copy ascii int to finumhexb
        lea     AX,finumhexb      ; return pointer to finumhexb in
        mov     SI,AX
        mov     AX,aitohexptr
        mov     DI,AX
        strncpy DI,SI,4
        mov     AX,finumhexptr

        ret

AFINUMHEX ENDP

        END

;-------------------------------------
```

Fig. 11-13 ends.

ITOA and ITOHEX (COM Version)   Figure 11-14 presents the COM version macro listing to ITOA and ITOHEX. Figures 11-15 and 11-16 present the COM version source code listings to ITOA.ASM and ITOHEX.ASM.

Figure 11-17 presents the source code listing to EPROG25.ASM. This ITOA EXE demonstration program prints a box using the '−' and '+' characters and fills the box with integers and pointers to text held in 'messtab'. Figure 11-18 presents the source code listing to the ITOA COM version demonstration program CPROG25.ASM.

Fig. 11-14. The COM macro listing to ITOA and ITOHEX.

```
;-------------------------------------
;
; Macro: ITOA val, buffer, justify
;
; Description - signed integer to ascii
;

ITOA MACRO val,string,just
        pushbcd
    IFDIFI <AX>,<val>
        mov     AX,val
    ENDIF
    IFDIFI <BX>,<string>
        lea     BX,string
    ENDIF
        PUBLIC  AITOA
        call    AITOA
    IFB <just>
        popbcd
    ELSE
        mov     AX,just
        finum   BX,AX
        popbcd
    ENDIF
        ENDM

;-------------------------------------
;
; Macro: FINUM buffer,lead
;
; Description: Place an ascii buffer
;  holding an integer right justified
;  into a field of width of 6 spaces with
;  leading chars of (0) spaces or (1) zeros.
;

FINUM MACRO buffer,lead
        push    SI
        push    DI
        pushbcd
    IFDIFI <BX>,<buffer>
        lea     BX,buffer
    ENDIF
    IFDIFI <AX>,<lead>
        mov     AX,lead
    ENDIF
        PUBLIC  AFINUM
        call    AFINUM
        popbcd
        pop     DI
        pop     SI
        ENDM

;-------------------------------------
;
; Macro: ITOHEX val, buffer, justify
;
; Description - signed integer to ascii
;
```

```
ITOHEX MACRO val,string,just
        pushbcd
   IFDIFI <AX>,<val>
        mov     AX,val
   ENDIF
   IFDIFI <BX>,<string>
        lea     BX,string
   ENDIF
        PUBLIC  AITOHEX
        call    AITOHEX
   IFB <just>
        popbcd
   ELSE
        mov     AX,just
        finumhex BX,AX
        popbcd
   ENDIF
        ENDM
;-----------------------------------
;
; Macro: FINUMHEX buffer,lead
;
; Description: Place an ascii buffer
;  holding an integer right justified
;  into a field of width of 6 spaces with
;  leading chars of (0) spaces or (1) zeros.
;
;
FINUMHEX MACRO buffer,lead
        push    SI
        push    DI
        pushbcd
   IFDIFI <BX>,<buffer>
        lea     BX,buffer
   ENDIF
   IFDIFI <AX>,<lead>
        mov     AX,lead
   ENDIF
        PUBLIC  AFINUMHEX
        call    AFINUMHEX
        popbcd
        pop     DI
        pop     SI
        ENDM
```

Fig. 11-14 ends.

Fig. 11-15. The COM source code listing to ITOA.ASM.

```
;-----------------------------------
;
; File Name: ITOA.ASM
;
; Integer to ascii -> no greater than unsigned 8FFFF
;
; On entry: AX holds 16 bit number
;           BX holds offset to buffer at least 8 bytes
;           DX holds 0: no block format
;                    1: block format
;
```

Fig. 11-15 continued.

```
BPROCEDURE aitoa

        jmp aitoa_1
aitoaptr DW     0
aitoaax  DW     0
aitoaneg DB     0
aitoabuf DB     10 DUP(0)
finumtog DW     0
finumptr DW     0
finumb  DB      8 DUP(0)
finumlen DW     0

aitoa_1:

        xor     DX,DX       ; 0 => DX
        mov     aitoaneg,0 ; clear flag
        mov     aitoaptr,BX ; save pointer to buffer
        mov     aitoaax,AX ; save 16 bit value
        lea     BX,aitoabuf ; set pointer to local buffer
;
        cmp     AX,0        ; is AX negative
        jge     isposi1     ; jump on positive
        neg     AX          ; AX is hegative so turn positive
        mov     aitoaneg,1 ; set negative flag
isposi1:

        add     BX,6        ; adjust pointer in aitoabuf
        mov     CX,10       ; divisor
        cmp     AX,0        ; special case of 0
        je      itoa_0      ; place '0' in buffer
aitoa1:
        cmp     AX,0        ; At last digit?
        je      aitoa2      ; yes do pickup and exit
        div     CX          ; divide by 10
        add     DX,'0'      ; make binary ascii
        mov     BYTE PTR [BX],DL ; move ascii digit to buffer
        dec     BX          ; back up pointer
        xor     DX,DX       ; clear DX
        jmp     aitoa1      ; get next digit
aitoa2:
        cmp     aitoaneg,0
        je      isposi2
        mov     BYTE PTR [BX],'-'
        jmp     exit_aitoa
isposi2:
        inc     BX
        jmp     exit_aitoa
itoa_0:
        mov     BYTE PTR [BX],'0'
exit_aitoa:
        mov     AX,aitoaptr
        mov     DI,AX
        mov     SI,BX
        strcpy  DI,SI
        mov     AX,aitoaptr
        ret
EPROCEDURE aitoa

; Name: FINUM
;
```

```
; Description: (F)ormat (I)nteger (NUM)ber
;   Take an integer number and right justify
;   into buffer with leading 0s or spaces
;

AFINUM  PROC    NEAR
        mov     finumptr,BX     ; save ptr to ascii int
        mov     finumtog,AX     ; save fill toggle
        strlen  BX              ; get length of ascii int to AX
        mov     finumlen,AX     ; and save
        cmp     finumtog,1      ; toggle set to ' ' fill
        je      finum2          ; yes -> jump
        memset  finumb,'0',6    ; otherwise '0' fill
        mov     finumb,' '      ; for minus
        jmp     finum3

finum2:
        memset  finumb,' ',6    ; ' ' fill

finum3:
        mov     BX,finumptr     ; left justify minus
        cmp     BYTE PTR [BX],'-' ; Negative number?
        jne     finum4          ; NO -> jump
        mov     finumb,'-'      ; place '-' at left column
        inc     finumptr        ; bypass '-' in string &
        sub1    finumlen        ; decrease ascii num len

finum4:
        lea     CX,finumb       ; set DI ptr to finumb
        mov     DI,CX
        add     DI,6            ; DI points to end of finumb
        sub     DI,finumlen     ; right just ascii int in finumb
        mov     BX,finumptr     ; move ptr to ascii int to SI
        mov     SI,BX
        strcpy  DI,SI           ; copy ascii int to finumb
        lea     CX,finumb       ; return pointer to finumb in
        mov     SI,CX
        mov     CX,aitoaptr
        mov     DI,CX
        strncpy DI,SI,6
        mov     AX,aitoaptr     ; AX reg

        ret
AFINUM  ENDP
```

;-------------------------------------

Fig. 11-15 ends.

Fig. 11-16. The COM source code listing to ITOHEX.ASM.

;-------------------------------------
;
; File Name: ITOHEX.ASM
;
; Integer to HEX ascii
;
; On entry: AX holds 16 bit number
;   BX holds offset to buffer at least 8 bytes

Fig. 11-16 continued.

```
;              DX holds 0: no block format
;                      1: block format
;


BPROCEDURE aitohex
        jmp       itohex_1
aitohexptr DW     0
aitohexax  DW     0
aitohexb   DB     10 DUP(0)
ihextab    DB     '0123456789ABCDEF',0
finumhextog DW    0
finumhexptr DW    0
finumhexb         DB 10 DUP(0)
finumhexlen DW    0

itohex_1:
        memset    aitohexb,0,10
        xor       DX,DX
        mov       aitohexptr,BX
        mov       aitohexax,AX
        lea       BX,aitohexb

        add       BX,4       ; adjust pointer in buffer
        mov       CX,16      ; divisor
        cmp       AX,0       ; special case of 0
        je        itohex_0    ; place '0' in buffer

aitohex1:
        cmp       AX,0       ; At last digit?
        je        aitohex2    ; yes do pickup and exit
        div       CX         ; divide by 10
        push      AX
        push      BX
        xor       AX,AX
        lea       BX,ihextab
        mov       AL,DL
        xlat                 ; ascii hex to AL
        pop       BX
        mov       BYTE PTR [BX],AL ; move ascii digit to buffer
        pop       AX
        dec       BX         ; back up pointer
        xor       DX,DX      ; clear DX
        jmp       aitohex1    ; get next digit

aitohex2:
        inc       BX
        jmp       exit_aitohex

itohex_0:
        mov       BYTE PTR [BX],'0'

exit_aitohex:
        mov       AX,aitohexptr
        mov       DI,AX
        mov       SI,BX
        strcpy    DI,SI
        mov       AX,aitohexptr
        ret
EPROCEDURE aitohex
```

```
;
; Name: FINUMHEX
;
; Description: (F)ormat (I)nteger (NUM)ber int (HEX)idecimal
;   Take an integer number and right justify
;   into buffer with leading 0s or spaces

AFINUMHEX       PROC    NEAR
        memset  finumhexb,0,10
        mov     finumhexptr,BX    ; save ptr to ascii int
        mov     finumhextog,AX    ; save fill toggle
        strlen  BX                ; get length of ascii int to AX
        mov     finumhexlen,AX    ; and save
        cmp     finumhextog,1     ; toggle set to ' ' fill
        je      finumhex2         ; yes -> jump
        memset  finumhexb,'0',4   ; otherwise '0' fill
;       mov     finumhexb,' '     ; for minus
        jmp     finumhex3

finumhex2:
        memset  finumhexb,' ',4   ; ' ' fill

finumhex3:
        lea     CX,finumhexb      ; set DI ptr to finumhexb
        mov     DI,CX
        add     DI,3              ; DI points to end of finumhexb
        sub     DI,finumhexlen    ; right just ascii int in finumhexb
        mov     BX,finumhexptr    ; move ptr to ascii int to SI
        mov     SI,BX
        inc     DI
        strcpy  DI,SI             ; copy ascii int to finumhexb
        lea     AX,finumhexb      ; return pointer to finumhexb in
        mov     SI,AX
        mov     AX,aitohexptr
        mov     DI,AX
        strncpy DI,SI,4
        mov     AX,finumhexptr

        ret

AFINUMHEX ENDP

;-------------------------------------
```

Fig. 11-16 ends.

Fig. 11-17. The source code listing to EPROG25.ASM.

```
;-------------------------------------
;
; File Name: EPROG25.ASM
;
INCLUDE SMALL.MAC

        PROG_EXE

        PROG_DATA

row     DW      5                 ; set row to 5
```

```
col      DW      10                      ; set column to 5
messtab DW       mess1                   ; table of pointers - message 1
         DW      75                      ; Value attached to message 1
         DW      mess2                   ; pointer to message 2
         DW      25867                   ; value attached to messgae 2
         DW      mess3                   ; pointer to message 3
         DW      -853                    ; value attached to message 3
         DW      mess4                   ; pointer to message 4
         DW      0                       ; value attached to message 4
         DW      mess5                   ; pointer to message 5
         DW      -31985                  ; data attached to message 5
mess1    DB      'The value of VAL1 variable is:    ',0
mess2    DB      'The value of AX general register is: ',0
mess3    DB      'The value of SI index register is:   ',0
mess4    DB      'The value of BP base pointer reg. is: ',0
mess5    DB      'The value of VAL5 variable is:       ',0
titlet   DB      '+---------------------------------------------+',0
title0   DB      '|            TABLE OF  MADE UP VALUES          |',0
title1   DB      '| ------------------------------------------- |',0
title2   DB      '|                                             |',0
buffer   DB      10 DUP(0)

         PROG_CODE

         vidinit
         clrscreen                  ; clear the screen
         swrite  2,8,titlet         ; and print the box
         swrite  3,8,title0         ;
         swrite  4,8,title1
         swrite  5,8,title2
         swrite  6,8,title2
         swrite  7,8,title2
         swrite  8,8,title2
         swrite  9,8,title2
         swrite  10,8,titlet
         setptr  DBASE_PTR,messtab ; set DBASE_PTR to table of pointers
BLOOP    report,5                  ; report LOOP for 5 iterations
         memset  buffer,0,10        ; clear buffer
         mvcur   row,col            ; move cursor
         getptr  SI,DBASE_PTR       ; get pointer from table of pointers
         puts    SI                 ; print first message
         add2    DBASE_PTR          ; adjust pointer by + 2
         mov     AX,WORD PTR [DBASE_PTR] ; integer value to AX
         itoa    AX,buffer,1        ; ASCII right justify with SPACE pad
         puts                       ; puts string of returned ptr to scrn
         add2    DBASE_PTR          ; adjust pointer by + 2
         add1    row                ; print next row
ELOOP    report                    ; END of report loop
         mvcur   23,0               ; move cursor screen bottom
         END_EXE

         END

;-------------------------------------
```

Fig. 11-17 ends.

Fig. 11-18. The source code listing to CPROG25.ASM.

```
;-----------------------------------
;
; File Name: CPROG25.ASM
;

INCLUDE SMALL.MAC

          PROG_COM

row      DW     5                   ; set row to 5
col      DW     10                  ; set column to 5
messtab  DW     mess1               ; table of pointers - message 1
         DW     75                  ; Value attached to message 1
         DW     mess2               ; pointer to message 2
         DW     25867               ; value attached to messgae 2
         DW     mess3               ; pointer to message 3
         DW     -853                ; value attached to message 3
         DW     mess4               ; pointer to message 4
         DW     0                   ; value attached to message 4
         DW     mess5               ; pointer to message 5
         DW     -31985              ; data attached to message 5
mess1    DB     'The value of VAL1 variable is:       ',0
mess2    DB     'The value of AX general register is: ',0
mess3    DB     'The value of SI index register is:   ',0
mess4    DB     'The value of BP base pointer reg. is: ',0
mess5    DB     'The value of VAL5 variable is:       ',0
titlet   DB     '+-------------------------------------------------+',0
title0   DB     '|            TABLE OF  MADE UP VALUES             |',0
title1   DB     '| ------------------------------------------------- |',0
title2   DB     '|                                                 |',0
buffer   DB     10 DUP(0)

program:

          vidinit
          clrscreen                 ; clear the screen
          swrite  2,8,titlet        ; and print the box
          swrite  3,8,title0        ;
          swrite  4,8,title1
          swrite  5,8,title2
          swrite  6,8,title2
          swrite  7,8,title2
          swrite  8,8,title2
          swrite  9,8,title2
          swrite  10,8,titlet
          setptr  DBASE_PTR,messtab ; set DBASE_PTR to table of pointers
BLOOP     report,5                  ; report LOOP for 5 iterations
          memset  buffer,0,10       ; clear buffer
          mvcur   row,col           ; move cursor
          getptr  SI,DBASE_PTR      ; get pointer from table of pointers
          puts    SI                ; print first message
          add2    DBASE_PTR         ; adjust pointer by + 2
          mov     AX,WORD PTR [DBASE_PTR] ; integer value to AX
          itoa    AX,buffer,1       ; ASCII right justify with SPACE pad
          puts                      ; puts string of returned ptr to scrn
          add2    DBASE_PTR         ; adjust pointer by + 2
          add1    row               ; print next row
ELOOP     report                    ; END of report loop
          mvcur   23,0              ; move cursor screen bottom
```

```
              COM_TO_DOS

     L_VIDINIT
     L_MVCUR
     L_PUTS
     L_PUTCHAR
     L_ITOA
     L_STRCPY
     L_STRNCPY
     L_STRLEN
     L_MEMSET
     L_CLRSCREEN

              END_COM

;-------------------------------------
```

Fig. 11-18 ends.

12

Reading a Text String from the Keyboard

Although DOS provides an interrupt function to read a string from the keyboard, I never felt satisfied with its performance. In this chapter a procedure named PROMPT will be presented in Fig. 12-7 (EXE version) and Fig. 12-9 (COM version). PROMPT allows the user to place the cursor at a screen location and then enter a text string of n bytes in length. This text string is placed in a buffer. The Enter key and Escape key are used to terminate the PROMPT procedure. If Enter is pressed, PROMPT returns a value of 1 (TRUE) in RET_VAL (AX register). If Escape is pressed then PROMPT returns a value of 0 (FALSE) in RET_VAL (AX register).

Before the PROMPT procedure is presented, three instructive and preparatory procedures must be presented. GETKEY is a procedure that waits for a key press and then returns both the character and scan codes. Having the key's scan code available allows for very easy processing of non-ASCII key selections (Function keys, Enter, Escape, etc. . .).

The ISPRINT procedure tests to see if the character value falls between ' ' and '~'. If the value tested falls between the stated parameters then the value is returned in RET_VAL (AX register) and remains unchanged. If the tested value falls outside the boundaries then a value of 0 (FALSE) is returned in RET_VAL (AX register). Note that PROMPT may easily be modified to permit the entry of, say, numerical digits or hex digits. All you need to do to change PROMPT to an INPUT_NUMBER procedure is simply change the boundary values in ISPRINT to '0' and '9' and rename ISPRINT to ISDIGIT.

The WTOBYTE procedure takes a word value contained in memory and casts it to a BYTE also held in memory.

TEXT STRING READ PROCEDURES

The following sections describe the CHUCK procedures used to read a text string from the keyboard.

GETKEY

GETKEY waits for a key press and returns the key's character and scan code values. The syntax is:

getkey   *key*

where *key* = memory

If GETKEY is invoked without any parameters the character code is returned in AL and the scan code is returned in AH (RET_VAL is AH and AL). If GETKEY is invoked with a parameter (as in the syntax example) then the scan and character values are returned in the WORD sized parameter (*key* in the syntax example).

Because GETKEY does not call a subroutine from within the macro, the EXE version and the COM version for GETKEY are identical. Figure 12-1 presents the macro listing to GETKEY. Remember to place the GETKEY macro in your KEYBOARD.MAC file.

Fig. 12-1. The EXE and COM macro listing to GETKEY.

```
;;--------------------------------------
;;
;; Macro: GETKEY
;;
;; Descritpion: Use BIOS to
;;   wait and get a character's
;;   char (AL) & scan code (AH)
;;
GETKEY MACRO key_val
    IFB <key_val>
            mov     AX,0
            int     16h
    ELSE
            mov     AX,0
            int     16h
            mov     key_val,AX
    ENDIF
            ENDM
```

ISPRINT

ISPRINT tests to see if a WORD value falls between ' ' and '~'. The syntax is:

isprint   *value*

where *value* = memory

ISPRINT is useful for determining if a WORD in memory holds a legal printable character. If the WORD in memory holds a legal printable character then the unchanged WORD value is returned in RET_VAL. If the value held in memory fall outside the boundaries of ' ' and '~' then a value of 0 (FALSE) is returned in RET_VAL.

Create a file named CTYPE.MAC and place the ISPRINT macro in that file. Also, modify the SMALL.MAC file to now include CTYPE.MAC.

ISPRINT (EXE Version) Figure 12-2 presents the EXE version of the macro listing for ISPRINT and Fig. 12-3 presents the EXE version of the listing to ISPRINT.ASM.

Fig. 12-2. The EXE macro listing to ISPRINT.

```
;;------------------------------------
;;
;; Macro: ISPRINT cval
;;
;; Description:
;;
;;  Checks to see if cval is located in the
;;  sets of: ' '...'~'  Returns
;;  the character if TRUE and a 0 if FALSE
;;

ISPRINT MACRO cval
   IFNB <cval>
      IFDIFI <AX>,<cval>
        mov     AX,cval
      ENDIF
   ENDIF
        EXTRN   AISPRINT:NEAR
        call    aisprint
        ENDM
```

Fig. 12-3. The EXE source code listing to ISPRINT.ASM.

```
;------------------------------------
;
; File Name: ISPRINT.ASM
;
; Description:
;  Checks to see if AX value lies in the
;  set of 'A' to 'Z'
;

INCLUDE SMALL.MAC

        DOSSEG

        .MODEL  SMALL

        PROG_CODE

        PUBLIC  AISPRINT

AISPRINT PROC NEAR
        BIFEGT  isprint1,AX,' '
                GOTO    isprint1a
        EIF     isprint1
        jmp     notisprint
```

```
isprint1a:
        BIFELT  isprint2,AX,'~'
                GOTO    yesisprint
        EIF     isprint2

notisprint:
        mov     AX,0
yesisprint:
        ret

AISPRINT ENDP

        END

;-------------------------------------
```

Fig. 12-3 ends.

ISPRINT (COM Version)

Figure 12-4 presents the COM version listing for the ISPRINT macro and Fig. 12-5 presents the listing to the COM version of ISPRINT.ASM.

Fig. 12-4. The COM macro listing to ISPRINT.

```
;-------------------------------------
;
; Macro: ISPRINT cval
;
; Description:
;
;   Checks to see if cval is located in the
;   sets of: ' '...'~' Returns
;   the character if TRUE and a 0 if FALSE
;
ISPRINT MACRO cval
    IFNB <cval>
        IFDIFI <AX>,<cval>
            mov     AX,cval
        ENDIF
    ENDIF
            PUBLIC  AISPRINT
            call    aisprint
            ENDM
```

Fig. 12-5. The COM source code listing to ISPRINT.ASM.

```
;-------------------------------------
;
; File Name: ISPRINT.ASM
;
; Description:
;   Checks to see if AX value lies in the
;   set of 'A' to 'Z'
;
AISPRINT PROC NEAR
```

```
            BIFEGT  isprint1,AX,' '
                    GOTO    isprint1a
            EIF     isprint1
            jmp     notisprint
isprint1a:
            BIFELT  isprint2,AX,'~'
                    GOTO    yesisprint
            EIF     isprint2
notisprint:
            mov     AX,0
yesisprint:
            ret
AISPRINT ENDP

;---------------------------------------
```

Fig. 12-5 ends.

WTOBYTE

WTOBYTE moves the least significant byte of a WORD held in memory to a BYTE held in memory. The syntax is:

wtobyte   *byte_val,word_val*

where *byte_val* = memory
      word_val = memory

As WTOBYTE does not call a subroutine from within the macro the EXE version and the COM version of WTUBYTE are identical. Figure 12-6 presents the macro listing of WTOBYTE.

Fig. 12-6. The EXE and COM macro listing to WTOBYTE.

```
;;----------------------------------------
;; Macro: WTOBYTE byte_val,word_val
;;
;; Description:
;;  Places LSB of word_val into byte_val
;;
;; Cautions: AX register may not be used
;;   to hold source or dest data
WTOBYTE MACRO   byte_val,word_val
        push    AX
        mov     AX,word_val
        mov     byte_val,AL
        pop     AX
        ENDM
```

PROMPT

PROMPT moves the cursor to a specified screen location and then gets a string from the keyboard. The syntax is:

prompt   *row,col,string,length*

where *row*   = immediate
     col   = immediate
   string = legal label name
  length = immediate

PROMPT places the cursor at row, col and then allows the user to enter a text string of length bytes. The user may terminate PROMPT by pressing the Enter key or Escape key. Enter returns a value of 1 (TRUE) in RET_VAL and Escape returns a value of 0 (FALSE) in RET_VAL.

PROMPT (EXE Version)   Figure 12-7 presents the EXE version of the macro listing to PROMPT and Fig. 12-8 presents the EXE version listing to PROMPT.ASM.

Fig. 12-7. The EXE macro listing to PROMPT.

```
;;-------------------------------------
;; Macro: PROMPT row,col,buffer,length
;;
;; Description:
;;  Moves the cursor to row,col and
;;  allows the user to enter a string
;;  of length bytes into buffer
PROMPT MACRO row,col,buffer,length
        pushbcd
   IFDIFI <AX>,<row>
        mov       AX,row
   ENDIF
   IFDIFI <DX>,<col>
        mov       DX,col
   ENDIF
   IFDIFI <BX>,<buffer>
        lea       BX,buffer
   ENDIF
   IFDIFI <CX>,<length>
        mov       CX,length
   ENDIF
        EXTRN     APROMPT:NEAR
        call      aprompt
        popbcd
        ENDM
```

Fig. 12-8. The EXE source code listing to PROMPT.ASM.

```
;-------------------------------------
;
; File Name: PROMPT.ASM
;

INCLUDE SMALL.MAC

        DOSSEG

        .MODEL SMALL
```

Fig. 12-8 continued.

```
            PROG_DATA

apcol   DW      0
aprow   DW      0
apstart DW      0
apstop  DW      0
apkey   DW      0
apexit  DW      0
apval   DW      0
apbyte  DB      0,0


            PROG_CODE

            PUBLIC  APROMPT

BPROCEDURE aprompt
;
;   relocate parameters to memory
;
        mov     [aprow],AX
        mov     [apcol],DX
        mov     [apstart],DX
        mov     [apstop],DX
        add     [apstop],CX
        setv0   [apexit]
BELOOP  apromptl1
;
; adjust cursor location
;
        mvcur   [aprow],[apcol]
;
; get scan and character code
;
        getkey  [apkey]
;
; filter key stroke
;
        SWITCH      swprompt1,[apkey]
;
; call procedure 'prisenter' on ENTER key selected
;
            CASE    swprompt1,prisenter,E_CR
;
; call procedure 'prisescape' on ESCAPE key selected
;
            CASE    swprompt1,prisescape,ESCAPE
;
; otherwise call procedure 'priskey' on other keys
;
            DEFAULT swprompt1,priskey

            ESWITCH swprompt1
;
; exit loop on exit flag set
;
        BIFE    aprompte1,[apexit],1
            EBREAK  apromptl1
        EIF     aprompte1
EELOOP  apromptl1
;
```

Fig. 12-8 continued.

```
; return prompt status value
;

        RETURN   [apval]

EPROCEDURE aprompt


;
; ENTER key selected so exit and return 1 (TRUE)
;

BPROCEDURE prisenter
        setv    [apexit],1
        setv    [apval],1
EPROCEDURE prisenter


;
; ESCAPE key selected so exit and return 0 (FALSE)
;

BPROCEDURE prisescape
        setv    [apexit],1
        setv    [apval],0
EPROCEDURE prisescape


;
; Evaluate key press
;

BPROCEDURE priskey
;
; mask scan code
;

        and     [apkey],00FFh
;
; is the code printable character?
;

        isprint [apkey]
;
; if character is printable
;

        BIFTRUE apcomp1,ax
;
; if column is less than right max
;

        BIFLT apcomp3,[apcol],[apstop]
;
; adjust cursor
;

                mvcur   [aprow],[apcol]
;
; putchar the character to the screen
;

                putchar [apkey]
;
; case WORD (in memory) value to BYTE (in memory)
;

                WTOBYTE [apbyte],[apkey]
;
```

```
; ASCII value to buffer
;
                setv    AL,[apbyte]
                mov     BYTE PTR[BX],AL
;
; adjust pointer in buffer
;
                add1    BX
;
; adjust column counter
;
                add1    [apcol]
        EIF     apcomp3
        EIF     apcomp1
;
; if the key is backspace
;
        BIFE    acomp4,[apkey],8
;
; and not at column start
;
            BIFGT acomp5,[apcol],[apstart]
;
; decrement column
;
                sub1    [apcol]
;
; decrement pointer
;
                sub1    BX
;
; adjust cursor
;
                mvcur   [aprow],[apcol]
;
; put SPACE to screen
;
                putchar ' '
;
; NULL to text buffer at col location
;
                mov     BYTE PTR[BX],0

        EIF     acomp5

        EIF     acomp4

EPROCEDURE priskey

        END

;-------------------------------------
```

Fig. 12-8 ends.

PROMPT (COM Version)   Figure 12-9 presents the COM version macro listing to PROMPT and Fig. 12-10 presents the COM version macro listing to PROMPT.ASM.

Fig. 12-9. The COM macro listing to PROMPT.

```
;----------------------------------------
; Macro: PROMPT row,col,buffer,length
;
; Description:
;  Moves the cursor to row,col and
;  allows the user to enter a string
;  of length bytes into buffer
PROMPT MACRO row,col,buffer,length
        pushbcd
   IFDIFI <AX>,<row>
        mov     AX,row
   ENDIF
   IFDIFI <DX>,<col>
        mov     DX,col
   ENDIF
   IFDIFI <BX>,<buffer>
        lea     BX,buffer
   ENDIF
   IFDIFI <CX>,<length>
        mov     CX,length
   ENDIF
        PUBLIC  APROMPT
        call    aprompt
        popbcd
        ENDM
```

Fig. 12-10. The COM source code listing to PROMPT.ASM.

```
;----------------------------------------
;
; File Name: PROMPT.ASM
;
BPROCEDURE aprompt
        jmp     a??p1
a?p?col   DW    0
a?p?row   DW    0
a?p?start DW    0
a?p?stop  DW    0
a?p?key   DW    0
a?p?exit  DW    0
a?p?val   DW    0
a?p?byte  DB    0,0
a??p1:
        mov     [a?p?row],AX
        mov     [a?p?col],DX
        mov     [a?p?start],DX
        mov     [a?p?stop],DX
        add     [a?p?stop],CX
        setv0   [a?p?exit]
BELOOP  a?p?romptl1
        mvcur   [a?p?row],[a?p?col]
        getkey  [a?p?key]
        SWITCH  swprompt1,[a?p?key]
           CASE    swprompt1,prisenter,E_CR
           CASE    swprompt1,prisesca?p?e,ESCAPE
          DEFAULT swprompt1,priskey
          ESWITCH swprompt1
        BIFE    a?p?rompte1,[a?p?exit],1
```

```
            EBREAK  a?p?romptl1
        EIF     a?p?rompte1
EELOOP  a?p?romptl1
        RETURN  [a?p?val]
EPROCEDURE aprompt

BPROCEDURE prisenter
        setv    [a?p?exit],1
        setv    [a?p?val],1
EPROCEDURE prisenter

BPROCEDURE prisesca?p?e
        setv    [a?p?exit],1
        setv    [a?p?val],0
EPROCEDURE prisesca?p?e

BPROCEDURE priskey
        and     [a?p?key],00FFh
        isprint [a?p?key]
        BIFTRUE a?p?comp1,ax
          BIFLT a?p?comp3,[a?p?col],[a?p?stop]
                mvcur   [a?p?row],[a?p?col]
                putchar [a?p?key]
                WTOBYTE [a?p?byte],[a?p?key]
                setv    AL,[a?p?byte]
                mov     BYTE PTR[BX],AL
                add1    BX
                add1    [a?p?col]
          EIF   a?p?comp3
        EIF     a?p?comp1
        BIFE    acomp4,[a?p?key],8 ; backspace
          BIFGT acomp5,[a?p?col],[a?p?start]
                sub1    [a?p?col]
                sub1    BX
                mvcur   [a?p?row],[a?p?col]
                putchar ' '
                mov     BYTE PTR[BX],0
          EIF   acomp5
        EIF     acomp4
EPROCEDURE priskey


;------------------------------------
```

Fig. 12-12 ends.

Figure 12-11 presents the EXE version of a program which demonstrates the use of PROMPT. Figure 12-12 presents the COM version example program of PROMPT.

Fig. 12-11. The source code listing to EPROG26.ASM.

```
;------------------------------------
;
; File Name: EPROG26.ASM
;

INCLUDE SMALL.MAC
```

```
        PROG_EXE

        PROG_DATA

mess0 DB    'Test of:  PROMPT 5,0,buff,25 ',0
mess3 DB    10,13,10,13,'ESCAPE key pressed...no action...',0
mess4 DB    10,13,'Size of response is ',0
mess5 DB    10,13,'Input response is: ',0
buff  DB    80 DUP (0),0
blen  DB    10 DUP (0)

        PROG_CODE

        vidinit
        clrscreen          ; clear the screen
        puts    mess0      ; print prompt message
        prompt  2,0,buff,25 ; get string from keyboard
        mvcur   4,0        ; move the cursor

BIFTRUE d6,RET_VAL         ; IF ENTER KEY selected
        strlen  buff       ;  get length of buffer
        itoa    RET_VAL,blen ; & place ascii in blen buffer
        printf  mess4,blen ;  print mess4 & length
        printf  mess5,buff ;  print mess5 and keyboard response
BELSE   d6                 ; ELSE ESCAPE KEY selected
        puts    mess3      ;  so print mess3
EIFELSE d6
        mvcur   23,0       ; move the cursor

        END_EXE

        END
```

;-------------------------------------

Fig. 12-11 ends.

Fig. 12-12. The source code listing to CPROG26.ASM.

;-------------------------------------
;
; File Name: CPROG26.ASM
;

```
INCLUDE SMALL.MAC

        PROG_COM

mess0 DB    'Test of:  PROMPT 5,0,buff,25 ',0
mess3 DB    10,13,10,13,'ESCAPE key pressed...no action...',0
mess4 DB    10,13,'Size of response is ',0
mess5 DB    10,13,'Input response is: ',0
buff  DB    80 DUP (0),0
blen  DB    10 DUP (0)

program:
        vidinit
        clrscreen          ; clear the screen
        puts    mess0      ; print prompt message
```

```
        prompt  2,0,buff,25   ; get string from keyboard
        mvcur   4,0            ; move the cursor

BIFTRUE d6,RET_VAL            ; IF ENTER KEY selected
        strlen  buff           ;  get length of buffer
        itoa    RET_VAL,blen ; & place ascii in blen buffer
        printf  mess4,blen     ;  print mess4 & length
        printf  mess5,buff     ;  print mess5 and keyboard response
BELSE   d6                     ; ELSE ESCAPE KEY selected
        puts    mess3          ;  so print mess3
EIFELSE d6
        mvcur   23,0           ; move the cursor

        COM_TO_DOS
L_VIDINIT
L_ITOA
L_PUTS
L_STRLEN
L_CLRSCREEN
L_MVCUR
L_PROMPT
L_PUTCHAR
L_ISPRINT
L_MEMSET
L_STRCPY
L_STRNCPY
        END_COM

;-------------------------------------
```

Fig. 12-12 ends.

13

Disk Drive Procedures

DOS happily provides the facilities for communication with disk drives. In this chapter procedures are presented to create a file, open a file, write to a file, read from a file and close a file. Note that all the macro procedures do not call a subroutine and consequently Fig. 13-1 will be used for EXE and COM file development. Figure 13-2 presents the source code listing to EPROG27.ASM, the EXE version CHUCK Input/Output (I/O) demonstration program and Fig. 13-3 presents the source code listing to CPROG27.ASM, the COM version demonstration program.

Create a file named IO.MAC and add Figure 13-1 to it. Remember to append the EXE and COM SMALL.MACs to include IO.MAC.

One last thought before Fig. 13-1 is presented. As you read the CHUCK I/O procedure operations you'll quickly note that the carry flag is set on an I/O error after a disk I/O operation. The conditional branch mnemonic "jc" allows you to jump to an error message if the carry flag is set. Now, take a moment to look at the BIFE CHUCK macro (located in CHUCK.MAC) and modify it as follows:

```
BIFERROR      name
          statement
EIF           name
```

Can you figure out how to do this? Figure 13-4 presented at the end of Chapter 13 provides one solution.

INTRODUCTION

The following sections discuss the disk drive procedures in detail.

Fig. 13-1. The EXE and COM listing to disk I/O macros.

```
;;----------------------------------------
;;
;; Macro: CLOSE handle
;;
;; Description:
;; Close an open file
;;

CLOSE   MACRO   handle
        pushbcd
    IFDIFI <BX>,<handle>
        mov     BX,handle
    ENDIF
        mov     AH,3Eh
        int     21h
        popbcd
        ENDM

;;----------------------------------------
;;
;; Macro: CREATE fname,access
;;
;; Description:
;; Creates a file and truncates file ptr
;; to 0
;;

CREATE  MACRO   fname,access
        pushbcd
    IFDIFI <DX>,<fname>
        lea     DX,fname
    ENDIF
    IFDIFI <CX>,<access>
        mov     CX,access
    ENDIF
        mov     AH,3Ch
        int     21h
        popbcd
        ENDM

;;----------------------------------------
;;
;; Macro: OPEN fname,access
;;
;; Description:
;; Opens a file and returns handle
;; in RET_VAL. CF set if error.
;;

OPEN    MACRO   fname,access
        pushbcd
    IFDIFI <DX>,<fname>
        lea     DX,fname
    ENDIF
    IFDIFI <CX>,<access>
        mov     AL,access
    ENDIF
        mov     AH,3Dh
        lea     DX,fname
```

```
        int     21h
        popbcd
        ENDM

;;-------------------------------------
;;
;; Macro: READ handle, buffer, number
;;
;; Description:
;; Read an open file of number bytes
;; to buffer
;;

READ    MACRO   handle,buffer,number
        pushbcd
   IFDIFI <AX>,<handle>
        mov     BX,handle
   ELSE
        mov     BX,AX
   ENDIF
   IFDIFI <DX>,<buffer>
        lea     DX,buffer
   ENDIF
   IFDIFI <CX>,<number>
        mov     CX,number
   ENDIF
        mov     AH,3Fh
        int     21h
        popbcd
        ENDM

;;-------------------------------------
;;
;; Macro: WRITE handle, buffer, number
;;
;; Description:
;; Write an open file of number bytes
;; from buffer
;;

WRITE   MACRO   handle,buffer,number
        pushbcd
   IFDIFI <AX>,<handle>
        mov     BX,handle
   ELSE
        mov     BX,AX
   ENDIF
   IFDIFI <DX>,<buffer>
        lea     DX,buffer
   ENDIF
   IFDIFI <CX>,<number>
        mov     CX,number
   ENDIF
        mov     AH,40H
        int     21h
        popbcd
        ENDM
```

Fig. 13-1 ends.

CLOSE

CLOSE closes a previously opened file. The syntax is:

close   *handle*

where *handle* = memory

CLOSE closes a previously opened file using DOS interrupt 12h, function 3Eh. The memory location *handle* must hold the handle created when the file was previously opened. On exit the Carry Flag will be set if there is an error and AX will hold the error code.

CREATE

CREATE creates the designated file if it does not already exist and truncates its length to 0 if it does. The syntax is:

create   *file_name,file_attr*

where   *file_name*   = legal label name
          file_attr   = immediate

CREATE uses DOS interrupt 21h, function 3Ch to create a file. There are four file attributes used by CREATE. They are:

Attribute	Description
00	Create Normal File
02	Create Hidden File
04	Create System File
06	Create Hidden and System file

CREATE returns with the carry flag set if there is an error. AX holds the error codes. The error codes are:

Code	Description
03	Path Not Found
04	No File Handles Available
05	File Access Denied

OPEN

OPEN opens a file and returns its handle. The syntax is:

open   *file_name,file_access*

where *file_name*   = legal label name
          file_access = immediate

OPEN uses DOS function 21h, function 3Dh to open a file. Upon successful open, the carry flag is not set and the handle is returned in RET_VAL (AX). If an OPEN error occurs the carry flag is set and the error value is placed in RET_VAL (AX). The OPEN error codes are:

Code	Description
01	Invalid function
02	File is not found
03	Path is nor found
04	No File Handles Available
05	File Access Denied
12	Invalid File Access Code

READ

READ reads data from an open file. The syntax is:

read   *file_handle,io_buff,num_bytes*

where *file_handle* = memory
      io_buff   = legal label name
      num_bytes = immediate

READ uses the interrupt 21h, function 3Fh to read data from a disk file. The *num_bytes* of data from the disk file specified by *handle* is read into *io_buff*. After a successful file read the carry flag is not set and the number of bytes is returned in RET_VAL (AX). On READ error the carry flag is set and the READ error codes are:

Code	Description
05	File Access Denied
06	File Handle Invalid

WRITE

Write writes data to a file. The syntax is:

write   *file_handle,io_buffer,byte_num*

where *file_handle* = memory
      io_buffer   = legal label name
      byte_num = immediate

WRITE uses interrupt 21h, function 40h to write *byte_num* number of bytes in *io_buffer* to the disk file specified by *file_handle*. On a successful write the carry flag is clear and the number of bytes is returned in RET_VAL (AX). On a write error the carry flag is set and the write error codes are:

Code	Description
02	File Not Found
05	File Access Denied

Figure 13-2 presents the source code listing to EPROG27.ASM, the EXE version IO demonstration program. Figure 13-3 presents the source code listing to CPROG27.ASM, the COM version IO demonstration program.

Fig. 13-2. The source code listing to EPROG27.ASM.

```
;------------------------------------
;
; File Name: EPROG27.ASM
;
INCLUDE SMALL.MAC

        PROG_EXE

; defines

ACCESS    equ  O_RDWR
F_ATTR    equ  F_NORMAL

        PROG_DATA

handle  DW   0
messa   DB   'Creating HELLO.TXT',10,13,0
messb   DB   'Writing HELLO.TXT: ',0
messd   DB   ' bytes written.',10,13,0
messc   DB   'HELLO WORLD!',10,13,0
mess2   DB   'Read ',0
mess3   DB   10 DUP (0)
mess4   DB   ' bytes in HELLO.TXT.',10,13,0
mess5   DB   'Press any key to display HELLO.TXT...',10,13,0
mess6   DB   'Error on open HELLO.TXT',10,13,0
iobuff  DB   20 DUP (0),0
fname   DB   'HELLO.TXT',0

        PROG_CODE
;
; initialize video
;
        vidinit
;
; clear the screen
;
        clrscreen
;
; put message to screen
;
        puts    messa
;
; Create file named HELLO.TXT with normal attribute
;
        create fname,F_ATTR
```

Fig. 13-2 continued.

```
;
; open HELLO.TXT
;
        open    fname,ACCESS
;
; move handle returned by OPEN to memory
;
        setv    [handle],RET_VAL
;
; print message messb
;
        puts    messb
;
; write 14 bytes of data in messc buffer to
; disk file HELLO.TXT
;
        write   [handle],messc,14
;
; save regs
;
        pushx
;
; convert number of bytes written to ASCII
;
        itoa    RET_VAL,mess3
;
; restore regs
;
        popx
;
; print mess3 & messd
;
        printf mess3,messd
;
; close the HELLO.TXT file
;
        close   [handle]
;
; open HELLO.TXT for read / write
;
        open    fname,ACCESS
;
; if OPEN returns no error branch to 'open_ok'
;
        jnc     open_ok
;
; else error in open and jmp to 'bad_open'
;
        jmp     bad_open

open_ok:
;
; read 14 bytes from HELLO.TXT into iobuff
;
        read    [handle],iobuff,14
;
; convert bytes read to ASCII
;
        itoa    RET_VAL,mess3
```

```
;
; close HELLO.TXT
;
        close    [handle]
;
; Print messages
;
        printf   mess2,mess3,mess4,mess5
;
; wait for key press
;
        getkey
;
; put iobuff to screen
;
        puts     iobuff
;
; go to end of demo 5
;
        goto     end_demo5
bad_open:
;
; beep on error
;
        beep
;
; put error message
;
        puts     mess6
end_demo5:
;
; to DOS
;
        END_EXE

        END

;------------------------------------
```

Fig. 13-2 ends.

Fig. 13-3. The source code listing to CPROG27.ASM.

```
;------------------------------------
;
; File Name: CPROG27.ASM
;
INCLUDE SMALL.MAC

; defines

ACCESS    equ   O_RDWR
F_ATTR    equ   F_NORMAL
```

```
               PROG_COM

handle  DW    0
messa   DB    'Creating HELLO.TXT',10,13,0
messb   DB    'Writing HELLO.TXT: ',0
messd   DB    ' bytes written.',10,13,0
messc   DB    'HELLO WORLD!',10,13,0
mess2   DB    'Read ',0
mess3   DB    10 DUP (0)
mess4   DB    ' bytes in HELLO.TXT.',10,13,0
mess5   DB    'Press any key to display HELLO.TXT...',10,13,0
mess6   DB    'Error on open HELLO.TXT',10,13,0
iobuff  DB    20 DUP (0),0
fname   DB    'HELLO.TXT',0

program:

        vidinit
        clrscreen
        puts    messa
        create  fname,F_ATTR
        open    fname,ACCESS
        setv    [handle],RET_VAL
        puts    messb
        write   [handle],messc,14
        pushx
        itoa    AX,mess3
        popx
        printf  mess3,messd
        close   [handle]

        open    fname,ACCESS
        jnc     open_ok
        jmp     bad_open
open_ok:
        read    [handle],iobuff,14
        itoa    AX,mess3
        close   [handle]
        printf  mess2,mess3,mess4,mess5
        getkey
        puts    iobuff
        goto    end_demo5
bad_open:
        beep
        puts    mess6
end_demo5:
        COM_TO_DOS
L_VIDINIT
L_ITOA
L_CLRSCREEN
L_PUTS
L_PUTCHAR
L_STRCPY
L_STRNCPY
L_MEMSET
L_STRLEN
        END_COM

;-------------------------------------
```

Fig. 13-3 ends.

BIFERROR Macro

Figure 13-4 presents the macro listing to BIFERROR (Begin IF ERROR). This macro should be added to your EXE and COM version CHUCK.MAC files.

Fig. 13-4. The EXE and COM macro listing to BIFERROR.

```
;;----------------------------------------
;; Macro BIFERROR name
;;
;; Description:
;;   Carry Flag set on error.
;;   If CF set then continue,
;;   otherwise jump to bypass
;;   error code
;;
BIFERROR MACRO name
         LOCAL   err_set
         jc      err_set
         jmp     &name&
err_set:
         ENDM
```

14

Window Procedures

Windows, an oft-used computer buzzword, can be defined as an outlined rectangular region of the screen. Windows are usually surrounded by borders and come in a variety of styles. At their simplest levels, windows present information. At more sophisticated levels, windows allow the user to conveniently input specific information.

A program's *User Interface* defines how the user sees information and makes selections or inputs information to the program. For the last few years the Drop-Down Window, Pop-Up Window, and Dialog Box have all become part of the programmer's vocabulary. In Chapter 14 four window creation routines are presented. These four routines allow the CHUCK or assembly programs to pop up and remove an information window.

Chapter 16, though, extends the window procedures presented in this chapter to permit you to create overlapping pop-up windows. The menu demonstration program presented in Chapter 16 clearly demonstrates how to create vertical scroll bar menus, Lotus style menus and Grid style menus. A functionally similar menu demonstration program is presented in C in Windcrest's *C Libraries: Menus and User Interfaces* and weighed in at 8986 bytes. The 8986-byte Turbo C menu demonstration program used the efficient coding algorithms underlying the 'C'erious Tools Plus C utility package.

The CHUCK menu demonstration program weighs in at 5523 bytes. This represents approximately a 40 percent reduction in code size over an assembly optimized C utility library.

Chapter 17, the final chapter in the book, presents the primarily CHUCK slightly assembly hybrid program for an ancient board game Wari. This program sports a menu bar, drop-down window, and pop-up window interface. By the time you've chomped on Chapter 17, writing slick user interfaces in CHUCK should not be difficult.

CHUCK'S WINDOW STRUCTURE

A structure is a convenient data arrangement which permits easy access to related information. Both MicroSoft's MASM and Borland's TASM provide the STRUC directive. Figure 14-1 presents the WINDOW structure listing contained in DEFINES.MAC.

Fig. 14-1. The listing to CHUCK's window structure.

```
;;-------------------------------------;;
;; WINDOW    Screen Window Structure  ;;
;;-------------------------------------;;

WINDOW    STRUC
    ulrow    DB    ?    ;; upper left row
    ulcol    DB    ?    ;; upper left col
    lrrow    DB    ?    ;; lower right row
    lrcol    DB    ?    ;; lower right col
    attr     DB    ?    ;; window attribute
    scrnimg  DW    ?    ;; pointer to screen image
    windimg  DW    ?    ;; pointer to rect image
WINDOW    ENDS
```

This version of the WINDOW structure holds space for the upper left and lower right window screen coordinates. The main window video attribute is also held along with pointers (really offsets) to dynamically allocated memory where screen and window data is temporarily stored.

The WINDOW structure is referred to in all CHUCK window procedures. As there is a synergy between the four window creation procedures in this chapter, all four EXE and COM version procedures will be presented before the EXE and COM demonstration programs.

Create a file named WINDOW.MAC and add the appropriate macro listings to your EXE and COM directory. Note that three of the four window creation procedures presented in this chapter call subroutines from within the macro. Add the following macro to your COM.MAC file:

```
L_WINDOW MACRO
         INCLUDE CLRRECT.ASM
         INCLUDE DRAWBOX.ASM
         INCLUDE WRITEBOX.ASM
         ENDM
```

CLRWINDOW

CLRWIND clears a window using its screen attribute. The syntax is:

clrwindow   window_name

where   window_name   =   legal label name

CLRWINDOW is most often invoked from within the WDISPLAY (Window DISPLAY) procedure.

CLRWINDOW (EXE Version)   Figure 14-2 presents the EXE version macro listing to CLRWINDOW and Fig. 14-3 presents the listing to CLRRECT.ASM.

Fig. 14-2. The EXE macro listing to CLRWINDOW.

```
;------------------------------------
; Macro: CLRWINDOW
;
; Descritpion: Clears a window with WINDOW's
;   attribute
;
CLRWINDOW MACRO wind

    IFDIFI <AX>,<WIND>
         lea      AX,WIND
    ENDIF

         EXTRN    CLRRECT:NEAR
         call     clrrect

         ENDM
```

Fig. 14-3. The EXE source code listing to CLRRECT.ASM.

```
;------------------------------------
;
; File Name CLRRECT.ASM
;
; Description: Clears a rectangle
; described by the WINDOW structure
;

INCLUDE SMALL.MAC


        DOSSEG

        .MODEL SMALL

        PUBLIC clrrect

        .CODE

clrrect PROC NEAR
;       push     BX
;       push     CX
;       push     DX

        push     AX
        mov      BX,AX
        mov      CH,[BX.ulrow]
        mov      CL,[BX.ulcol]
        mov      DH,[BX.lrrow]
        mov      DL,[BX.lrcol]
        mov      BH,[BX.attr]
        mov      AL,0
        mov      AH,6
        int      10h
        pop      AX
;       pop      DX
;       pop      CX
;       pop      BX
        ret
```

```
clrrect ENDP

        END

;-------------------------------------
;
```

Fig. 14-3 ends.

CLRWINDOW (COM Version)

Figure 14-4 presents the COM version macro listing to CLRWINDOW and Fig. 14-5 presents the COM version source code listing to CLRRECT.ASM.

Fig. 14-4. The COM macro listing to CLRWINDOW.

```
;-------------------------------------
; Macro: CLRWINDOW
;
; Descritpion: Clears a window with WINDOW's
;  attribute
;
CLRWINDOW MACRO wind

    IFDIFI <AX>,<WIND>
        lea     AX,WIND
    ENDIF

        PUBLIC  CLRRECT
        call    clrrect

        ENDM
```

Fig. 14-5. The COM source code listing to CLRRECT.ASM.

```
;-------------------------------------
;
; File Name CLRRECT.ASM
;
; Description: Clears a rectangle
; described by the WINDOW structure
;
clrrect PROC NEAR
        pushx
        mov     BX,AX
        mov     CH,[BX.ulrow]
        mov     CL,[BX.ulcol]
        mov     DH,[BX.lrrow]
        mov     DL,[BX.lrcol]
        mov     BH,[BX.attr]
        mov     AL,0
        mov     AH,6
        int     10h
        popx
        ret

clrrect ENDP

;-------------------------------------
```

WDISPLAY

WDISPLAY displays the window described in the window structure. The syntax is:

wdisplay   *window_name,border_type*

where *window_name* = legal label name
      border_type = immediate

The WDISPLAY procedure displays the window described by the structure associated with *window_name*. In this book, only one border type (single sided on all four sides) is presented. The constant S_S_S_S (single side border) is defined in DEFINES.MAC. You can easily modify DRAWBOX.ASM to permit any mixture of single line and double line window borders. Do you see how?

WDISPLAY (EXE Version)   Figure 14-6 presents the EXE version of the WDISPLAY macro listing and Fig. 14-7 presents the EXE version of DRAWBOX.ASM, the subroutine called from within WDISPLAY.

Fig. 14-6. The EXE macro listing to WDISPLAY.

```
;------------------------------------;
; Macro: WDISPLAY wind,box
;
; Description: Pop up the window described in
;   the WINDOW structure. This call is used for
;   the first time the window is dosplayed. Subsequent
;   times you should use WHIDE to remove a window and
;   WSHOW to Pop up the window.

WDISPLAY MACRO wind,box

    IFDIFI <AX>,<wind>
        lea     AX,wind
    ENDIF

    IFDIFI <DX>,<box>
        mov     DX,box
    ENDIF

        clrwindow AX

        EXTRN   DRAWBOX:NEAR
        call    drawbox

        ENDM
```

Fig. 14-7. The EXE source code listing to DRAWBOX.ASM.

```
;------------------------------------
;
;
; File Name: DRAWBOX.ASM
;
; Description: Draws a border around
```

Fig. 14-7 continued.
```
;  a WINDOW using the ROM's box characters

INCLUDE SMALL.MAC

        DOSSEG

        .MODEL SMALL

        .DATA
        EXTRN PAG_NUM:BYTE

        .CODE

        PUBLIC DRAWBOX

drawbox PROC NEAR
        jmp     db1

topbot  DW      196
leftrt  DW      179
ulcor   DW      218
urcor   DW      191
llcor   DW      192
lrcor   DW      217
dbrow   DW      0
dbcol   DW      0

db1:
        pushx
        mov     BX,AX

; draw top of box
        xor     CX,CX

        push    BX
        xor     AX,AX           ; move currsor
        xor     DX,DX           ; to
        mov     AL,[BX.ulrow]   ; upper left corner
        mov     DL,[BX.ulcol]
        mvcur   AX,DX
        mov     CL,[BX.lrcol]
        sub     CL,[BX.ulcol]
        mov     AL,[BX.attr]
        mov     BL,AL
        mov     BH,PAG_NUM
        mov     AX,topbot
        mov     AH,9
        int     10h
        pop     BX


        push    BX
        xor     AX,AX           ; move currsor
        xor     DX,DX           ; to
        mov     AL,[BX.lrrow]   ; lower left corner
        mov     DL,[BX.ulcol]
        mvcur   AX,DX
        mov     CL,[BX.lrcol]
        sub     CL,[BX.ulcol]
        mov     AL,[BX.attr]
```

Fig. 14-7 continued.

```
        mov     BL,AL
        mov     BH,PAG_NUM
        mov     AX,topbot
        mov     AH,9
        int     10h
        pop     BX


        xor     DX,DX
        mov     DL,[BX.ulcol]
        mov     dbcol,DX
        mov     DL,[BX.ulrow]
        mov     dbrow,DX
        mov     DL,[BX.lrrow]
        sub     DL,[BX.ulrow]
        BLOOP   dolcol,DX
           mvcur    dbrow,dbcol
           putchar leftrt
           add1    dbrow
        ELOOP   dolcol

        xor     DX,DX
        mov     DL,[BX.lrcol]
        mov     dbcol,DX
        mov     DL,[BX.ulrow]
        mov     dbrow,DX
        mov     DL,[BX.lrrow]
        sub     DL,[BX.ulrow]

        BLOOP   dorcol,DX
           mvcur    dbrow,dbcol
           putchar leftrt
           add1    dbrow
        ELOOP   dorcol


        xor     AX,AX
        xor     DX,DX
        mov     AL,[BX.ulrow] ; upper left corner
        mov     DL,[BX.ulcol]
        mvcur   AX,DX
        putchar ulcor
        mov     AL,[BX.ulrow] ; upper right corner
        mov     DL,[BX.lrcol]
        mvcur   AX,DX
        putchar urcor

        mov     AL,[BX.lrrow] ; lower left corner
        mov     DL,[BX.ulcol]
        mvcur   AX,DX
        putchar llcor
        mov     AL,[BX.lrrow] ; lower right corner
        mov     DL,[BX.lrcol]
        mvcur   AX,DX
        putchar lrcor
        popx

        ret

drawbox ENDP
```

```
        END

;---------------------------------------
```

Fig. 14-7 ends.

WDISPLAY (COM Version)   Figure 14-8 presents the COM version macro listing to WDISPLAY and Fig. 14-9 presents the COM version listing to DRAWBOX.ASM.

Fig. 14-8. The COM macro listing to WDISPLAY.

```
;------------------------------------------;
; Macro: WDISPLAY wind,box
;
; Description: Pop up the window described in
;   the WINDOW structure. This call is used for
;   the first time the window is dosplayed. Subsequent
;   times you should use WHIDE to remove a window and
;   WSHOW to Pop up the window.

WDISPLAY MACRO wind,box

    IFDIFI <AX>,<wind>
        lea    AX,wind
    ENDIF

    IFDIFI <DX>,<box>
        mov    DX,box
    ENDIF

        clrwindow AX

        PUBLIC  DRAWBOX
        call    drawbox

        ENDM
```

Fig. 14-9. The COM source code listing to DRAWBOX.ASM.

```
;
; File Name: DRAWBOX.ASM
;
; Description: Draws a border around
;   a WINDOW using the ROM's box characters

drawbox PROC NEAR
        jmp    db1
topbot  DW     196
leftrt  DW     179
ulcor   DW     218
urcor   DW     191
llcor   DW     192
lrcor   DW     217
dbrow   DW     0
dbcol   DW     0
db1:
```

Fig. 14-9 continued.

```
        pushx
        mov     BX,AX

; draw top of box
        xor     CX,CX

        push    BX
        xor     AX,AX           ; move currsor
        xor     DX,DX           ; to
        mov     AL,[BX.ulrow]   ; upper left corner
        mov     DL,[BX.ulcol]
        mvcur   AX,DX
        mov     CL,[BX.lrcol]
        sub     CL,[BX.ulcol]
        mov     AL,[BX.attr]
        mov     BL,AL
        mov     BH,PAG_NUM
        mov     AX,topbot
        mov     AH,9
        int     10h
        pop     BX


        push    BX
        xor     AX,AX           ; move currsor
        xor     DX,DX           ; to
        mov     AL,[BX.lrrow]   ; lower left corner
        mov     DL,[BX.ulcol]
        mvcur   AX,DX
        mov     CL,[BX.lrcol]
        sub     CL,[BX.ulcol]
        mov     AL,[BX.attr]
        mov     BL,AL
        mov     BH,PAG_NUM
        mov     AX,topbot
        mov     AH,9
        int     10h
        pop     BX


        xor     DX,DX
        mov     DL,[BX.ulcol]
        mov     dbcol,DX
        mov     DL,[BX.ulrow]
        mov     dbrow,DX
        mov     DL,[BX.lrrow]
        sub     DL,[BX.ulrow]
        BLOOP   dolcol,DX
            mvcur   dbrow,dbcol
            putchar leftrt
            add1    dbrow
            ELOOP   dolcol

        xor     DX,DX
        mov     DL,[BX.lrcol]
        mov     dbcol,DX
        mov     DL,[BX.ulrow]
        mov     dbrow,DX
        mov     DL,[BX.lrrow]
        sub     DL,[BX.ulrow]
```

```
        BLOOP   dorcol,DX
            mvcur   dbrow,dbcol
            putchar leftrt
            add1    dbrow
            ELOOP   dorcol

        xor     AX,AX
        xor     DX,DX
        mov     AL,[BX.ulrow] ; upper left corner
        mov     DL,[BX.ulcol]
        mvcur   AX,DX
        putchar ulcor
        mov     AL,[BX.ulrow] ; upper right corner
        mov     DL,[BX.lrcol]
        mvcur   AX,DX
        putchar urcor

        mov     AL,[BX.lrrow] ; lower left corner
        mov     DL,[BX.ulcol]
        mvcur   AX,DX
        putchar llcor
        mov     AL,[BX.lrrow] ; lower right corner
        mov     DL,[BX.lrcol]
        mvcur   AX,DX
        putchar lrcor
        popx
        ret
drawbox ENDP
```

Fig. 14-9 ends.

WSWRITE

WSWRITE writes a string to a window in teletype fashion. The syntax is:

wswrite   *window_name,window_row,window_col,string_name*

where *window_name* = legal label name
     window_row = memory|immediate
     window_col = memory|immediate
     string_name = legal label name

The WSWRITE procedure writes a string to a window at *window_row* and *window_col* where position 0,0 is the upper left-hand corner of the window border. The string is written using the window attribute held in the window structure.

WSWRITE (EXE Version)   Figure 14-10 presents the EXE version macro listing to WSWRITE and Fig. 14-11 presents the EXE version source code listing to WRITEBOX.ASM, the subroutine called from within the WSWRITE macro.

Fig. 14-10. The EXE macro listing to WSWRITE.

```
;----------------------------------------
;
; Macro: WSWRITE wind,row,col,string
;
; Description: Writes a string in teletype
;   fashion to a window using the window's
;   upper left hand corner as origin (0,0)
WSWRITE MACRO wind,row,col,string

    IFDIFI <AX>,<wind>
        lea     AX,wind
    ENDIF

    IFDIFI <DX>,<row>
        mov     DX,row
    ENDIF

    IFDIFI <BX>,<col>
        mov     BX,col
    ENDIF

    IFDIFI <CX>,<string>
        lea     CX,string
    ENDIF

        EXTRN   WRITEBOX:NEAR
        call    writebox

        ENDM
```

Fig. 14-11. The EXE source code listing to WRITEBOX.ASM.

```
;----------------------------------------
;
; File Name: WRITEBOX.ASM
;
; Description: Writes a string to
;   a window using the existing
;   screen attributes.
;

INCLUDE SMALL.MAC

        DOSSEG

        .MODEL SMALL

        .DATA

w_row   DB      0
w_col   DB      0

        .CODE

        PUBLIC writebox

writebox PROC NEAR
        push    SI
```

```
        push    CX
        mov     w_row,DL
        mov     w_col,BL
        mov     BX,AX
        xor     AX,AX
        xor     DX,DX
        mov     AL,[BX.ulrow]
        add     AL,w_row
        mov     DL,[BX.ulcol]
        add     DL,w_col
        mvcur   AX,DX
        pop     SI
        puts    SI
        pop     SI
        ret

writebox ENDP

        END

;-------------------------------------
;
```

Fig. 14-11 ends.

WSWRITE (COM Version)   Figure 14-12 presents the COM version macro listing to WSWRITE and Fig. 14-13 presents the COM version source code listing to WRITEBOX.ASM.

Fig. 14-12. The COM macro listing to WSWRITE.

```
;-------------------------------------
;
;
; Macro: WSWRITE wind,row,col,string
;
; Description: Writes a string in teletype
;   fashion to a window using the window's
;   upper left hand corner as origin (0,0)
WSWRITE MACRO wind,row,col,string

    IFDIFI <AX>,<wind>
        lea     AX,wind
    ENDIF

    IFDIFI <DX>,<row>
        mov     DX,row
    ENDIF

    IFDIFI <BX>,<col>
        mov     BX,col
    ENDIF

    IFDIFI <CX>,<string>
        lea     CX,string
    ENDIF

        PUBLIC  WRITEBOX
        call    writebox

        ENDM
```

Fig. 14-13. The COM source code listing to WRITEBOX.ASM.

```
;----------------------------------------
;
; File Name: WRITEBOX.ASM
;
; Description: Writes a string to
;   a window using the existing
;   screen attributes.
;

writebox PROC NEAR
        pushx
        jmp ??wb1

w_row   DB      0
w_col   DB      0

??wb1:
        push    SI
        push    CX
        mov     w_row,DL
        mov     w_col,BL
        mov     BX,AX
        xor     AX,AX
        xor     DX,DX
        mov     AL,[BX.ulrow]
        add     AL,w_row
        mov     DL,[BX.ulcol]
        add     DL,w_col
        mvcur   AX,DX
        pop     SI
        puts    SI
        pop     SI
        popx
        ret

writebox ENDP

;----------------------------------------
```

WSETATTR

WSETATTR sets the window structure attribute byte. The syntax is:

wsetattr   *window_name,window_attr*

where *window_name* = legal label name
    window_attr = memory|RET_VAL|immediate

The WSETATTR procedure takes a previously calculated attribute value and places it within the window's structure. As there is no subroutine called from within this macro you may add it to both your COM and EXE versions of WINDOW.MAC.

WSETATTR (EXE and COM Version)   Figure 14-14 presents the EXE and COM version macro listing to WSETATTR. Figure 14-15 presents the EXE version source code listing to the simple window demonstration program, EPROG28.ASM. Figure 14-16 presents the source code listing to CPROG28.ASM, the WINDOW COM demonstration program.

Fig. 14-14. The EXE and COM macro listing to WSETATTR.

```
;------------------------------------
; Macro WSETATTR wind,attr
;
; Description: Set the WINDOW structure
;   attribute.
;
WSETATTR MACRO wind,attr

    IFDIFI <BX>,<wind>
         lea     BX,wind
    ENDIF

    IFDIFI <AX>,<attr>
         mov     AX,attr
    ENDIF

         mov     [BX.attr],AL

         ENDM
```

Fig. 14-15. The source code listing to EPROG28.ASM.

```
;------------------------------------
;
; File Name: EPROG28.ASM
;
INCLUDE SMALL.MAC

        PROG_EXE

        PROG_DATA

wind1   WINDOW <5,5,11,38,7,,>   ; Initialize window structure
bytes_free DW 0,0
disk_val   DW 0
mess0 DB     'Sectors per cluster:    ',0
mess1 DB     'Clusters available:     ',0
mess2 DB     'Bytes per sector:       ',0
mess3 DB     'Total clusters:         ',0
mess4 DB     'Free bytes on drive ',0

buff  DB     15 DUP(0)

        PROG_CODE
;
; initialize video
;
        vidinit
```

```
;
; save current cursor location
;
        savecurloc
;
; save the screen image
;
        savescrn
;
; turn the cursor off
;
        offcursor
;
; make window attribute
;
        makeattr    WHITE,RED,ON_INTEN,OFF_BLINK
;
; set wind1 screen attribute in structure
;
        wsetattr    wind1,AX
;
; display wind1
;
        wdisplay    wind1,S_S_S_S
;
; write window messages
;
        wswrite     wind1,1,1,mess0
        wswrite     wind1,2,1,mess1
        wswrite     wind1,3,1,mess2
        wswrite     wind1,4,1,mess3
        wswrite     wind1,5,1,mess4
;
; wait for key press
;
        getkey
;
; restore screen image
;
        restscrn
;
; restore cursor location
;
        restcurloc
;
; turn the cursor on
;
        oncursor
;
; to DOS
;
        END_EXE
;
; end of source
;
        END
;
;-------------------------------------
```

Fig. 14-15 ends.

Fig. 14-16. The source code listing to CPROG28.ASM.

```
;----------------------------------------
;
; File Name: CPROG28.ASM
;
INCLUDE SMALL.MAC

        PROG_COM

wind1   WINDOW <5,5,11,38,7,,>   ; Initialize window structure
bytes_free DW 0,0
disk_val  DW 0
mess0 DB    'Sectors per cluster:  ',0
mess1 DB    'Clusters available:   ',0
mess2 DB    'Bytes per sector:     ',0
mess3 DB    'Total clusters:       ',0
mess4 DB    'Free bytes on drive ',0

buff  DB    15 DUP(0)

program:
;
; initialize video
;
        vidinit
;
; save current cursor location
;
        savecurloc
;
; save the screen image
;
        savescrn
;
; turn the cursor off
;
        offcursor
;
; make window attribute
;
        makeattr    WHITE,RED,ON_INTEN,OFF_BLINK
;
; set wind1 screen attribute in structure
;
        wsetattr    wind1,AX
;
; display wind1
;
        wdisplay    wind1,S_S_S_S
;
; write window messages
;
        wswrite     wind1,1,1,mess0
        wswrite     wind1,2,1,mess1
        wswrite     wind1,3,1,mess2
        wswrite     wind1,4,1,mess3
        wswrite     wind1,5,1,mess4
;
; wait for key press
;
        getkey
```

```
;
; restore screen image
;
        restscrn
;
; restore cursor location
;
        restcurloc
;
; turn the cursor on
;
        oncursor
;
; to DOS
;
        COM_TO_DOS

L_VIDINIT
L_PUTS
L_PUTCHAR
L_ONCURSOR
L_SAVECURLOC
L_MAKEATTR
L_WINDOW
L_MVCUR

L_SAVESCRN

;
; end of source
;
        END_COM

;-------------------------------------
```

Fig. 14-16 ends.

FINAL WORDS

Part III's mission was to add additional procedures to your CHUCK arsenal. This was accomplished by presenting a sprinkling of procedures for direct video access, cursor control, sound, string handling, code conversion, keyboard input, disk control, and window management.

Part IV presents three demonstration programs. Chapter 15 presents a COM terminate and stay resident pop-up window printer utility program. Chapter 16 presents a few more window procedures and a useful menu demonstration program. Chapter 17 uses virtually every procedure presented in this book to present an applications program.

PART IV
Demonstration Programs

Chapters 15, 16, and 17 present the source code listings to three demonstration programs.

Chapter 16 shows how to use the CHUCK COM program macros and procedures to create a terminate and stay resident program. This TSR program uses the Print Screen key as a hot key. When Print Screen is selected, a window containing a vertical scroll bar menu appears. The three choices are to print the screen, turn Epson condense on, or turn Epson condense off.

Chapter 17 demonstrates how to create a program with overlapping pop-up windows while using Lotus style, vertical bar style or grid style windows.

Chapter 18 presents the final and longest program in the text: the CHUCK and assembly source code to an implementation of the African board game Wari.

15

COM Programs Become TSR

Terminate and stay resident (TSR) programs have become very popular for the PC. A terminate and stay resident COM program stays in the computer, in a sense, asleep until some signal pushes it to action. In our demonstration TSR program, the Print Screen key invokes the terminate and stay resident utility.

Early on in the text I described my need to turn on the Epson printer's condense mode and wrote a small EXE and COM program to fulfill the task. In truth, though, there are times when I would like to turn the condense mode on or off in the same programming session.

Also, the other day I was at TSR Systems Ltd office and used the standard print screen to dump a screen to the laser printer. As there is no default form feed following the screen print I had to switch the laser printer off line, do a form feed manually, and then get the laser printer back on line. I decided to add a form feed at the end of the print screen vector.

Figure 15-3 presents the source code listing to CPROG29.ASM. CPROG29.COM terminates and stays resident when invoked. Once CPROG29 is loaded, a print screen key press will pop up a window with three choices. They are:

- *Print Screen* Prints screen with form feed
- *Condense On* Turns on Epson condense mode
- *Condense Off* Turns off Epson condense mode

COM TSR PROGRAM STRUCTURE

For purposes of this brief discussion, there are basically two sections to the code of the terminate and stay resident program. The first section could be called the resident section of code. The resident section of code contains all the routines, which permit the TSR program to work as billed.

The second section, the non-resident code, helps to install the TSR program and print installation messages. It is very easy to set up these two sections of a TSR program using CHUCK and structured assembly.

The print screen TSR program in this chapter begins by jumping over the resident section and going to the installation (non-resident) section of the program. Once there, the video structure is initialized (vidinit procedure), the installation message is printed to the screen, and then the program is made TSR. The memory holding the non-resident section of the code is freed.

Figure 15-1 is the COM macro listing to COM_TO_TSR, Fig. 15-2 is the source code listing to SETPSVEC.ASM and Fig. 15-3 is the source code listing to CPROG29.ASM.

COM_TO_TSR

COM_TO_TSR makes a COM program terminate and stay resident (TSR). The syntax is:

COM_TO_TSR   *install*

where   *install*   =   legal label name

The COM_TO_TSR macro makes your COM program terminate and stay resident while freeing up all memory after the install label. In other words, any code or data coming after install should be in the non-resident section of the TSR program. All code and data before install should comprise all of the TSR resident code.

COM_TO_TSR (COM Version)   Figure 15-1 presents the COM_TO_TSR macro.

Fig. 15-1. The COM macro listing to COM_TO_TSR.

```
;;----------------------------------------
;;
;; Macro: COM_TO_TSR
;;
;; Description: Terminate the
;;    com program and return to
;;    DOS
;;
COM_TO_TSR MACRO name

        lea     DX,name
        mov     CL,4
        shr     DX,CL
        inc     DX
        mov     AL,0
        mov     AH,49
        int     21h

        ENDM
```

SETPSVEC

SETPSVEC redirects print screen vector to 'newps' procedure. The syntax is:

```
cproc    setpsvec
```

Calling SETPSVEC takes care of all the necessary interrupt handling for the print screen vector (05h). After it's called, pressing the print screen key calls a procedure in your program named NEWPS. Remember that NEWPS must not violate any rules of COM TSR programming. You can't address multiple segments or dynamically allocate memory.

SETPSVEC (COM Version)   Figure 15-2 is the COM source code listing to SETPSVEC.ASM. Figure 15-3 is the source code listing to CPROG29.ASM, the TSR program that my AUTOEXEC.BAT file invokes every boot up.

Note that the CPROG29.COM is 2973 bytes on disk and takes up 3040 bytes inside my AT clone. Keeping the program's size in memory as close as possible to the executable program's disk size is a desirable goal. As you can see, CHUCK handles that task fairly well.

Fig. 15-2. The COM source code listing to SETPSVVEC.ASM.

```
;********************
; Source Code Start
;
; File Name:    SETPSVEC.ASM
;
; Synopsis:     setPSvec(id)
;
; int id        PRTSCRN identification
;               value MUST MATCH id VALUE
;               used in psfind(id)
;
;
; Description: Redirects the print screen
;               key to point to a routine
;               called by default newPS().
;               Note that this print screer
;               int handler also saves and
;               restores the DTA along with
;               the PSP.
;
; Returns:      Nothing
;
;           dw        100h dup (0ffh)
;tsrSTACK:
;
;
; Set the start of the function
;

setpsvec PROC NEAR

            jmp       ps1

old5     DW       0,0
oldDS    DW       0
oldES    DW       0
oldSS    DW       0
oldSP    DW       0
newDS    DW       0
newES    DW       0
newSS    DW       0
newSP    DW       0
```

Fig. 15-2 continued.

```
tsrPSP    DW      0
curPSP    DW      0
offDTA    DW      0
segDTA    DW      0

ps1:
          push    AX
          push    BX
          push    CX
          push    DX
          push    DS
          push    ES

          mov     oldDS,DS
          mov     oldES,ES
          mov     oldSS,SS
          mov     oldSP,SP

;
; Get the segment and register of
; the existing INT 05h vector...
;

          mov     AX,3505h ; get int 5 vec
          int     21h

;
; ... and store it in memory
;

          mov     old5,BX
          mov     old5+2,ES

;
; Set new INT 05h vector to
; ANEWPS
;

          mov     DX,offset ANEWPS
          mov     AX,2505h
          int     21H

;
; Relocate vector info data
; in code segment
;

          call    rem_vecs

;
; Clear interrupt flag
;

          cli

;
; Get tsr PSP ...
;
```

Fig. 15-2 continued.

```
                mov     AH,51H
                int     21H

;
; ... and save in memory
;

                mov     tsrPSP,BX

;
; Enable interrupts
;
                sti

;
; Pop REGS from stack
;

                pop     ES
                pop     DS
                pop     DX
                pop     CX
                pop     BX
                pop     AX

                ret
setpsvec ENDP

;
; Far call for new int 05h
;

ANEWPS PROC FAR
;
; Jump over data in code segment
;

                jmp     byp ; uses 3 bytes
;
; The data here is accessed by psremv()
; and rps.com to restore the old print
; screen vector and free the memory
;

id      DW      313 ; default value
o5      DW      0,0 ; uses four bytes
oldCS   DW      0
progon  DB      0

;

byp:
;
; Save regs
;

                push    BP
                mov     BP,SP

                push    AX
```

Fig. 15-2 continued.

```
        push    BX
        push    CX
        push    DX
        push    DI
        push    SI
        push    DS
        push    ES


;
; Restore NON-INTERRUPT reg values
;

        mov     newSS,SS
        mov     newSP,SP

        mov     DS,oldDS
        mov     ES,oldES

        mov     SS,oldSS
        mov     SP,oldSP


;
; find current PSP
;

        mov     AH,51H
        int     21H
        mov     curPSP,BX


;
; set PSP to original tsrPSP
;

        mov     BX,tsrPSP
        mov     AH,50H
        int     21H


;
; set original DTA
;

        mov     AH,2fH
        int     21H
        mov     offDTA,BX
        mov     segDTA,ES
        push    DS
        mov     DS,tsrPSP
        mov     DX,80H
        mov     AH,1aH
        int     21H
        pop     DS


;
; Is busy flag on?
;

        cmp     progon,1


;
; Jump on YES to prevent re-entering
```

Fig. 15-2 continued.

```
; currently executing 05h code
;

        je      nops

;
; Set busy flag ON
;

        mov     progon,1

;
; Call ASMplus function
;

        call    newps

;
; C function has returned so
; clear the busy flag
;

        mov     progon,0

nops:

;
; reset PSP
;

        mov     BX,curPSP
        mov     AH,50H
        int     21H

;
; reset DTA
;

        push    DS
        push    AX
        mov     AX,offDTA
        mov     DX,AX
        mov     AX,segDTA
        mov     DS,AX
        mov     AH,1aH
        int     21H
        pop     AX
        pop     DS

;
; restore regs
;

        mov     SS,newSS
        mov     SP,newSP

        pop     ES
        pop     DS
        pop     SI
        pop     DI
```

```
        pop     DX
        pop     CX
        pop     BX
        pop     AX

        mov     SP,BP
        pop     BP
        iret
ANEWPS ENDP

;
; relocate seg data -
; for future use
;

rem_vecs PROC NEAR
;
; Relocate original int 5 offset
;

        mov     AX,old5
        mov     o5,AX


;
; Relocate original int 5 segment
;

        mov     AX,old5+2
        mov     o5+2,AX


;
; Relocate original int 5 CODE
; segment
;


        mov     AX,CS
        mov     oldCS,AX
        ret
rem_vecs ENDP

;
; End of source listing
;***********************
```

Fig. 15-2 ends.

Fig. 15-3. The source code listing to CPROG29.ASM.

```
;-------------------------------------
;
; File Name: CPROG29.ASM
;
; Description: .COM test file
;
INCLUDE SMALL.MAC

;-------------------------------------
;
; ***** Resident section of the *****
; ***** code begins here        *****
;
;-------------------------------------

;
; Define window coordinates
;
W1_ULR   equ      5
W1_ULC   equ      10
W1_LRR   equ      9
W1_LRC   equ      25

;
; Define window size
;
W1_SIZE equ      (W1_LRR-W1_ULR+1)*(W1_LRC-W1_ULC+1)

;
; Invoke COM program directives and setup
;
         PROG_COM

;
; Declare window screen buffer
;
w1_buff DW       W1_SIZE DUP(0)

;
; Declare window structure
;
W1    WINDOW      <W1_ULR,W1_ULC,W1_LRR,W1_LRC,7,,>

;
; Program data
;
key     DW       0
token   DW       0

k_resp  DW       ?
w1attr  DW       ?
w1inv   DW       ?
```

Fig. 15-3 continued.

```
w2attr  DW      ?
w2inv   DW      ?

first_row  DW   1
first_exit DW   0
act_flag   DW   0
handle  DW      ?
io_len  DW      ?

top     DB 201,205,205,205,205,205,205,205,205,205,205,205,205,187,0
side    DB 186,32,32,32,32,32,32,32,32,32,32,32,32,186,0
bot     DB 200,205,205,205,205,205,205,205,205,205,205,205,205,188,0
mess1   DB 'Print Screen',0
mess2   DB 'Condense ON ',0
mess3   DB 'Condense OFF',0


program:
;
; Jump over TSR program code
;

        jmp     install


;
; New Print Screen call
;

BPROCEDURE newps
;
; set proper page segment in video structure
;

        vidinit


;
; Save screen image under window
;

        call    save_scrn


;
; Write window to screen
;

        vdwrite     5,10,14,top,[w1attr]
BFORLTE pcDB1,6,8
        vdwrite     v1pcDB1,10,14,side,[w1attr]
EFOR    pcDB1
        vdwrite     9,10,14,bot,[w1attr]


;
; Set variables
;

        setv    first_row,1
        setv0   first_exit
        setv0   act_flag

; main keyboard loop
```

Fig. 15-3 continued.

```
BELOOP  EL1
;
; Clear highlight bar
;

        vdwrite     W1_ULR+1,W1_ULC+1,12,mess1,[w1attr]
        vdwrite     W1_ULR+2,W1_ULC+1,12,mess2,[w1attr]
        vdwrite     W1_ULR+3,W1_ULC+1,12,mess3,[w1attr]


;
; Draw highlight bar
;

        wvdattr     W1,[first_row],1,12,[w1inv]


;
; Wait for key press and get key
;

        getkey      [key]


;
; Evaluate key press
;

        switch      sw1,[key]
           case     sw1,first_au,UP_ARROW
           case     sw1,first_ad,DOWN_ARROW
           case     sw1,first_cr,E_CR
           default  sw1,first_esc
        eswitch     sw1


;
; If first_exit is true then exit
; endless loop
;

        BIFTRUE ISE1,[first_exit]
           EBREAK  EL1
        EIF     ISE1

EELOOP  EL1


;
; restore screen image under window
;

        call    rest_scrn


;
; If ESCAPE key selected then bypass action
;

BIFFALSE L2,act_flag
        goto    no_cond
EIF     L2


;
; Select procedure based on highlight bar's row
;
```

Fig. 15-3 continued.

```
        switch      sw2,[first_row]
          case      sw2,prt_scrn,1
          case      sw2,cond_on,2
          case      sw2,cond_off,3
        eswitch     sw2

no_cond:
;
; Exit from new Print Screen code
;
EPROCEDURE NEWPS

;-------------------------------------
; Up Arrow key selected
;

BPROCEDURE first_au
BIFE    FA1,first_row,1
        setv    first_row,3
BELSE   FA1
        sub1    first_row
EIFELSE FA1
EPROCEDURE first_au

;-------------------------------------
; Down Arrow key selected
;

BPROCEDURE first_ad
BIFE    FA2,first_row,3
        setv    first_row,1
BELSE   FA2
        add1    first_row
EIFELSE FA2
EPROCEDURE first_ad

;-------------------------------------
; ENTER Key has been selected
;

BPROCEDURE first_cr
        setv    act_flag,1
        setv    first_exit,1
EPROCEDURE first_cr

;-------------------------------------
; ESCAPE key has been selected
;

BPROCEDURE first_esc
        setv0   act_flag
        setv    first_exit,1
EPROCEDURE first_esc

;-------------------------------------
; Print the screen
;

BPROCEDURE prt_scrn
```

Fig. 15-3 continued.

```
BFORLTE PRT1,0,24
   BFORLTE PRT2,0,79
        vdrdchar    v1PRT1,v1PRT2
        setv0       AH
        prchar      0,RET_VAL
   EFOR    PRT2
        prchar  0,10
        prchar  0,13
   EFOR      PRT1
        prchar      0,12
EPROCEDURE prt_scrn

;-------------------------------------
;
; Send EPSON Condense ON to printer
;
BPROCEDURE cond_on
        prchar  0,15
EPROCEDURE cond_on


;
; Send EPSON Condense ON to printer
;


BPROCEDURE cond_off
        prchar  0,18
EPROCEDURE cond_off

;-------------------------------------
; Save the screen image under window
;

BPROCEDURE save_scrn
        lea     BX,w1_buff
BFORLTE SL1,W1_ULR,W1_LRR
   BFORLTE SL2,W1_ULC,W1_LRC
        vdrdchar       v1SL1,v1SL2
        mov            WORD PTR [BX],RET_VA
        add2           BX
   EFOR    SL2
EFOR    SL1
EPROCEDURE save_scrn

;-------------------------------------
;
; Restore the screen image under window
;

BPROCEDURE rest_scrn


        lea     BX,w1_buff
BFORLTE RL1,W1_ULR,W1_LRR
   BFORLTE RL2,W1_ULC,W1_LRC
        mov            AX, WORD PTR [BX]
        setv           [token],RET_VAL
        vdtoken        v1RL1,v1RL2,[token]
        add2           BX
   EFOR    RL2
EFOR    RL1
EPROCEDURE rest_scrn


;-------------------------------------
```

```
L_VIDINIT
L_MAKEATTR
L_TOKEN
L_WVDATTR
L_VDCHAR
L_SETPSVEC
;------------------------------------
;
; ***** Non-Resident section of *****
; ***** the code begins here     *****
;
;------------------------------------


install:
;
; set proper page segment in video structure
;

        vidinit

;
; Create window attribute
;

        makeattr    BLACK,CYAN,OFF_INTEN,OFF_BLINK
        setv        w1attr,RET_VAL
        makeattr    CYAN,BLACK,ON_INTEN,OFF_BLINK
        setv        w1inv,RET_VAL
        wsetattr    W1,[w1attr]

;
; Print intro buffer to screen
;

        puts        intro


;
; Re-direct Int 5
;

        cproc       setpsvec

;
; Make COM program TSR and free memory
; after 'install' label
;

        COM_TO_TSR install

;
; Procedures and data not needed by this
; TSR program
;

intro DB 10,13,'EPSON Printer Condense Program now installed.',13,10
      DB 'PRINT SCREEN Key is hot key',13,10,0

L_PUTS
L_PUTCHAR
L_MVCUR
        END_COM
```
_____

Fig. 15-3 ends.

16

Menu Demonstration

In this chapter you add four macro procedures to your EXE WINDOW.MAC file. WSETMEM dynamically allocates memory for the screen image that lies under the window. The DOS memory allocate function returns a segment, consequently this function may never be used in a COM file (COM files have only one segment). WVDATTR changes the video attributes for a string of text on a screen row. WSCRNSAVE and WSCRNREST save and restore the screen image under the window. These procedures are useful for overlapping windows.

EPROG30.ASM, the menu demonstration program, shows how to create Lotus style, vertical scroll bar style, and grid style windows using CHUCK. The method for memory allocation is explained in the source code. CPROG30.ASM is a substantial CHUCK demonstration program and is worth carefully exploring to increase your understanding of memory allocation.

CHUCK MENU PROCEDURES

The following sections discuss the CHUCK menu procedures in detail.

WSETMEM

WSETMEM allocates memory for windows. The syntax is:

    wsetmem   *seg_address, total_size*

where *seg_address* = memory
      total_size   = immediate

The WSETMEM procedure allocates all the dynamically allocated memory for your program at one time. You calculate how much memory you need to dynamically allocate and then allocate the memory using DOS. The segment of the allocated memory is placed in *seg_address* and the window images are held at differing offsets within the allocated memory.

Remember that WSETMEM should only be added to your EXE version WINDOW.MAC file and should never be called from a COM program.

WSETMEM (EXE Version)   Figure 16-1 presents the macro listing to WSETMEM.

Fig. 16-1. The EXE macro listing to WSETMEM.

```
;-----------------------------------
; Macro: WSETMEM wind,size
;
; Description: Allocates memory for WINDOW
;  scratch pads
;

WSETMEM MACRO seg_addr,size
        mov     BX,size ; num of 16 byte para to BX
        mov     AH,48h  ; DOS allocate me function
        int     21           ; Invoke DOS
        mov     [seg_addr],AX ; save block segment
        ENDM
```

WVDATTR

WVDATTR changes *n* bytes of window video attributes. The syntax is:

wvdattr   *wind1,row,col,length,attr*

where *wind1*   = legal label name
      row   = memory|immediate
      col   = memory|immediate
      length = immediate
      attr   = memory

The WVDATTR procedure changes the video attributes of *length* number of positions within the *wind1* window starting at *row, col*. The new screen attribute is *attr*.

WVDATTR (EXE Version)   Figure 16-2 presents the EXE version of the WVDATTR macro listing and Fig. 16-3 presents the source code listing of WVDATTR.ASM.

Fig. 16-2. The EXE macro listing to WVDATTR.

```
;-----------------------------------
; Macro: WVDATTR wind,row,col,len,attr
;
; Description: Writes attribute to
;  window without changing characters
; ** length must be immediate
```

```
WVDATTR MACRO wind,row,col,len,attr
        pushbcd
        lea     BX,wind

        mov     CX,attr
        mov     CH,len
        mov     AX,row
        mov     DX,col

        EXTRN   AWVDATTR:NEAR
        call    awvdattr
        popbcd
        ENDM
```

Fig. 16-2 ends.

Fig. 16-3. The EXE source code listing to WVDATTR.ASM.

```
;----------------------------------------
;
; vdAttr.asm
;
; vdAttr(row,col,len,attr)
;
; int row     row of string write
; int col     column of string write
; int len     number of bytes to write
; int attr    attribute of screen write
;

INCLUDE SMALL.MAC

        DOSSEG

        .MODEL SMALL

        EXTRN   SCRNSEG:WORD

        .DATA

avdpattr DB     7

        .CODE

        PUBLIC  awvdattr

awvdattr PROC NEAR
        xchg    CL,CH

        mov     avdpattr,CH
        xor     CH,CH

        push    ES

        push    CX      ; save length to stack

        mov     CL,[BX.ulrow]
        add     AL,CL

        mov     CL,[BX.ulcol]
        add     DL,CL
```

```
        mov     CX,SCRNSEG
        mov     ES,CX           ; reset extra seg

        mov     BL,160          ; 80 chars wide * 2
        mul     BL              ; row * scrn width  -> AX
        mov     CL,DL           ; column to CL
        xor     CH,CH           ; 0 -> CH
        shl     CX,1            ; col * 2
        add     AX,CX           ; column + (row * scrn width)
        mov     DI,AX           ; point DI to scrn

        cld                     ; direction increment
        pop     CX              ; string length parameter
vdr1:
        inc     DI              ; bypass character byte
        mov     AL,[avdpattr]   ; attribute to AL
        stosb                   ; AL -> screen
        loop    vdr1
        pop     ES
        ret

awvdattr ENDP

        END
```

;-------------------------------------

Fig. 16-3 ends.

WSCRNSAVE
WSCRNREST

WSCRNSAVE saves the screen image under the window. WSCRNREST restores the screen image to window area. The syntax is:

```
wscrnsave    window_name,seg_address
wscrnrest    window_name,seg_address
```

where *window_name* = legal label name
      seg_address = memory

The WSCRNSAVE procedure saves the screen image under the window before the window is drawn to the screen. Note that *seg_address* must have previously been allocated using the WSETMEM procedure. The WSCRNREST procedure restores the previously saved screen image over the window, making it disappear.

WSCRNSAVE and WSCRNREST (EXE Version)   Figure 16-4 presents the EXE version macro listing of WSCRNSAVE and WSCRNREST and Fig. 16-5 presents the source code listing of WSCRNRS.ASM, the subroutines called from within the WSCRNSAVE and WSCRNREST macros.

Fig. 16-4. The EXE macro listing to WSCRNSAVE and WSCRNREST.

```
;-------------------------------------
;
; WSCRNSAVE      wind,seg_addr
;
; Description
;  Save the screen image which is under
;  the window to a previously allocated
;  buffer in [BX.scrnimg]

WSCRNSAVE MACRO wind,seg_addr

        lea     BX,&wind

        push    ES
        push    DI

        push    [BX.scrnimg]
        pop     DI
        push    [seg_addr]
        pop     ES

        EXTRN   AWSSAVE:NEAR
        call    awssave

        pop     DI
        pop     ES

        ENDM

;-------------------------------------


;-------------------------------------
;
; WSCRNREST      wind,seg_addr
;
; Description
;  Restore the screen image which is under
;  the window from a previously allocated
;  buffer in [BX.scrnimg]

WSCRNREST MACRO wind,seg_addr

        lea     BX,wind

        push    ES
        push    DI

        push    [BX.scrnimg]
        pop     DI
        push    [seg_addr]
        pop     ES

        EXTRN   AWSREST:NEAR
        call    awsrest

        pop     DI
        pop     ES

        ENDM

;-------------------------------------
```

Fig. 16-5. The EXE source code listing to WSCRNRS.ASM.

```
;----------------------------------------
;
; File Name: WSCRNRS.ASM
;
;  Subroutine to WSCRNREST / WSCRNSAVE
;

INCLUDE SMALL.MAC

        DOSSEG

        .MODEL  SMALL

        .DATA

wrulcol DW      ?
wrulrow DW      ?
wrlrrow DW      ?
wrlrcol DW      ?

tokensr DW      ?

        .CODE

        PUBLIC AWSREST,AWSSAVE

AWSREST PROC NEAR

        mov     AL,[BX.ulrow]
        mov     [wrulrow],AX
        mov     AL,[BX.ulcol]
        mov     [wrulcol],AX
        mov     AL,[BX.lrrow]
        mov     [wrlrrow],AX
        mov     AL,[BX.lrcol]
        mov     [wrlrcol],AX


BFORLTE L0,[wrulrow],[wrlrrow]
   BFORLTE L1,[wrulcol],[wrlrcol]
        mov     AX,WORD PTR ES:[DI]
        mov     [tokensr],AX
        vdtoken v1L0,v1L1,[tokensr]
        add2    DI
   EFOR    L1
EFOR    L0

        ret

AWSREST ENDP

AWSSAVE PROC NEAR

        mov     AL,[BX.ulrow]
        mov     [wrulrow],AX
        mov     AL,[BX.ulcol]
```

```
            mov      [wrulcol],AX
            mov      AL,[BX.lrrow]
            mov      [wrlrrow],AX
            mov      AL,[BX.lrcol]
            mov      [wrlrcol],AX


BFORLTE L00,[wrulrow],[wrlrrow]
   BFORLTE L11,[wrulcol],[wrlrcol]
            vdrdchar v1L00,v1L11
            mov      WORD PTR ES:[DI],RET_VAL
            add2     DI
      EFOR     L11
EFOR    L00
            ret

AWSSAVE ENDP

            END


;----------------------------------------
```

Fig. 16-5 ends.

WINDOW DEMONSTRATION EXAMPLE

The source code listing to EPROG30.ASM is presented in Fig. 16-6.

Fig. 16-6. The source code listing to EPROG30.ASM.

```
;----------------------------------------
;
; File Name: EPROG30.ASM
;
; Description:
;  MENU demonstration program source
;


;
; No print of include files in listing
;

%NOINCL


;
; Include ASMplus files
;

INCLUDE SMALL.MAC

; Calculate window offsets within
; window_pad
;
; FIRST offset = 0 byte paragraphs
;       First size =
;
```

Fig. 16-6 continued.

```
; FIRST window size = ((10-1)*(34-3)) = 279 screen chars
;       279 bytes * 2 = 558 bytes for image tokens
;       offset 0 & allocate 560 bytes
;
; INFORM window size = ((17-6)*(44-14)) = 330 screen chars
;       330 bytes * 2 = 560 bytes for image tokens
;       offset 560 & allocate 672 bytes
;
; LOTUS window size = ((9-5)*(68-19)) = 196 screen chars
;       196 bytes * 2 = 392 bytes for image tokens
;       offset 1232 & allocate 400 bytes
;
; GRID window size = ((18-9)*(32-9)) =  207 screen chars
;       207 bytes * 2 = 414 bytes for image tokens
;       offset 1632 & allocate 416 bytes
;
; TOTAL_PAD = (last offset + allocated bytes) / 16
;

TOTAL_PAD equ 128

FIRST_OFF   equ 0
INFORM_OFF  equ 560
LOTUS_OFF   equ 1232
GRID_OFF    equ 1632

        PROG_EXE

        PROG_DATA
;-------------------------------------
; Segment address for window
; pad. This segment is dynamically
; allocated using 'wsetmem'

window_pad DW   0


;-------------------------------------

FIRST   WINDOW < 2,4,10,34,7,FIRST_OFF,>
INFORM  WINDOW < 7,15,17,44,7,INFORM_OFF,>
LOTUS   WINDOW < 6,20,9,68,7,LOTUS_OFF,>
GRID    WINDOW < 10,10,18,32,7,GRID_OFF,>

i_bar   DB      195
        DB      29 DUP(196)
        DB      180,0

; Main window screen data
fname   DB      ' TSR ASMplus  (c) 1989 ',0
ftitle  DB      '     ASMplus  Ver. 1.0',0
item1   DB      ' Lotus Style Menu',0
item2   DB      ' Grid Style Menu',0
item3   DB      ' Some Historical Information',0
item5   DB      ' Quit ASMplus Demo',0

; Lotus style window screen data
l_title DB      ' Lotus Style Window ',0
menu1   DB      ' Mean  Mode  Median  Range  Standard Deviation ',0
mess1   DB      ' Mean is the Average score of the distribution ',0
mess2   DB      ' Mode is the most frequent score               ',0
```

Fig. 16-6 continued.

```
mess3    DB        ' Median in the middle score of the sample      ',0
mess4    DB        ' Range is the distance from highest to lowest   ',0
mess5    DB        ' Standard dev. is the avg. distance from mean   ',0

; Grid style window screen data
g_title DB         ' Grid Style Window ',0
gmenu    DB        '    SELECT A NUMBER',0
grid1    DB        '       1  2  3',0
grid2    DB        '       4  5  6',0
grid3    DB        '       7  8  9',0
grid4    DB        ' Press ENTER to Exit',0

; History information screen data
i_title DB         ' Esoteric Information ',0
speed1   DB        '    TSRs ASMplus  History',0
speed2   DB        195
         DB        28 DUP(196)
         DB        180,0
speed3   DB        '         TSR SYSTEMS LTD',0
speed4   DB        ' -------------------------',0
speed5   DB        '   ASMplus by Len Dorfman',0
speed6   DB        '    & Chuckie & Friskie',0

speed8   DB        '    Press ANY KEY to Exit',0


inverse DW        0
hl_tense DW       0
intense DW        0
fattr    DW       0
lattr    DW       0
l_inv    DW       0
iattr    DW       0
i_inv    DW       0
gattr    DW       0
g_blink DW        0

token    DW       0
key      DW       0
lotus_key DW      0
lotus_col DW      0
grid_key DW       0
grid_col DW       0
first_exit DW     0
first_row  DW     3


; Start of code segment

        PROG_CODE

        vidinit        ; CHUCK video initialization

; allocate window pad memory

        wsetmem    [window_pad],TOTAL_PAD

; set inverse video

        makeattr  BLACK,WHITE,OFF_INTEN,OFF_BLINK
```

Fig. 16-6 continued.

```
        setv      [inverse],RET_VAL

; set hl_tense video

        makeattr  WHITE,WHITE,ON_INTEN,OFF_BLINK
        setv      [hl_tense],RET_VAL

; set intense video

        makeattr  WHITE,MAGENTA,ON_INTEN,OFF_BLINK
        setv      [hl_tense],RET_VAL

; set fattr video

        makeattr  WHITE,MAGENTA,OFF_INTEN,OFF_BLINK
        setv      [fattr],RET_VAL

; set lattr video

        makeattr  WHITE,BLUE,ON_INTEN,OFF_BLINK
        setv      [lattr],RET_VAL

        makeattr  MAGENTA,BLUE,ON_INTEN,OFF_BLINK
        setv      [l_inv],RET_VAL

; set gattr video

        makeattr  WHITE,RED,OFF_INTEN,OFF_BLINK
        setv      [gattr],RET_VAL

        makeattr  WHITE,RED,OFF_INTEN,ON_BLINK
        setv      [g_blink],RET_VAL

; set iattr video & i_inv

        makeattr  BLACK,CYAN,OFF_INTEN,OFF_BLINK
        setv      [iattr],RET_VAL

        makeattr  CYAN,BLACK,OFF_INTEN,OFF_BLINK
        setv      [i_inv],RET_VAL

; turn off the cursor

        offcursor

; save cursor location

        savecurloc

; initialize FIRST window structure and display

        wsetattr   FIRST,[fattr]
        wscrnsave  FIRST,[window_pad]
        wdisplay   FIRST,S_S_S_S

; initialize LOTUS window attribute

        wsetattr   LOTUS,[lattr]

; initialize GRID window attribute
```

Fig. 16-6 continued.

```
        wsetattr    GRID,[gattr]

; initialize INFORM window attribute

        wsetattr    INFORM,[iattr]

; print window title

        wswrite     FIRST,0,4,fname
        wswrite     FIRST,1,1,ftitle
        wvdattr     FIRST,1,1,29,[inverse]
        wswrite     FIRST,2,0,i_bar
        wswrite     FIRST,3,1,item1
        wswrite     FIRST,4,1,item2
        wswrite     FIRST,5,1,item3
        wswrite     FIRST,6,0,i_bar
        wswrite     FIRST,7,1,item5


; main keyboard loop

BELOOP  EL1
        call        clr_first
        wvdattr     FIRST,[first_row],1,29,[inverse]
        getkey      [key]
        switch      sw1,[key]
           case     sw1,first_up,UP_ARROW
           case     sw1,first_dn,DOWN_ARROW
           case     sw1,first_cr,E_CR
           default  sw1,first_key
        eswitch     sw1

        BIFTRUE ISE1,[first_exit]
           EBREAK  EL1
        EIF     ISE1

EELOOP  EL1

; restore screen image under first window

        wscrnrest  FIRST,[window_pad]

; restore cursor location

        restcurloc

; turn on the cursor

        oncursor

        END_EXE             ; DOS EXE terminate

;-----------------------------------

;-----------------------------------
;***********************************
;
; Procedures from sw1 switch / case
;
```

Fig. 16-6 continued.

```
;----------------------------------------
;
BPROCEDURE first_up

BIFE   fu3,[first_row],3
         setv    [first_row],7
         return
EIF    fu3

BIFE   fu2,[first_row],7
         setv    [first_row],5
         return
EIF    fu2

         sub1    [first_row]

up_done:
EPROCEDURE first_up

;----------------------------------------
;
BPROCEDURE first_dn

BIFE   fd3,[first_row],7
         setv    [first_row],3
         return
EIF    fd3

BIFE   fd2,[first_row],5
         setv    [first_row],7
         return
EIF    fd2

         add1    [first_row]

dn_done:
EPROCEDURE first_dn

;----------------------------------------
;
BPROCEDURE first_cr
         switch  sw2,[first_row]
            case sw2,do_lotus,3
            case sw2,do_grid,4
            case sw2,do_inform,5
            case sw2,to_dos,7
         eswitch sw2
EPROCEDURE first_cr

;----------------------------------------
;
; Handles default in sw1

BPROCEDURE first_key
         and     [key],0FFh ; mask scan code
BIFGT  fk0,[key],'Z'        ; if lower case then..
         sub     [key],20h  ; make upper case
EIF    fk0

BIFE   fk1,[key],'L'
```

Fig. 16-6 continued.

```
        setv    [first_row],3
EIF     fk1

BIFE    fk2,[key],'G'
        setv    [first_row],4
EIF     fk2

BIFE    fk3,[key],'S'
        setv    [first_row],5
EIF     fk3

BIFE    fk4,[key],'Q'
        beep
        setv    [first_row],7
EIF     fk4

EPROCEDURE first_key

;-------------------------------------

;-------------------------------------
;*************************************
;
; Procedures from sw2 switch / case
;
;-------------------------------------
;

BPROCEDURE to_dos
        setv    [first_exit],1
EPROCEDURE to_dos

;-------------------------------------
;
; Clear highlight bar and highlight
; first letters of main menu items
;

BPROCEDURE clr_first

BFORLTE clrf1,3,7
        wvdattr    FIRST,v1clrf1,1,29,[fattr]
EFOR    clrf1

BFORLTE clrf2,3,5
        wvdattr    FIRST,v1clrf2,2,1,[hl_tense]
EFOR    clrf2

        wvdattr    FIRST,7,2,1,[hl_tense]

EPROCEDURE clr_first

;-------------------------------------
;
; LOTUS Style window
;

BPROCEDURE do_lotus
```

Fig. 16-6 continued.

```
          wscrnsave  LOTUS,[window_pad]

          wdisplay   LOTUS,S_S_S_S
          wswrite    LOTUS,0,14,l_title
          wswrite    LOTUS,1,1,menu1

BELOOP  LEL1
          wvdattr    LOTUS,1,1,47,lattr
          call       lotus_hilite

          wvdattr    LOTUS,2,1,47,l_inv

          getkey     [lotus_key]
          switch  sw4,[lotus_key]
             case sw4,l_is_ra,RIGHT_ARROW
             case sw4,l_is_la,LEFT_ARROW
          eswitch sw4


          BIFE       LEL2,[lotus_key],E_CR
             EBREAK  LEL1
          EIF        LEL2

EELOOP  LEL1

          wscrnrest  LOTUS,[window_pad]

EPROCEDURE  do_lotus

;---------------------------------------
;***************************************
;
; Procedures called from sw4 switch / case
;

;---------------------------------------
; LOTUS left arrow key press
;

BPROCEDURE  l_is_la
BIFE     LLA4,[lotus_col],0
          setv    [lotus_col],4
BELSE    LLA4
          sub1    [lotus_col]
EIFELSE LLA4
EPROCEDURE  l_is_la

;---------------------------------------
; LOTUS right arrow key press
;

BPROCEDURE  l_is_ra
BIFE     LRA4,[lotus_col],4
             setv0 [lotus_col]
BELSE    LRA4
          add1   [lotus_col]
EIFELSE LRA4
EPROCEDURE  l_is_ra

;---------------------------------------
```

Fig. 16-6 continued.

```
; Highlight top row item selected
;

BPROCEDURE lotus_hilite

BIFFALSE LH0,[lotus_col]
        wvdattr    LOTUS,1,1,6,[inverse]
        wswrite    LOTUS,2,1,mess1
        return
EIF     LH0

BIFE    LH1,[lotus_col],1
        wvdattr    LOTUS,1,7,6,[inverse]
        wswrite    LOTUS,2,1,mess2
        return
EIF     LH1

BIFE    LH2,[lotus_col],2
        wvdattr    LOTUS,1,13,8,[inverse]
        wswrite    LOTUS,2,1,mess3
        return
EIF     LH2

BIFE    LH3,[lotus_col],3
        wvdattr    LOTUS,1,21,7,[inverse]
        wswrite    LOTUS,2,1,mess4
        return
EIF     LH3

        wvdattr    LOTUS,1,28,20,[inverse]
        wswrite    LOTUS,2,1,mess5

EPROCEDURE lotus_hilite

;------------------------------------

;------------------------------------

;------------------------------------
;
; GRID Style window
;

BPROCEDURE do_grid
        wscrnsave  GRID,[window_pad]

        wdisplay   GRID,S_S_S_S
        wswrite    GRID,0,2,g_title
        wvdattr    GRID,1,1,21,[inverse]
        wswrite    GRID,1,1,gmenu
        wswrite    GRID,3,1,grid1
        wswrite    GRID,4,1,grid2
        wswrite    GRID,5,1,grid3
        wswrite    GRID,7,1,grid4
        wvdattr    GRID,7,8,5,[g_blink]

BELOOP  GEL1
        call       grid_hilite

        getkey     [grid_key]
```

Fig. 16-6 continued.

```
        switch  sw5,[grid_key]
           case sw5,g_is_ra,RIGHT_ARROW
           case sw5,g_is_la,LEFT_ARROW
           case sw5,g_is_ua,UP_ARROW
           case sw5,g_is_da,DOWN_ARROW
        eswitch sw5


        BIFE       GEL2,[grid_key],E_CR
           EBREAK  GEL1
        EIF        GEL2

EELOOP  GEL1

        wscrnrest  GRID,[window_pad]

EPROCEDURE do_grid

;-------------------------------------

;-------------------------------------
; GRID left arrow key press
;

BPROCEDURE g_is_la
BIFE GLA4,[grid_col],0
        setv    [grid_col],2
        return
EIF  GLA4

BIFE GLA5,[grid_col],3
        setv    [grid_col],5
        return
EIF  GLA5

BIFE GLA6,[grid_col],6
        setv    [grid_col],8
        return
EIF  GLA6

        sub1    [grid_col]

EPROCEDURE g_is_la

;-------------------------------------
; GRID right arrow key press
;

BPROCEDURE g_is_ra
BIFE GRA4,[grid_col],2
        setv0   [grid_col]
        return
EIF  GRA4

BIFE GRA5,[grid_col],5
        setv    [grid_col],3
        return
EIF  GRA5

BIFE GRA6,[grid_col],8
```

Fig. 16-6 continued.

```
        setv    [grid_col],6
        return
EIF  GRA6

        add1    [grid_col]

EPROCEDURE g_is_ra

;------------------------------------

;------------------------------------
; GRID up arrow key press
;

BPROCEDURE g_is_ua
BIFE GUA4,[grid_col],0
        setv    [grid_col],6
        return
EIF  GUA4

BIFE GUA5,[grid_col],1
        setv    [grid_col],7
        return
EIF  GUA5

BIFE GUA6,[grid_col],2
        setv    [grid_col],8
        return
EIF  GUA6

        sub     [grid_col],3

EPROCEDURE g_is_ua

;------------------------------------

;------------------------------------
; GRID down arrow key press
;

BPROCEDURE g_is_da
BIFE GDA4,[grid_col],6
        setv0   [grid_col]
        return
EIF  GDA4

BIFE GDA5,[grid_col],7
        setv    [grid_col],1
        return
EIF  GDA5

BIFE GDA6,[grid_col],8
        setv    [grid_col],2
        return
EIF  GDA6

        add     [grid_col],3

EPROCEDURE g_is_da
```

Fig. 16-6 continued.

```
;-------------------------------------
;-------------------------------------

BPROCEDURE grid_hilite

BFORLTE  GF1,3,5
         wvdattr    GRID,v1GF1,7,9,[gattr]
EFOR     GF1
BIFFALSE GH0,[grid_col]
         wvdattr    GRID,3,7,3,[inverse]
         return
EIF      GH0

BIFE     GH1,[grid_col],1
         wvdattr    GRID,3,10,3,[inverse]
         return
EIF      GH1

BIFE     GH2,[grid_col],2
         wvdattr    GRID,3,13,3,[inverse]
         return
EIF      GH2

BIFE     GH3,[grid_col],3
         wvdattr    GRID,4,7,3,[inverse]
         return
EIF      GH3

BIFE     GH4,[grid_col],4
         wvdattr    GRID,4,10,3,[inverse]
         return
EIF      GH4

BIFE     GH5,[grid_col],5
         wvdattr    GRID,4,13,3,[inverse]
         return
EIF      GH5

BIFE     GH6,[grid_col],6
         wvdattr    GRID,5,7,3,[inverse]
         return
EIF      GH6

BIFE     GH7,[grid_col],7
         wvdattr    GRID,5,10,3,[inverse]
         return
EIF      GH7

         wvdattr    GRID,5,13,3,[inverse]
EPROCEDURE grid_hilite

;-------------------------------------

;-------------------------------------
;
; INFORM Style window
;

BPROCEDURE do_inform
```

```
          wscrnsave   INFORM, [window_pad]

          wdisplay    INFORM,S_S_S_S

          wswrite     INFORM,0,4,i_title
          wswrite     INFORM,1,1,speed1
          wvdattr     INFORM,1,1,28,i_inv
          wswrite     INFORM,2,0,speed2
          wswrite     INFORM,3,1,speed3
          wswrite     INFORM,4,1,speed4
          wswrite     INFORM,5,1,speed5
          wswrite     INFORM,6,1,speed6
          wswrite     INFORM,7,1,speed4
          wswrite     INFORM,8,0,speed2
          wswrite     INFORM,9,1,speed8

          getkey

          wscrnrest   INFORM, [window_pad]

EPROCEDURE do_inform

          END

;
; End of Source Listing
;----------------------------------------
```

Fig. 16-6 ends.

17

Wari Demonstration

Wari. What a wonderful game. Wari is a board game that appears to have roots in ancient Egypt although currently the game is most well known in Africa and Asia. In a way, Wari appears to have a flavor of backgammon. Wari's rules are simple, but the play is deliciously tricky.

THE GAME OF WARI

Wari is played on a game board where six cups are on your side and six cups are on your opponents side. The game starts with four stones in each cup.

Players alternately move by taking the stones in one of their cups and then dropping them in a counter clockwise direction around the board. If the last stone you drop falls in one of your opponent's cups and there are two or three stones in that cup, you may capture those stones. After your capture you may then look at the opponents's cup containing the next to last stone you dropped. If there are two or three stones in that cup then you may capture again, etc. You may not, though, capture stones on your side of the board.

The CHUCK Wari game ends if you or the computer get a majority of stones (or jewels as they're called in the TAB game) on the board (25 or more stones).

Your square cups are at the screen's bottom and are clearly numbered one through six. You make your choice by pressing the keyboard number below the cup.

Now, when I was coding the computer logic, the path I took stood positional in nature. After your move, CHUCK (your computer opponent) does the following:

1. Simulates dropping all the stones in his cups and remembers the captures for each selection, the number of vulnerable stones to capture on his side and your side

2. If

   CHUCK can capture any stones he makes the capture

else if

vulnerable cups on CHUCK's side is not equal then CHUCK moves to create the fewest vulnerable cups on his side (defensive move)

else

CHUCK moves to create most vulnerable cups on your side (offensive)

I'm a long-time chess fan and my teenage respect for Aron Nimzovitch's positional notions still run deep. I suppose I could have simply laid out a tree calculating all the possible variations a few move sequences deep, but that mechanical approach didn't appeal to me here. I wanted to work on CHUCK's positional nuances. When CHUCK uses his beginner level he makes some very dumb guesses and when you are learning the game I suggest you keep CHUCK at beginner until you beat him severely every time.

CHUCK's Wari skill will provide nice entertainment for children who can count from one to thirty and up. Teens have also enjoyed playing this version of the game.

Note that there is a menu bar drop-down window interface. Wari's drop-down windows are invoked by pressing the Alt key and the first letter of the menu item. Drop-down window items may be selected by moving the highlight bar and then pressing the Enter key. Wari's rules are embedded in the program and can be called from the Play window.

Game Code

Figure 17-1 presents the source code to TABWARI.ASM, Fig. 17-2 presents the source code listing to TABWARI1.ASM, Fig. 17-3 presents the source code listing to TABWARI2.ASM and Fig. 17-4 presents the source code listing to WARIDATA.ASM.

To create an executable copy of TABWARI simply assemble TABWARI.ASM and then link it with TAB.LIB. TABWARI1, TABWARI2, and WARIDATA are all included from TABWARI.

Fig. 17-1. The source code listing to TABWARI.ASM.

```
;----------------------------------------
; File Name:   TABWARI.ASM
; Description: Simple Demonstration of ASMplus Language
;----------------------------------------
;

include SMALL.MAC        ; ASMplus include files

PROG_EXE 200h              ; Create .EXE program with stack=200h

PROG_DATA                  ; Start PROGram DATA segment


buff10  DB      10 DUP(0)
blank   DB  '   ',0
ecell_val DW    0
emax_cell DW    0
emax_val DW     0
```

Fig. 17-1 continued.

```
include WARIDATA.ASM      ; AWARi Data


;---------------------------------------
;
PROG_CODE                 ; Start PROGram CODE segment
        vidinit
        offcursor
        makeattr    BLUE,WHITE,OFF_INTEN,OFF_BLINK
        setv        [inverse],RET_VAL
        makeattr    WHITE,BLUE,OFF_INTEN,OFF_BLINK
        setv        [hili_attr],RET_VAL
        wsetattr    playw,[hili_attr]
        wsetattr    filew,[hili_attr]
        makeattr    WHITE,RED,OFF_INTEN,OFF_BLINK
        setv        [cell_attr],RET_VAL
        makeattr    BLUE,RED,ON_INTEN,OFF_BLINK
        setv        [ston_attr],RET_VAL
        makeattr    BLACK,WHITE,OFF_INTEN,OFF_BLINK
        setv        [scrn_attr],RET_VAL
        wsetattr    scrnw,[scrn_attr]
        makeattr    BLUE,WHITE,OFF_INTEN,OFF_BLINK
        setv        [choo_attr],RET_VAL
        wsetattr    gowind,[choo_attr]
        clrwindow   scrnw
        swrite      0,0,menubar
        swrite      1,0,hbar
        swrite      23,0,hbar
        scwrite     0,31,17,wname1,[choo_attr]
        wsetattr    wind11,[cell_attr]
        wsetattr    wind10,[cell_attr]
        wsetattr    wind9,[cell_attr]
        wsetattr    wind8,[cell_attr]
        wsetattr    wind7,[cell_attr]
        wsetattr    wind6,[cell_attr]
        wsetattr    wind0,[cell_attr]
        wsetattr    wind1,[cell_attr]
        wsetattr    wind2,[cell_attr]
        wsetattr    wind3,[cell_attr]
        wsetattr    wind4,[cell_attr]
        wsetattr    wind5,[cell_attr]
        wsetattr    wbord,[choo_attr]
        wdisplay    wbord,S_S_S_S
        scwrite     21,8,63,choose,[choo_attr]
        wdisplay    wind11,S_S_S_S
        wdisplay    wind10,S_S_S_S
        wdisplay    wind9,S_S_S_S
        wdisplay    wind8,S_S_S_S
        wdisplay    wind7,S_S_S_S
        wdisplay    wind6,S_S_S_S
        wdisplay    wind0,S_S_S_S
        wdisplay    wind1,S_S_S_S
        wdisplay    wind2,S_S_S_S
        wdisplay    wind3,S_S_S_S
        wdisplay    wind4,S_S_S_S
        wdisplay    wind5,S_S_S_S


        cproc       show_score
BELOOP  keyboard


        BIFGT    gamo1,[p_score],24
```

Fig. 17-1 continued.

```
          savescrn
          wdisplay    gowind,S_S_S_S
          wswrite     gowind,2,1,pwins
          wswrite     gowind,3,1,wkey
          cproc       newgame
          GOTO        nomove
        EIF    gamo1

        BIFGT   gamo2,[c_score],24
          savescrn
          wdisplay    gowind,S_S_S_S
          wswrite     gowind,2,1,cwins
          wswrite     gowind,3,1,wkey
          cproc       newgame
          GOTO        nomove
        EIF    gamo2

        BIFE    kb0,[level],0
          scwrite   0,31,17,wname2,[choo_attr]
        BELSE   kb0
          scwrite   0,31,17,wname1,[choo_attr]
        EIFELSE kb0
        call    show_board

        cproc   draw_board

        swrite  3,31,yt_mess

        cproc   filter_key

        BIFE    kb1,RET_VAL,1
          EBREAK    keyboard        ; BREAK from loop
        EIF    kb1

        BIFLT   kb2,[key_num],1     ; on key_num < 1
          GOTO      nomove          ; bypass game play
        EIF    kb2

        BIFGT   kb3,[key_num],6     ; on key_num > 6
          GOTO      nomove          ; bypass game play
        EIF    kb3

        cmp     [key_num],1
        jne     kb4
        cmp     [board],0
        jne     kbok
        jmp     inomove
kb4:
        cmp     [key_num],2
        jne     kb5
        cmp     [board+2],0
        jne     kbok
        jmp     inomove
kb5:
        cmp     [key_num],3
        jne     kb6
        cmp     [board+4],0
        jne     kbok
        jmp     inomove
kb6:
```

Fig. 17-1 continued.

```
                cmp     [key_num],4
                jne     kb7
                cmp     [board+6],0
                jne     kbok
                jmp     inomove
kb7:
                cmp     [key_num],5
                jne     kb8
                cmp     [board+8],0
                jne     kbok
                jmp     inomove
kb8:
                cmp     [key_num],6
                jne     kbok
                cmp     [board+10],0
                jne     kbok
                jmp     inomove
kbok:

                sub1    [key_num]

                setv    AX,[key_num]
                cproc   drop_jewels
                cproc   grab_play
                cproc   draw_board
                cproc   show_score

;               call    show_board

                swrite  3,31,ct_mess

                cproc   delay

;               push    AX
;               getkey
;               pop     AX

BIFE    ml1,[level],0           ; beginner level?
                cproc   beg_chuck       ; yes => call dumb max cell
BELSE   ml1                             ; else
                cproc   int_chuck       ; advanced level
EIFELSE ml1

                cproc   drop_jewels
                cproc   grab_chuck
                cproc   show_score
;               call    show_board
                GOTO    nomove
inomove:
        beep
nomove:
EELOOP  keyboard
        clrscreen
        oncursor
        END_EXE
;-------------------------------------------

BPROCEDURE newgame
                onsound 10000
                cproc   delay
```

Fig. 17-1 continued.

```
        offsound
        getkey
        restscrn
        cproc      init_board
        setv0      [p_score]
        setv0      [c_score]
        cproc      show_score
EPROCEDURE newgame

;------------------------------------
BPROCEDURE grab_play
        BIFE      gpa,AX,11
           GOTO  gp11
        EIF       gpa
        BIFE      gpb,AX,10
           GOTO  gp10
        EIF       gpb
        BIFE      gpc,AX,9
           GOTO  gp9
        EIF       gpc
        BIFE      gpd,AX,8
           GOTO  gp8
        EIF       gpd
        BIFE      gpe,AX,7
           GOTO  gp7
        EIF       gpe
        BIFE      gpf,AX,6
           GOTO  gp6
        EIF       gpf
        GOTO      exit_gp
gp11:
        mov       AX,[board+22]
        BIFGT     gp11a,AX,3
           GOTO   exit_gp
        EIF       gp11a
        BIFLT     gp11b,AX,2
           GOTO   exit_gp
        EIF       gp11b
        add       [p_score],AX
        mov       [board+22],0
        cproc     bleep
        cproc     show_score
gp10:
        mov       AX,[board+20]
        BIFGT     gp10a,AX,3
           GOTO   exit_gp
        EIF       gp10a
        BIFLT     gp10b,AX,2
           GOTO   exit_gp
        EIF       gp10b
        add       [p_score],AX
        mov       [board+20],0
        cproc     bleep
        cproc     show_score
gp9:
        mov       AX,[board+18]
        BIFGT     gp9a,AX,3
           GOTO   exit_gp
        EIF       gp9a
        BIFLT     gp9b,AX,2
```

Fig. 17-1 continued.

```
              GOTO    exit_gp
       EIF    gp9b
       add    [p_score],AX
       mov    [board+18],0
       cproc  bleep
       cproc  show_score
gp8:
       mov    AX,[board+16]
       BIFGT  gp8a,AX,3
         GOTO   exit_gp
       EIF    gp8a
       BIFLT  gp8b,AX,2
         GOTO   exit_gp
       EIF    gp8b
       add    [p_score],AX
       mov    [board+16],0
       cproc  bleep
       cproc  show_score
gp7:
       mov    AX,[board+14]
       BIFGT  gp7a,AX,3
         GOTO   exit_gp
       EIF    gp7a
       BIFLT  gp7b,AX,2
         GOTO   exit_gp
       EIF    gp7b
       add    [p_score],AX
       mov    [board+14],0
       cproc  bleep
       cproc  show_score
gp6:
       mov    AX,[board+12]
       BIFGT  gp6a,AX,3
         GOTO   exit_gp
       EIF    gp6a
       BIFLT  gp6b,AX,2
         GOTO   exit_gp
       EIF    gp6b
       add    [p_score],AX
       mov    [board+12],0
       cproc  bleep
       cproc  show_score
exit_gp:
EPROCEDURE  grab_play

;-------------------------------------
BPROCEDURE grab_chuck
       BIFE   gca,AX,5
         GOTO gc5
       EIF    gca
       BIFE   gcb,AX,4
         GOTO gc4
       EIF    gcb
       BIFE   gcc,AX,3
         GOTO gc3
       EIF    gcc
       BIFE   gcd,AX,2
         GOTO gc2
       EIF    gcd
       BIFE   gce,AX,1
```

Fig. 17-1 continued.

```
              GOTO   gc1
       EIF    gce
       BIFE   gcf,AX,0
          GOTO  gc0
       EIF    gcf
       GOTO   exit_gc
gc5:
       mov    AX,[board+10]
       BIFGT  gc11a,AX,3
          GOTO   exit_gc
       EIF    gc11a
       BIFLT  gc11b,AX,2
          GOTO   exit_gc
       EIF    gc11b
       add    [c_score],AX
       mov    [board+10],0
       cproc  bleep
       cproc  show_score
gc4:
       mov    AX,[board+8]
       BIFGT  gc10a,AX,3
          GOTO   exit_gc
       EIF    gc10a
       BIFLT  gc10b,AX,2
          GOTO   exit_gc
       EIF    gc10b
       add    [c_score],AX
       mov    [board+8],0
       cproc  bleep
       cproc  show_score
gc3:
       mov    AX,[board+6]
       BIFGT  gc9a,AX,3
          GOTO   exit_gc
       EIF    gc9a
       BIFLT  gc9b,AX,2
          GOTO   exit_gc
       EIF    gc9b
       add    [c_score],AX
       mov    [board+6],0
       cproc  bleep
       cproc  show_score
gc2:
       mov    AX,[board+4]
       BIFGT  gc8a,AX,3
          GOTO   exit_gc
       EIF    gc8a
       BIFLT  gc8b,AX,2
          GOTO   exit_gc
       EIF    gc8b
       add    [c_score],AX
       mov    [board+4],0
       cproc  bleep
       cproc  show_score
gc1:
       mov    AX,[board+2]
       BIFGT  gc7a,AX,3
          GOTO   exit_gc
       EIF    gc7a
       BIFLT  gc7b,AX,2
```

Fig. 17-1 continued.

```
              GOTO    exit_gc
        EIF       gc7b
        add       [c_score],AX
        mov       [board+2],0
        cproc   bleep
        cproc   show_score
gc0:
        mov       AX,[board]
        BIFGT   gc6a,AX,3
          GOTO    exit_gc
        EIF       gc6a
        BIFLT   gc6b,AX,2
          GOTO    exit_gc
        EIF       gc6b
        add       [c_score],AX
        mov       [board],0
        cproc   bleep
        cproc   show_score
exit_gc:
EPROCEDURE  grab_chuck


;--------------------------------------------

BPROCEDURE grab_tree
        setv0   [t_score]
        BIFE      gta,AX,5
          GOTO  gt5
        EIF       gta
        BIFE      gtb,AX,4
          GOTO  gt4
        EIF       gtb
        BIFE      gtc,AX,3
          GOTO  gt3
        EIF       gtc
        BIFE      gtd,AX,2
          GOTO  gt2
        EIF       gtd
        BIFE      gte,AX,1
          GOTO  gt1
        EIF       gte
        BIFE      gtf,AX,0
          GOTO  gt0
        EIF       gtf
        GOTO    exit_gt
gt5:
        mov       AX,[tree1+10]
        BIFGT   gt11a,AX,3
          GOTO    exit_gt
        EIF       gt11a
        BIFLT   gt11b,AX,2
          GOTO    exit_gt
        EIF       gt11b
        add       [t_score],AX
        mov       [tree1+10],0
gt4:
        mov       AX,[tree1+8]
        BIFGT   gt10a,AX,3
          GOTO    exit_gt
        EIF       gt10a
        BIFLT   gt10b,AX,2
          GOTO    exit_gt
```

Fig. 17-1 continued.

```
        EIF     gt10b
        add     [t_score],AX
        mov     [tree1+8],0
gt3:
        mov     AX,[tree1+6]
        BIFGT   gt9a,AX,3
          GOTO  exit_gt
        EIF     gt9a
        BIFLT   gt9b,AX,2
          GOTO  exit_gt
        EIF     gt9b
        add     [t_score],AX
        mov     [tree1+6],0
gt2:
        mov     AX,[tree1+4]
        BIFGT   gt8a,AX,3
          GOTO  exit_gt
        EIF     gt8a
        BIFLT   gt8b,AX,2
          GOTO  exit_gt
        EIF     gt8b
        add     [t_score],AX
        mov     [tree1+4],0
gt1:
        mov     AX,[tree1+2]
        BIFGT   gt7a,AX,3
          GOTO  exit_gt
        EIF     gt7a
        BIFLT   gt7b,AX,2
          GOTO  exit_gt
        EIF     gt7b
        add     [t_score],AX
        mov     [tree1+2],0
gt0:
        mov     AX,[tree1]
        BIFGT   gt6a,AX,3
          GOTO  exit_gt
        EIF     gt6a
        BIFLT   gt6b,AX,2
          GOTO  exit_gt
        EIF     gt6b
        add     [t_score],AX
        mov     [tree1],0
exit_gt:
EPROCEDURE  grab_tree

;------------------------------------
BPROCEDURE drop_tree
BBLOCK   treea
treestart       DW      0
treetemp        DW      0
treeval DW      0
EBLOCK treea
        setv    treestart,AX
        setv    treetemp,AX
        setptr  DBASE_PTR,tree1
        shl     AX,1
        add     DBASE_PTR,AX
        mov     CX,WORD PTR[DBASE_PTR]
        setv    treeval,CX
```

Fig. 17-1 continued.

```
        mov     WORD PTR[DBASE_PTR],0
BLOOP   tree2,CX
        BIFE     tree3,treetemp,11
          setv0  treetemp
          setptr DBASE_PTR,tree1
        BELSE    tree3
          add2   DBASE_PTR
          add1   treetemp
        EIFELSE tree3
        BIFE     tree5,treetemp,treestart
          BIFE       tree6,treetemp,11
            setv0  treetemp
            setptr DBASE_PTR,tree1
          BELSE      tree6
            add2     DBASE_PTR
            add1     treetemp
          EIFELSE    tree6
        EIF     tree5
        mov     AX,WORD PTR[DBASE_PTR]
        add1    AX
        mov     WORD PTR[DBASE_PTR],AX
ELOOP   tree2
        RETURN  treetemp
EPROCEDURE drop_tree
;------------------------------------


;------------------------------------
BPROCEDURE adj_tree
        setv0   OFFTEMP
BIFE at02,[tree1+0],2
        add     OFFTEMP,2
EIF  at02
BIFE at01,[tree1+0],1
        add     OFFTEMP,1
EIF  at01
BIFE at12,[tree1+2],2
        add     OFFTEMP,2
EIF  at12
BIFE at11,[tree1+2],1
        add     OFFTEMP,1
EIF  at11
BIFE at22,[tree1+4],2
        add     OFFTEMP,2
EIF  at22
BIFE at21,[tree1+4],1
        add     OFFTEMP,1
EIF  at21
BIFE at32,[tree1+6],2
        add     OFFTEMP,2
EIF  at32
BIFE at31,[tree1+6],1
        add     OFFTEMP,1
EIF  at31
BIFE at42,[tree1+8],2
        add     OFFTEMP,2
EIF  at42
BIFE at41,[tree1+8],1
        add     OFFTEMP,1
EIF  at41
BIFE at52,[tree1+10],2
```

Fig. 17-1 continued.

```
          add      OFFTEMP,2
EIF   at52
BIFE at51,[tree1+10],1
          add      OFFTEMP,1
EIF   at51


          setv0    DEFTEMP
BIFE dat02,[tree1+12],2
          add      DEFTEMP,2
EIF   dat02
BIFE dat01,[tree1+12],1
          add      DEFTEMP,1
EIF   dat01
BIFE dat12,[tree1+14],2
          add      DEFTEMP,2
EIF   dat12
BIFE dat11,[tree1+14],1
          add      DEFTEMP,1
EIF   dat11
BIFE dat22,[tree1+16],2
          add      DEFTEMP,2
EIF   dat22
BIFE dat21,[tree1+16],1
          add      DEFTEMP,1
EIF   dat21
BIFE dat32,[tree1+18],2
          add      DEFTEMP,2
EIF   dat32
BIFE dat31,[tree1+18],1
          add      DEFTEMP,1
EIF   dat31
BIFE dat42,[tree1+20],2
          add      DEFTEMP,2
EIF   dat42
BIFE dat41,[tree1+20],1
          add      DEFTEMP,1
EIF   dat41
BIFE dat52,[tree1+22],2
          add      DEFTEMP,2
EIF   dat52
BIFE dat51,[tree1+22],1
          add      DEFTEMP,1
EIF   dat51
EPROCEDURE adj_tree

BPROCEDURE board_to_tree1
          setmv    [tree1+0],[board+0]
          setmv    [tree1+2],[board+2]
          setmv    [tree1+4],[board+4]
          setmv    [tree1+6],[board+6]
          setmv    [tree1+8],[board+8]
          setmv    [tree1+10],[board+10]
          setmv    [tree1+12],[board+12]
          setmv    [tree1+14],[board+14]
          setmv    [tree1+16],[board+16]
          setmv    [tree1+18],[board+18]
          setmv    [tree1+20],[board+20]
          setmv    [tree1+22],[board+22]

EPROCEDURE board_to_tree1
```

Fig. 17-1 continued.

```
;----------------------------------------
BPROCEDURE int_eval
        setv0    emax_cell
        setv0    emax_val

BIFGT   ie1,[EVAL11],55
        setv     emax_cell,11
        GOTO     exit_ie
EIF     ie1

BIFGT   ie2,[EVAL10],55
        setv     emax_cell,10
        GOTO     exit_ie
EIF     ie2

BIFGT   ie3,[EVAL9],55
        setv     emax_cell,9
        GOTO     exit_ie
EIF     ie3

BIFGT   ie4,[EVAL8],55
        setv     emax_cell,8
        GOTO     exit_ie
EIF     ie4

BIFGT   ie5,[EVAL7],55
        setv     emax_cell,7
        GOTO     exit_ie
EIF     ie5

BIFGT   ie6,[EVAL6],55
        setv     emax_cell,6
        GOTO     exit_ie
EIF     ie6

BIFGT   ie130,[EVAL11],53
        setv     emax_cell,11
        GOTO     exit_ie
EIF     ie130

BIFGT   ie23,[EVAL10],53
        setv     emax_cell,10
        GOTO     exit_ie
EIF     ie23

BIFGT   ie33,[EVAL9],53
        setv     emax_cell,9
        GOTO     exit_ie
EIF     ie33

BIFGT   ie43,[EVAL8],53
        setv     emax_cell,8
        GOTO     exit_ie
EIF     ie43

BIFGT   ie53,[EVAL7],53
        setv     emax_cell,7
        GOTO     exit_ie
EIF     ie53

BIFGT   ie63,[EVAL6],53
```

Fig. 17-1 continued.

```
        setv    emax_cell,6
        GOTO    exit_ie
EIF     ie63

BIFGT   ie120,[EVAL11],50
        setv    emax_cell,11
        GOTO    exit_ie
EIF     ie120

BIFGT   ie22,[EVAL10],50
        setv    emax_cell,10
        GOTO    exit_ie
EIF     ie22

BIFGT   ie32,[EVAL9],50
        setv    emax_cell,9
        GOTO    exit_ie
EIF     ie32

BIFGT   ie42,[EVAL8],50
        setv    emax_cell,8
        GOTO    exit_ie
EIF     ie42

BIFGT   ie52,[EVAL7],50
        setv    emax_cell,7
        GOTO    exit_ie
EIF     ie52

BIFGT   ie62,[EVAL6],50
        setv    emax_cell,6
        GOTO    exit_ie
EIF     ie62


; specific cell attack defense

; cell 5 drop dangerous?

        setmv   [testit],[board+10]
;--------------------------------------
BIFGT   ied1,[testit],0
  BIFLT ied1a,[testit],7
        setptr  DBASE_PTR,[board+10]
        shl     [testit],1
        add     DBASE_PTR,[testit]
        mov     AX,WORD PTR [DBASE_PTR]
    BIFE  ied1b,AX,2
        shr     [testit],1
        add     [testit],5
        setmv   [emax_cell],[testit]
    EIF   ied1b
    BIFE  ied1c,AX,3
        shr     [testit],1
        add     [testit],5
        setmv   emax_cell,[testit]
    EIF   ied1c
  EIF   ied1a
EIF     ied1
```

Fig. 17-1 continued.

```
;-----------------------------------------

BIFE    ie12,[DEF6],0
 BIFGT  ie12a,[board+12],0
        setv    emax_cell,6
        GOTO    exit_ie
 EIF    ie12a
EIF     ie12

BIFE    ie11,[DEF7],0
 BIFGT  ie11a,[board+14],0
        setv    emax_cell,7
        GOTO    exit_ie
 EIF    ie11a
EIF     ie11

BIFE    ie7,[DEF11],0
 BIFGT  ie7a,[board+22],0
        setv    emax_cell,11
        GOTO    exit_ie
 EIF    ie7a
EIF     ie7

BIFE    ie8,[DEF10],0
 BIFGT  ie8a,[board+20],0
        setv    emax_cell,10
        GOTO    exit_ie
 EIF    ie8a
EIF     ie8

BIFE    ie9,[DEF9],0
 BIFGT  ie9a,[board+18],0
        setv    emax_cell,9
        GOTO    exit_ie
 EIF    ie9a
EIF     ie9

BIFE    ie10,[DEF8],0
 BIFGT  ie10a,[board+16],0
        setv    emax_cell,8
        GOTO    exit_ie
 EIF    ie10a
EIF     ie10


BIFE    ie13,[DEF11],1
 BIFGT  ie13a,[board+22],0
        setv    emax_cell,11
        GOTO    exit_ie
 EIF    ie13a
EIF     ie13

BIFE    ie14,[DEF10],1
 BIFGT  ie14a,[board+20],0
        setv    emax_cell,10
        GOTO    exit_ie
 EIF    ie14a
EIF     ie14
BIFE    ie15,[DEF9],1
 BIFGT  ie15a,[board+18],0
```

Fig. 17-1 continued.

```
        setv    emax_cell,9
        GOTO    exit_ie
 EIF    ie15a
EIF     ie15

BIFE    ie16,[DEF8],1
 BIFGT  ie16a,[board+16],0
        setv    emax_cell,8
        GOTO    exit_ie
 EIF    ie16a
EIF     ie16

BIFE    ie17,[DEF7],1
 BIFGT  ie17a,[board+14],0
        setv    emax_cell,7
        GOTO    exit_ie
 EIF    ie17a
EIF     ie17

BIFE    ie18,[DEF6],1
 BIFGT  ie18a,[board+12],0
        setv    emax_cell,6
        GOTO    exit_ie
 EIF    ie18a
EIF     ie18

BIFE    ie19,[board+12],1
        setv    emax_cell,6
        GOTO    exit_ie
EIF     ie19


BIFGT   ie20a,[board+22],0
        setv    emax_cell,11
        GOTO    exit_ie
EIF     ie20a

BIFGT   ie21a,[board+20],0
        setv    emax_cell,10
        GOTO    exit_ie
EIF     ie21a

        cproc   beg_chuck
        mov     emax_cell,AX

exit_ie:
        RETURN  emax_cell
EPROCEDURE int_eval


BPROCEDURE int_chuck
        setv0   OFF11
        setv0   OFF10
        setv0   OFF9
        setv0   OFF8
        setv0   OFF7
        setv0   OFF6
        setv0   DEF11
        setv0   DEF10
        setv0   DEF9
```

Fig. 17-1 continued.

```
              setv0    DEF8
              setv0    DEF7
              setv0    DEF6
              setv0    [EVAL11]
              setv0    [EVAL10]
              setv0    [EVAL9]
              setv0    [EVAL8]
              setv0    [EVAL7]
              setv0    [EVAL8]
; drop cell 11
BIFE     idc11,[board+22],0
              setv     [EVALTEMP],0
BELSE    idc11
              setv     [EVALTEMP],50
              setv0    [t_score]
              cproc    board_to_tree1
              setv     AX,11
              cproc    drop_tree
              cproc    grab_tree
              mov      AX,[t_score]
              add      [EVALTEMP],AX
              cproc    adj_tree
              setmv    [OFF11],[OFFTEMP]
              setmv    [DEF11],[DEFTEMP]
EIFELSE idc11
              setmv    [EVAL11],[EVALTEMP]


;        pushx
;        swrite   5,0,blank
;        memset   buff10,0,10
;        itoa     [EVALTEMP],buff10
;        swrite   5,0,buff10
;        popx


; drop cell 10
BIFE     idc10,[board+20],0
              setv     [EVALTEMP],0
BELSE    idc10
              setv     [EVALTEMP],50
              setv0    [t_score]
              cproc    board_to_tree1
              setv     AX,10
              cproc    drop_tree
              cproc    grab_tree
              mov      AX,[t_score]
              add      [EVALTEMP],AX
              cproc    adj_tree
              setmv    [OFF10],[OFFTEMP]
              setmv    [DEF10],[DEFTEMP]
EIFELSE idc10
              setmv    [EVAL10],[EVALTEMP]


;        pushx
;        swrite   6,0,blank
;        memset   buff10,0,10
;        itoa     [EVALTEMP],buff10
;        swrite   6,0,buff10
;        popx
```

Fig. 17-1 continued.

```
; drop cell 9
BIFE    idc9,[board+18],0
        setv    [EVALTEMP],0
BELSE   idc9
        setv    [EVALTEMP],50
        setv0   [t_score]
        cproc   board_to_tree1
        setv    AX,9
        cproc   drop_tree
        cproc   grab_tree
        mov     AX,[t_score]
        add     [EVALTEMP],AX
        cproc   adj_tree
        setmv   [OFF9],[OFFTEMP]
        setmv   [DEF9],[DEFTEMP]
EIFELSE idc9
        setmv   [EVAL9],[EVALTEMP]

;       pushx
;       swrite  7,0,blank
;       memset  buff10,0,10
;       itoa    [EVALTEMP],buff10
;       swrite  7,0,buff10
;       popx

; drop cell 8
BIFE    idc8,[board+16],0
        setv    [EVALTEMP],0
BELSE   idc8
        setv    [EVALTEMP],50
        setv0   [t_score]
        cproc   board_to_tree1
        setv    AX,8
        cproc   drop_tree
        cproc   grab_tree
        mov     AX,[t_score]
        add     [EVALTEMP],AX
        cproc   adj_tree
        setmv   [OFF8],[OFFTEMP]
        setmv   [DEF8],[DEFTEMP]
EIFELSE idc8
        setmv   [EVAL8],[EVALTEMP]

;       pushx
;       swrite  8,0,blank
;       memset  buff10,0,10
;       itoa    [EVALTEMP],buff10
;       swrite  8,0,buff10
;       popx

; drop cell 7
BIFE    idc7,[board+14],0
        setv    [EVALTEMP],0
BELSE   idc7
        setv    [EVALTEMP],50
        setv0   [t_score]
        cproc   board_to_tree1
        setv    AX,7
        cproc   drop_tree
        cproc   grab_tree
```

Fig. 17-1 continued.

```
                mov      AX,[t_score]
                add      [EVALTEMP],AX
                cproc    adj_tree
                setmv    [OFF7],[OFFTEMP]
                setmv    [DEF7],[DEFTEMP]
EIFELSE idc7
                setmv    [EVAL7],[EVALTEMP]

;               pushx
;               swrite   9,0,blank
;               memset   buff10,0,10
;               itoa     [EVALTEMP],buff10
;               swrite   9,0,buff10
;               popx


; drop cell 6
BIFE    idc6,[board+12],0
                setv     [EVALTEMP],0
BELSE   idc6
                setv     [EVALTEMP],50
                setv0    [t_score]
                cproc    board_to_tree1
                setv     AX,6
                cproc    drop_tree
                cproc    grab_tree
                mov      AX,[t_score]
                add      [EVALTEMP],AX
                cproc    adj_tree
                setmv    [OFF6],[OFFTEMP]
                setmv    [DEF6],[DEFTEMP]
EIFELSE idc6
                setmv    [EVAL6],[EVALTEMP]

;               pushx
;               swrite   10,0,blank
;               memset   buff10,0,10
;               itoa     [EVALTEMP],buff10
;               swrite   10,0,buff10
;               popx

                cproc    int_eval

;               pushx
;               swrite   12,0,blank
;               memset   buff10,0,10
;               itoa     AX,buff10
;               swrite   12,0,buff10
;               popx
;
;               pushx
;               memset   buff10,0,10
;               itoa     [OFF11],buff10
;               swrite   5,3,buff10
;               popx
;
;               pushx
;               memset   buff10,0,10
;               itoa     [OFF10],buff10
;               swrite   6,3,buff10
```

Fig. 17-1 continued.

```
;        popx
;
;        pushx
;        memset   buff10,0,10
;        itoa     [OFF9],buff10
;        swrite   7,3,buff10
;        popx
;
;        pushx
;        memset   buff10,0,10
;        itoa     [OFF8],buff10
;        swrite   8,3,buff10
;        popx
;
;        pushx
;        memset   buff10,0,10
;        itoa     [OFF7],buff10
;        swrite   9,3,buff10
;        popx
;
;        pushx
;        memset   buff10,0,10
;        itoa     [OFF6],buff10
;        swrite   10,3,buff10
;        popx
;
;
;        pushx
;        memset   buff10,0,10
;        itoa     [DEF11],buff10
;        swrite   12,3,buff10
;        popx
;
;        pushx
;        memset   buff10,0,10
;        itoa     [DEF10],buff10
;        swrite   13,3,buff10
;        popx
;
;        pushx
;        memset   buff10,0,10
;        itoa     [DEF9],buff10
;        swrite   14,3,buff10
;        popx
;
;        pushx
;        memset   buff10,0,10
;        itoa     [DEF8],buff10
;        swrite   15,3,buff10
;        popx
;
;        pushx
;        memset   buff10,0,10
;        itoa     [DEF7],buff10
;        swrite   16,3,buff10
;        popx
;
;        pushx
;        memset   buff10,0,10
;        itoa     [DEF6],buff10
```

```
;          swrite    17,3,buff10
;          popx
;
           RETURN   RET_VAL
EPROCEDURE int_chuck

INCLUDE TABWARI2.ASM

           END
```

Fig. 17-1 ends.

Fig. 17-2. The source code listing to TABWARI1.ASM.

```
;-------------------------------------
; TABWARI1.ASM

;----------------------------------------------------;
; Drop down play options window
;
BPROCEDURE  drop_play
        savescrn
        scwrite     0,0,6,playdat,[hili_attr]
        wdisplay    playw,S_S_S_S
        wswrite     playw,1,2,play1
        wswrite     playw,2,2,play2
        wswrite     playw,3,2,play3
        wswrite     playw,4,2,play4
BELOOP  lp1
        cproc       clr_play
        wvdattr     playw,[play_row],2,12,inverse
        getkey      [play_key]
        SWITCH      sw1,[play_key]
           CASE     sw1,play_isup,UP_ARROW
           CASE     sw1,play_isdn,DOWN_ARROW
           CASE     sw1,play_enter,E_CR
           CASE     sw1,play_escape,ESCAPE
        ESWITCH     sw1
        BIFE        lp1_exit,[case_flag],0
           EBREAK      lp1
        EIF         lp1_exit
EELOOP  lp1
        restscrn
EPROCEDURE  drop_play

BPROCEDURE  play_isup
        BIFE        piu,[play_row],1
           setv        [play_row],4
        BELSE       piu
           sub1        [play_row]
        EIFELSE     piu
        setv        [case_flag],1
EPROCEDURE  play_isup

BPROCEDURE  play_isdn
        BIFE        pid,[play_row],4
           setv        [play_row],1
        BELSE       pid
           add1        [play_row]
        EIFELSE     pid
        setv     [case_flag],1
```

Fig. 17-2 continued.

```
EPROCEDURE   play_isdn

BPROCEDURE   play_enter
        setv    [case_flag],0
        SWITCH      sw3,[play_row]
           CASE     sw3,play_advanced,1
           CASE     sw3,play_beginner,2
           CASE     sw3,play_rules,3
           CASE     sw3,play_chuck,4
        ESWITCH     sw3
EPROCEDURE   play_enter

BPROCEDURE   play_escape
        setv     [case_flag],0
EPROCEDURE   play_escape

BPROCEDURE  play_beginner
        setv    [level],0
EPROCEDURE  play_beginner

BPROCEDURE  play_advanced
        setv    [level],1
EPROCEDURE  play_advanced

BPROCEDURE  play_rules
        clrscreen
        puts     rules
        getkey
EPROCEDURE  play_rules

BPROCEDURE  play_chuck
        clrscreen
        puts     chuck
        getkey
EPROCEDURE  play_chuck

BPROCEDURE  clr_play
        setv        [temporary],1
BLOOP   clr_playl,4
        wvdattr     playw,[temporary],2,12,[hili_attr]
        add1        [temporary]
ELOOP   clr_playl
EPROCEDURE  clr_play
;-------------------------------------------------;


;-------------------------------------------------;
;
; This routine will be added by you
;
;BPROCEDURE   drop_file
;
;       savescrn
;       scwrite     0,7,6,filedat,[hili_attr]
;       wdisplay    filew,S_S_S_S
;       wswrite     filew,1,2,file1
;       wswrite     filew,2,2,file2
;       wvdattr     filew,[file_row],2,9,inverse
;BELOOP lf1
;       cproc       clr_file
```

Fig. 17-2 continued.

```
;       wvdattr     filew,[file_row],2,9,inverse
;       getkey      [file_key]
;       SWITCH      sw2,[file_key]
;          CASE     sw2,file_isup,UP_ARROW
;          CASE     sw2,file_isdn,DOWN_ARROW
;          CASE     sw2,file_enter,E_CR
;          CASE     sw2,file_escape,ESCAPE
;       ESWITCH     sw2
;       BIFE        lf1_exit,[case_flag],0
;          EBREAK      lf1
;       EIF         lf1_exit
;EELOOP lf1
;       restscrn
;EPROCEDURE  drop_file
;
;BPROCEDURE  file_isup
;       BIFE        fiu,[file_row],1
;          setv        [file_row],2
;       BELSE       fiu
;          sub1        [file_row]
;       EIFELSE     fiu
;       setv        [case_flag],1
;EPROCEDURE  file_isup
;
;BPROCEDURE  file_isdn
;       BIFE        fid,[file_row],2
;          setv        [file_row],1
;       BELSE       fid
;          add1        [file_row]
;       EIFELSE     fid
;       setv    [case_flag],1
;EPROCEDURE  file_isdn
;
;BPROCEDURE  file_enter
;       setv    [case_flag],0
;EPROCEDURE  file_enter
;
;BPROCEDURE  file_escape
;       setv    [case_flag],0
;EPROCEDURE  file_escape
;
;BPROCEDURE  clr_file
;       setv        [temporary],1
;BLOOP  clr_filel,2
;       wvdattr     filew,[temporary],2,9,[hili_attr]
;       add1        [temporary]
;ELOOP  clr_filel
;EPROCEDURE  clr_file
;----------------------------------------------------;

;----------------------------------------------------;
BPROCEDURE draw_board
        push    AX
        jmp     db1
dbBX    DW      0
db1:
; Fill Cell 0
        mov     AX,[board]
        shl     AX,1
        setptr  BX,table
```

Fig. 17-2 continued.

```
        add     BX,AX
        mov     AX,WORD PTR[BX]
        mov     dbBX,AX
        setptr  BX,windtable
        add     BX,0
        mov     DX,WORD PTR[BX]
        mov     BX,dbBX
        cproc   fill_cell
; Fill Cell 1
        mov     AX,[board+2]
        shl     AX,1
        setptr  BX,table
        add     BX,AX
        mov     AX,WORD PTR[BX]
        mov     dbBX,AX
        setptr  BX,windtable
        add     BX,2
        mov     DX,WORD PTR[BX]
        mov     BX,dbBX
        cproc   fill_cell
; Fill Cell 2
        mov     AX,[board+4]
        shl     AX,1
        setptr  BX,table
        add     BX,AX
        mov     AX,WORD PTR[BX]
        mov     dbBX,AX
        setptr  BX,windtable
        add     BX,4
        mov     DX,WORD PTR[BX]
        mov     BX,dbBX
        cproc   fill_cell
; Fill Cell 3
        mov     AX,[board+6]
        shl     AX,1
        setptr  BX,table
        add     BX,AX
        mov     AX,WORD PTR[BX]
        mov     dbBX,AX
        setptr  BX,windtable
        add     BX,6
        mov     DX,WORD PTR[BX]
        mov     BX,dbBX
        cproc   fill_cell
; Fill Cell 4
        mov     AX,[board+8]
        shl     AX,1
        setptr  BX,table
        add     BX,AX
        mov     AX,WORD PTR[BX]
        mov     dbBX,AX
        setptr  BX,windtable
        add     BX,8
        mov     DX,WORD PTR[BX]
        mov     BX,dbBX
        cproc   fill_cell
; Fill Cell 5
        mov     AX,[board+10]
        shl     AX,1
        setptr  BX,table
```

Fig. 17-2 continued.

```
        add     BX,AX
        mov     AX,WORD PTR[BX]
        mov     dbBX,AX
        setptr  BX,windtable
        add     BX,10
        mov     DX,WORD PTR[BX]
        mov     BX,dbBX
        cproc   fill_cell
; Fill Cell 6
        mov     AX,[board+12]
        shl     AX,1
        setptr  BX,table
        add     BX,AX
        mov     AX,WORD PTR[BX]
        mov     dbBX,AX
        setptr  BX,windtable
        add     BX,12
        mov     DX,WORD PTR[BX]
        mov     BX,dbBX
        cproc   fill_cell
; Fill Cell 7
        mov     AX,[board+14]
        shl     AX,1
        setptr  BX,table
        add     BX,AX
        mov     AX,WORD PTR[BX]
        mov     dbBX,AX
        setptr  BX,windtable
        add     BX,14
        mov     DX,WORD PTR[BX]
        mov     BX,dbBX
        cproc   fill_cell
; Fill Cell 8
        mov     AX,[board+16]
        shl     AX,1
        setptr  BX,table
        add     BX,AX
        mov     AX,WORD PTR[BX]
        mov     dbBX,AX
        setptr  BX,windtable
        add     BX,16
        mov     DX,WORD PTR[BX]
        mov     BX,dbBX
        cproc   fill_cell
; Fill Cell 9
        mov     AX,[board+18]
        shl     AX,1
        setptr  BX,table
        add     BX,AX
        mov     AX,WORD PTR[BX]
        mov     dbBX,AX
        setptr  BX,windtable
        add     BX,18
        mov     DX,WORD PTR[BX]
        mov     BX,dbBX
        cproc   fill_cell
; Fill Cell 10
        mov     AX,[board+20]
        shl     AX,1
        setptr  BX,table
```

Fig. 17-2 continued.

```
        add     BX,AX
        mov     AX,WORD PTR[BX]
        mov     dbBX,AX
        setptr  BX,windtable
        add     BX,20
        mov     DX,WORD PTR[BX]
        mov     BX,dbBX
        cproc   fill_cell
; Fill Cell 11
        mov     AX,[board+22]
        shl     AX,1
        setptr  BX,table
        add     BX,AX
        mov     AX,WORD PTR[BX]
        mov     dbBX,AX
        setptr  BX,windtable
        add     BX,+22
        mov     DX,WORD PTR[BX]
        mov     BX,dbBX
        cproc   fill_cell
        pop     AX
EPROCEDURE draw_board
;----------------------------------------------------;


;----------------------------------------------------;
BPROCEDURE show_score
        memset    p_buff,0,8
        memset    c_buff,0,8
        itoa      [p_score],p_buff,1
        swrite    24,12,p_buff
        swrite    24,4,p_mess
        itoa      [c_score],c_buff,1
        swrite    24,70,c_buff
        swrite    24,60,c_mess
EPROCEDURE show_score
;----------------------------------------------------;


;----------------------------------------------------;
BPROCEDURE fill_cell
        push    AX
        jmp     fc1
windptr DW      0
fc1:
setv    windptr,DX
setv    rowctr,1
setv    colctr,1
BLOOP   outer,4
   setv   colctr,1
   BLOOP  inner,8
      mov     AL,BYTE PTR[BX]
      xor     AH,AH
      mov     cval,AX
      add1    BX
      push    BX
      setv    BX,windptr
      wvdchar BX,[rowctr],[colctr],[cval],[ston_attr]
      pop     BX
      add1    colctr
   ELOOP   inner
   add1       rowctr
```

Fig. 17-2 continued.

```
ELOOP     outer
          pop     AX
EPROCEDURE fill_cell
;---------------------------------------------------------;

BPROCEDURE show_board
          pushx
          swrite  1,0,blank
          memset  buff10,0,10
          itoa    [board],buff10
          swrite  1,0,buff10
          popx

          pushx
          swrite  2,0,blank
          memset  buff10,0,10
          itoa    [board+2],buff10
          swrite  2,0,buff10
          popx

          pushx
          swrite  3,0,blank
          memset  buff10,0,10
          itoa    [board+4],buff10
          swrite  3,0,buff10
          popx

          pushx
          swrite  4,0,blank
          memset  buff10,0,10
          itoa    [board+6],buff10
          swrite  4,0,buff10
          popx

          pushx
          swrite  5,0,blank
          memset  buff10,0,10
          itoa    [board+8],buff10
          swrite  5,0,buff10
          popx

          pushx
          swrite  6,0,blank
          memset  buff10,0,10
          itoa    [board+10],buff10
          swrite  6,0,buff10
          popx

          pushx
          swrite  7,0,blank
          memset  buff10,0,10
          itoa    [board+12],buff10
          swrite  7,0,buff10
          popx

          pushx
          swrite  8,0,blank
          memset  buff10,0,10
          itoa    [board+14],buff10
          swrite  8,0,buff10
```

Fig. 17-2 continued.

```
        popx

        pushx
        swrite  9,0,blank
        memset  buff10,0,10
        itoa    [board+16],buff10
        swrite  9,0,buff10
        popx

        pushx
        swrite  10,0,blank
        memset  buff10,0,10
        itoa    [board+18],buff10
        swrite  10,0,buff10
        popx

        pushx
        swrite  11,0,blank
        memset  buff10,0,10
        itoa    [board+20],buff10
        swrite  11,0,buff10
        popx

        pushx
        swrite  12,0,blank
        memset  buff10,0,10
        itoa    [board+22],buff10
        swrite  12,0,buff10
        popx
EPROCEDURE show_board

BPROCEDURE show_tree1
        pushx
        swrite  1,0,blank
        memset  buff10,0,10
        itoa    [tree1],buff10
        swrite  1,0,buff10
        popx

        pushx
        swrite  2,0,blank
        memset  buff10,0,10
        itoa    [tree1+2],buff10
        swrite  2,0,buff10
        popx

        pushx
        swrite  3,0,blank
        memset  buff10,0,10
        itoa    [tree1+4],buff10
        swrite  3,0,buff10
        popx

        pushx
        swrite  4,0,blank
        memset  buff10,0,10
        itoa    [tree1+6],buff10
        swrite  4,0,buff10
        popx
```

```
        pushx
        swrite   5,0,blank
        memset   buff10,0,10
        itoa     [tree1+8],buff10
        swrite   5,0,buff10
        popx

        pushx
        swrite   6,0,blank
        memset   buff10,0,10
        itoa     [tree1+10],buff10
        swrite   6,0,buff10
        popx

        pushx
        swrite   7,0,blank
        memset   buff10,0,10
        itoa     [tree1+12],buff10
        swrite   7,0,buff10
        popx

        pushx
        swrite   8,0,blank
        memset   buff10,0,10
        itoa     [tree1+14],buff10
        swrite   8,0,buff10
        popx

        pushx
        swrite   9,0,blank
        memset   buff10,0,10
        itoa     [tree1+16],buff10
        swrite   9,0,buff10
        popx

        pushx
        swrite   10,0,blank
        memset   buff10,0,10
        itoa     [tree1+18],buff10
        swrite   10,0,buff10
        popx

        pushx
        swrite   11,0,blank
        memset   buff10,0,10
        itoa     [tree1+20],buff10
        swrite   11,0,buff10
        popx

        pushx
        swrite   12,0,blank
        memset   buff10,0,10
        itoa     [tree1+22],buff10
        swrite   12,0,buff10
        popx
EPROCEDURE show_tree1
```

Fig. 17-2 ends.

Fig. 17-3. The source code listing to TABWARI2.ASM.

```
;-------------------------------------
; TABWARI2.ASM


INCLUDE TABWARI1.ASM

;------------------------------------------------------;
; Name: FILTER_KEY
;
; Description: Read a key and filter
;   program responses

BPROCEDURE filter_key
        getkey    [key_val]
        cproc     set_key
        BIFE      fk1,[key_val],ALT_P
            cproc     drop_play
            RETURN    0
        EIF       fk1


;
; this code to be added by you for drop down window
;
;        BIFE      fk2,[key_val],ALT_F
;            cproc     drop_file
;            RETURN    0
;        EIF       fk2

        BIFE      fk3,[key_val],ALT_Q
            RETURN    1
        EIF       fk3
EPROCEDURE filter_key
;------------------------------------------------------;

;------------------------------------------------------;
; Name SET_KEY
;
; Description: Place binary of ASCII
;   number into [key_num]
BPROCEDURE  set_key
        push      AX
        mov       BX,AX
        xor       BH,BH
        sub       BL,'0'
        mov       [key_num],BX
        pop       AX
EPROCEDURE  set_key
;------------------------------------------------------;


;------------------------------------------------------;
BPROCEDURE drop_jewels
BBLOCK  pm1
pmstart DW        0
pmtemp  DW        0
pmval   DW        0
EBLOCK  pm1
        setv      pmstart,AX
        setv      pmtemp,AX
```

Fig. 17-3 continued.

```
          setptr  DBASE_PTR,board
          shl     AX,1
          add     DBASE_PTR,AX
          mov     CX,WORD PTR[DBASE_PTR]
          BIFE    pm4,CX,0
;                 beep
                  RETURN  12
          EIF     pm4
          setv    pmval,CX
          mov     WORD PTR[DBASE_PTR],0
BLOOP     pm2,CX
          BIFE    pm3,pmtemp,11
            setv0   pmtemp
            setptr DBASE_PTR,board
          BELSE   pm3
            add2  DBASE_PTR
            add1  pmtemp
          EIFELSE pm3
          BIFE    pm5,pmtemp,pmstart
             BIFE        pm6,pmtemp,11
                setv0  pmtemp
                setptr DBASE_PTR,board
             BELSE      pm6
                add2    DBASE_PTR
                add1    pmtemp
             EIFELSE    pm6
          EIF     pm5
          mov     AX,WORD PTR[DBASE_PTR]
          add1    AX
          mov     WORD PTR[DBASE_PTR],AX
ELOOP     pm2
          RETURN  pmtemp
EPROCEDURE drop_jewels
;-----------------------------------------------------;


;-----------------------------------------------------;
BPROCEDURE beg_chuck
BBLOCK    bc1
cell_val DW       0
max_cell DW       0
max_val  DW       0
EBLOCK    bc1
          setv0   max_cell
          setv0   max_val
          setv    cell_val,11
          setptr  DBASE_PTR,board
          add     DBASE_PTR,22
BLOOP     bc2,6
          mov     AX,WORD PTR[DBASE_PTR]
          BIFGT   bc3,AX,max_val
             mov     max_val,AX
             mov     AX,cell_val
             mov     max_cell,AX
          EIF     bc3
          sub1    cell_val
          sub2    DBASE_PTR
ELOOP     bc2
          RETURN  max_cell
EPROCEDURE beg_chuck
;-----------------------------------------------------;
```

```
BPROCEDURE bleep
        pushaa
        onsound 1000
        cproc   delay1
        cproc   delay1
        cproc   delay1
        onsound 2000
        cproc   delay1
        cproc   delay1
        cproc   delay1
        onsound 3000
        cproc   delay1
        cproc   delay1
        cproc   delay1
        onsound 4000
        cproc   delay1
        cproc   delay1
        cproc   delay1
        onsound 5000
        cproc   delay1
        cproc   delay1
        cproc   delay1
        offsound
        popaa
EPROCEDURE bleep

BPROCEDURE delay
        pushx
BLOOP dly1,200
   BLOOP dly2,800
   ELOOP dly2
ELOOP dly1
        popx
EPROCEDURE delay

BPROCEDURE delay1
        pushx
BLOOP dly1a,100
   BLOOP dly2a,100
   ELOOP dly2a
   ELOOP dly1a
          popx
   EPROCEDURE delay1

   BPROCEDURE init_board
          setv    [board],4
          setv    [board+2],4
          setv    [board+4],4
          setv    [board+6],4
          setv    [board+8],4
          setv    [board+10],4
          setv    [board+12],4
          setv    [board+14],4
          setv    [board+16],4
          setv    [board+18],4
          setv    [board+20],4
          setv    [board+22],4
   EPROCEDURE init_board
```

Fig. 17-3 ends.

Fig. 17-4. The source code listing to WARIDATA.ASM.

```
; File Name: WARIDATA.ASM
;------------------------------------------------------
table       DW      pat0,pat1,pat2,pat3,pat4,pat5,pat6
            DW      pat7,pat8,pat9,pat10,pat11,pat12
            DW      pat13,pat14,pat15,pat16,pat17,pat18,
            DW      pat19,pat20,pat21,pat22,pat23,pat24
            DW      pat25,pat26,pat27,pat28,pat29,pat30
            DW      pat31,pat32
windtable DW      wind0,wind1,wind2,wind3,wind4,wind5
            DW      wind6,wind7,wind8,wind9,wind10,wind11
t_score     DW      0
c_score     DW      0
c_buff      DB      8 DUP(0)
c_mess      DB      'Chucks Score: ',0
p_score     DW      0
p_buff      DB      8 DUP(8)
p_mess      DB      'Your Score: ',0
yt_mess     DB      '[ Your Turn Now ]',0
ct_mess     DB      '[ Chuck ....... ]',0
level       DW      1       ; advanced by default
cval        DW      0
rowctr      DW      1
colctr      DW      0
case_flag DW      1
play_key    DW      0
file_key    DW      0
play_row    DW      1
file_row    DW      1
cell_attr DW      0
ston_attr DW      0
scrn_attr DW      0
choo_attr DW      0
hili_attr DW      0
inverse     DW      0
temporary DW      0
counter     DW      0
testit      DW      0
gowind  WINDOW <6,20,18,60,7,,>
wind11  WINDOW <4,4,11,15,7,,>
wind10  WINDOW <4,16,11,27,7,,>
wind9   WINDOW <4,28,11,39,7,,>
wind8   WINDOW <4,40,11,51,7,,>
wind7   WINDOW <4,52,11,63,7,,>
wind6   WINDOW <4,64,11,75,7,,>
wind0   WINDOW <13,4,20,15,7,,>
wind1   WINDOW <13,16,20,27,7,,>
wind2   WINDOW <13,28,20,39,7,,>
wind3   WINDOW <13,40,20,51,7,,>
wind4   WINDOW <13,52,20,63,7,,>
wind5   WINDOW <13,64,20,75,7,,>
wbord   WINDOW <3,3,22,76,7,,>
scrnw   WINDOW <0,0,24,79,7,,>
playw   WINDOW <1,0,6,15,7,,>
filew   WINDOW <1,7,4,19,7,,>

;
; Menu bar for File Drop down options
;
;menubar        DB      ' Play  File
```

Fig. 17-4 continued.

```
;

menubar DB        ' Play                                         '
        DB        '                                    Quit      ',0
hbar    DB        80 DUP(196),0
choose  DB        '<1>         <2>         <3>         <4>'
        DB        '            <5>         <6>',0
key_val DW        0
key_num DW        0
wname1  DB        '[ Advanced WARI ]',0
wname2  DB        '[ Beginner WARI ]',0
playdat DB        ' Play ',0
filedat DB        ' File ',0
play1   DB        'Advanced',0
play2   DB        'Beginner',0
play3   DB        'WARI Rules',0
play4   DB        'ASMplus Info',0
file1   DB        'Save Game',0
file2   DB        'Load Game',0
cwins   DB        ' CHUCK Wins! Too bad.',0
wkey    DB        ' Any key gives you new game.',0
pwins   DB        ' YOU Win! Great job. '
buffer  DB        10 DUP(0)
pat0    DB 32,32,32,32,32,32,32,32
        DB 32,32,32,32,32,32,32,32
        DB 32,32,32,32,32,32,32,32
        DB 32,32,32,32,32,32,32,32
pat1    DB 32,32,32,32,32,32,32,32
        DB 32,32,32,9,32,32,32,32
        DB 32,32,32,32,32,32,32,32
        DB 32,32,32,32,32,32,32,32
pat2    DB 32,32,32,32,32,32,32,32
        DB 32,32,32,9,9,32,32,32
        DB 32,32,32,32,32,32,32,32
        DB 32,32,32,32,32,32,32,32
pat3    DB 32,32,32,32,32,32,32,32
        DB 32,32,32,9,9,32,32,32
        DB 32,32,32,9,32,32,32,32
        DB 32,32,32,32,32,32,32,32
pat4    DB 32,32,32,32,32,32,32,32
        DB 32,32,32,9,9,32,32,32
        DB 32,32,32,9,9,32,32,32
        DB 32,32,32,32,32,32,32,32
pat5    DB 32,32,32,32,32,32,32,32
        DB 32,32,9,9,9,32,32,32
        DB 32,32,32,9,9,32,32,32
        DB 32,32,32,32,32,32,32,32
pat6    DB 32,32,32,32,32,32,32,32
        DB 32,32,9,9,9,32,32,32
        DB 32,32,9,9,9,32,32,32
        DB 32,32,32,32,32,32,32,32
pat7    DB 32,32,32,32,32,32,32,32
        DB 32,32,9,9,9,9,32,32
        DB 32,32,9,9,9,32,32,32
        DB 32,32,32,32,32,32,32,32
pat8    DB 32,32,32,32,32,32,32,32
        DB 32,32,9,9,9,9,32,32
        DB 32,32,9,9,9,9,32,32
        DB 32,32,32,32,32,32,32,32
pat9    DB 32,32,32,32,32,32,32,32
```

Fig. 17-4 continued.

```
         DB  32,9,9,9,9,9,32,32
         DB  32,32,9,9,9,9,32,32
         DB  32,32,32,32,32,32,32,32
pat10    DB  32,32,32,32,32,32,32,32
         DB  32,9,9,9,9,9,32,32
         DB  32,9,9,9,9,9,32,32
         DB  32,32,32,32,32,32,32,32
pat11    DB  32,32,9,32,32,32,32,32
         DB  32,9,9,9,9,9,32,32
         DB  32,9,9,9,9,9,32,32
         DB  32,32,32,32,32,32,32,32
pat12    DB  32,32,9,32,32,32,32,32
         DB  32,9,9,9,9,9,32,32
         DB  32,9,9,9,9,9,32,32
         DB  32,32,9,32,32,32,32,32
pat13    DB  32,32,9,9,32,32,32,32
         DB  32,9,9,9,9,9,32,32
         DB  32,9,9,9,9,9,32,32
         DB  32,32,9,32,32,32,32,32
pat14    DB  32,32,9,9,32,32,32,32
         DB  32,9,9,9,9,9,32,32
         DB  32,9,9,9,9,9,32,32
         DB  32,32,9,9,32,32,32,32
pat15    DB  32,32,9,9,9,32,32,32
         DB  32,9,9,9,9,9,32,32
         DB  32,9,9,9,9,9,32,32
         DB  32,32,9,9,32,32,32,32
pat16    DB  32,32,9,9,9,32,32,32
         DB  32,9,9,9,9,9,32,32
         DB  32,9,9,9,9,9,32,32
         DB  32,32,9,9,9,32,32,32
pat17    DB  32,9,9,9,9,32,32,32
         DB  32,9,9,9,9,9,32,32
         DB  32,9,9,9,9,9,32,32
         DB  32,32,9,9,9,32,32,32
pat18    DB  32,9,9,9,9,32,32,32
         DB  32,9,9,9,9,9,32,32
         DB  32,9,9,9,9,9,32,32
         DB  32,9,9,9,9,32,32,32
pat19    DB  32,9,9,9,9,9,32,32
         DB  32,9,9,9,9,9,32,32
         DB  32,9,9,9,9,9,32,32
         DB  32,9,9,9,9,32,32,32
pat20    DB  32,9,9,9,9,9,32,32
         DB  32,9,9,9,9,9,32,32
         DB  32,9,9,9,9,9,32,32
         DB  32,9,9,9,9,9,32,32
pat21    DB  32,9,9,9,9,9,9,32
         DB  32,9,9,9,9,9,32,32
         DB  32,9,9,9,9,9,32,32
         DB  32,9,9,9,9,9,9,32
pat22    DB  32,9,9,9,9,9,9,32
         DB  32,9,9,9,9,9,9,32
         DB  32,9,9,9,9,9,32,32
         DB  32,9,9,9,9,9,32,32
pat23    DB  32,9,9,9,9,9,9,32
         DB  32,9,9,9,9,9,9,32
         DB  32,9,9,9,9,9,9,32
         DB  32,9,9,9,9,9,32,32
pat24    DB  32,9,9,9,9,9,9,32
```

Fig. 17-4 continued.

```
          DB  32,9,9,9,9,9,9,32
          DB  32,9,9,9,9,9,9,32
          DB  32,9,9,9,9,9,9,32
pat25     DB  32,9,9,9,9,9,9,32
          DB  9,9,9,9,9,9,9,32
          DB  32,9,9,9,9,9,9,32
          DB  32,9,9,9,9,9,9,32
pat26     DB  32,9,9,9,9,9,9,32
          DB  9,9,9,9,9,9,9,9
          DB  32,9,9,9,9,9,9,32
          DB  32,9,9,9,9,9,9,32
pat27     DB  32,9,9,9,9,9,9,32
          DB  9,9,9,9,9,9,9,9
          DB  9,9,9,9,9,9,9,32
          DB  32,9,9,9,9,9,9,32
pat28     DB  32,9,9,9,9,9,9,32
          DB  9,9,9,9,9,9,9,9
          DB  9,9,9,9,9,9,9,9
          DB  32,9,9,9,9,9,9,32
pat29     DB  9,9,9,9,9,9,9,32
          DB  9,9,9,9,9,9,9,9
          DB  9,9,9,9,9,9,9,9
          DB  32,9,9,9,9,9,9,32
pat30     DB  9,9,9,9,9,9,9,9
          DB  9,9,9,9,9,9,9,9
          DB  9,9,9,9,9,9,9,9
          DB  32,9,9,9,9,9,9,32
pat31     DB  9,9,9,9,9,9,9,9
          DB  9,9,9,9,9,9,9,9
          DB  9,9,9,9,9,9,9,9
          DB  9,9,9,9,9,9,9,32
pat32     DB  9,9,9,9,9,9,9,9
          DB  9,9,9,9,9,9,9,9
          DB  9,9,9,9,9,9,9,9
          DB  9,9,9,9,9,9,9,9
dummy     DW  0,0,0,0
board     DW  4,4,4,4,4,4,4,4,4,4,4,4,0
tree1     DW  0,0,0,0,0,0,0,0,0,0,0,0,0
rules     DB  'WARI Game Rules',10,13
          DB  '---------------',10,13,10,13
          DB  'Alternating turns, you (the player) and '
          DB  'CHUCK (the language) select a box',10,13
          DB  'containing jewels for play. Your jewel '
          DB  'boxes are numbered 1-6 and may be',10,13
          DB  'selected by pressing a number key.',10,13,10,13
          DB  'When a box is selected, the jewels are '
          DB  'dropped 1 by 1 in a counterclockwise ',10,13
          DB  'direction (skipping the original box '
          DB  'if there are more than 12 jewels in',10,13
          DB  'the selected box) on the game board. '
          DB  'If the last jewel dropped lands in',10,13
          DB  'opponents box which contains 2 or 3 '
          DB  'jewels, the jewels become yours and',10,13
          DB  'and are captured. Once a capture is '
          DB  'made, the player is permitted to take',10,13
          DB  'the jewels from the immediately preceding cup. ',10,13,10,13
          DB  'The game ends when all the jewel boxes '
          DB  'on one players side of the board are',10,13
          DB  'are empty and it is that players turn. '
          DB  'The player with the most jewels when',10,13
```

```
            DB 'the game ends WINS.',10,13,10,13
            DB 'Consult the documentation for more '
            DB 'information on WARI.',0

chuck       DB 'ASMplus Implementation of the CHUCK Programming Language',10,13
            DB '(c) 1989 by TSR SYSTEMS LTD, Port Jefferson, New York    ',10,13
            DB '--------------------------------------------------------'
            DB 10,13,10,13
            DB 'The ASMplus Development System is a full featured '
            DB 'implementation of the CHUCK ',10,13
            DB 'Programming Language. ASMplus retains '
            DB 'the structure of higher lever ',10,13
            DB 'languages (C, PASCAL, ADA) while  '
            DB 'permitting easy access to high-level ',10,13
            DB 'like procedures. The ASMplus Development '
            DB 'System has been shown to reduce ',10,13
            DB 'the .CODE size of C generated .EXE '
            DB 'files between the range of 40% to 60%.',10,13
            DB 'Pure Assembly code may be freely '
            DB 'co-mingled in the mid-level ASMplus ',10,13
            DB 'programming environment. This allows for '
            DB 'maximum flexibility where program',10,13
            DB 'size and execution speed are of '
            DB 'concern.',10,13,10,13
            DB 'We, at TSR SYSTEMS LTD, are VERY '
            DB 'excited about the power and convenience ',10,13
            DB 'of the ASMplus Program Development System. '
            DB 'Call us at:',10,13,10,13
            DB '  516 - 331 - 6336',10,13,10,13
            DB 'for more information about ASMplus or '
            DB 'an ASMplus demonstration disk.',0
EVALTEMP DW       0
EVAL11   DW       0
EVAL10   DW       0
EVAL9    DW       0
EVAL8    DW       0
EVAL7    DW       0
EVAL6    DW       0

OFFTEMP DW        0
OFF11    DW       0
OFF10    DW       0
OFF9     DW       0
OFF8     DW       0
OFF7     DW       0
OFF6     DW       0

DEFTEMP DW        0
DEF11    DW       0
DEF10    DW       0
DEF9     DW       0
DEF8     DW       0
DEF7     DW       0
DEF6     DW       0
```

Fig. 17-4 ends.

FINAL WORDS

Although structured assembly might not be for every programmer, I suspect it has a bright future. As shown in this book, CHUCK's program flow structures take some of the pain out of assembly programming without the price of the heavy code overhead of many high-level languages. Calling CHUCK procedures, at first glance, seems no more difficult than calling C, PASCAL, or ADA procedures and as CHUCK libraries evolve the utility of the language will flourish.

I believe CHUCK procedures and structured assembly will prove useful to commercial assembly programmers who have tight deadlines to meet or high-level language programmers who wish to dabble in assembly waters.

For those who have additional ideas on improving CHUCK and structured assembly or any other comments please feel free to write me at TAB BOOKS.

Index

Structured Assembly Language

If you are intrigued by the concepts of *Structured Assembly Language* (Windcrest book 3484), you should definitely consider having the companion disk containing both source and object code for all routines developed in the book. Not only will it save you time and typing effort, the disk eliminates the possibility of errors that can prevent the routines from working. Only $24.95 plus postage and handling.

Special Offer! Save 40 percent on *ASMplus*

ASMplus is a product designed to give assembly language programmers an even more dramatic productivity boost, and increase the ease of assembly code maintenance. Offered by special arrangement with leading library developer TSR Systems, *ASMplus* provides a much more extensive set of macros to add C – , Pascal – , or Ada-like control flow structure to assembly programs. In addition to the program control macros, *ASMplus* contains a library of 100 + functions for windows, screen handling, etc. *ASMplus* can easily be used in a mixed-language programming environment. It's a $100 value for only $59.95!

Both the companion disk and *ASMplus* support Borland Turbo Assembler (TASM) and Microsoft MASM, require DOS 3.0 or later, and are available in 5.25″ and 3.5″ versions. Both are guaranteed free from manufacturing defects. (Return the problem disk within 30 days and we'll send you a new one.)